I0887692

THE ASSASSINATION OF ABRAHAM LINCOLN

By the same author

Decapitating the Union: Jefferson Davis, Judah Benjamin and the Plot to Assassinate Lincoln (2015)

THE ASSASSINATION OF ABRAHAM LINCOLN:

FOUR SMOKING GUNS

JOHN C. FAZIO

PEN & SWORD
HISTORY
AN IMPRINT OF PEN & SWORD BOOKS LTD.
YORKSHIRE – PHILADELPHIA

First published in Great Britain in 2023 by
PEN AND SWORD HISTORY
An imprint of
Pen & Sword Books Ltd
Yorkshire – Philadelphia

ISBN 978 1 39904 681 7

A CIP catalogue record for this book is available from the British Library.

Typeset in Times New Roman 11.5/15 by
SJmagic DESIGN SERVICES, India.
Printed and bound in the UK by CPI Group (UK) Ltd.

Pen & Sword Books Limited incorporates the imprints of Atlas, Archaeology, Aviation, Discovery, Family History, Fiction, History, Maritime, Military, Military Classics, Politics, Select, Transport, True Crime, Air World, Frontline Publishing, Leo Cooper, Remember When, Seaforth Publishing, The Praetorian Press, Wharncliffe Local History, Wharncliffe Transport, Wharncliffe True Crime and White Owl.

For a complete list of Pen & Sword titles please contact
PEN & SWORD BOOKS LIMITED
George House, Units 12 & 13, Beevor Street, Off Pontefract Road,
Barnsley, South Yorkshire, S71 1HN, England

E-mail: enquiries@pen-and-sword.co.uk
Website: www.pen-and-sword.co.uk

Or
PEN AND SWORD BOOKS
1950 Lawrence Rd, Havertown, PA 19083, USA
E-mail: Uspen-and-sword@casematepublishers.com
Website: www.penandswordbooks.com

MIX
Paper | Supporting responsible forestry
FSC® C013604

To my wife, Mary,
and to the memory of all those, North and South, who perished at the crossroads to our true nationhood.

Contents

Acknowledgements

Once again, I must first thank my wife, Mary, who tolerated a husband who spent so much time and effort with his books, pamphlets, journals, magazines, newspapers, etc. Patience, it is said, is a virtue (impatience, by the way, is not a flower; it is a demand for attention), and she is indeed a virtuous woman. Fortunately, I found time to shop, cook, clean and walk the dog, which helped.

Second, and once again, I must thank my computer whiz-bang secretary, Linda Lester, without whose skills I would be the Robinson Crusoe of the literary world. She's so good at it, in fact, that a bunch of Brazilians paid all her expenses to fly to, live in and fly back from Sao Paulo to teach them how to tame the monsters.

Third, I must express my gratitude to those who, before I came along, gave so much time, thought and work to the subject of the Lincoln assassination and who therefore helped me, and many others, immensely. There is room only for those whose works were helpful to me in formulating and substantiating the thesis of this book, such as: Terry Alford, ed., *John Wilkes Booth: A Sister's Memoir* (1996); Samuel Arnold, *Memoirs of a Lincoln Conspirator*, ed. by Michael W. Kauffman (1995); David Homer Bates, *Lincoln in the Telegraph Office* (1907); Thomas Nelson Conrad, *A Confederate Spy* (1892); J. Marshall Crawford, *Mosby and His Men* (1867); Carman Cumming, *Devil's Game* (2004); William C. Edwards and Edward Steers, Jnr, eds., *The Lincoln Assassination: The Evidence* (2009); Eli N. Evans, *Judah P. Benjamin, The Jewish Confederate* (1989); David Goetz, *Ever the Gray Ghost: Colonel John Singleton Mosby and the Lincoln Conspiracies*; James O. Hall and Michael Malone, *John Wilkes Booth: Following the Money Trail* (2003); William Hanchett, *The Lincoln Murder Conspiracies* (1986); James D. Horan, *Confederate Agent*

(1954); Andrew C.A. Jampoler, *The Last Lincoln Conspirator: John Surratt's Flight from the Gallows* (2008); Thomas A. Jones, *J. Wilkes Booth* (1893); Michael W. Kauffman, *American Brutus: John Wilkes Booth and the Lincoln Conspiracies* (2004); Robert Lockwood Mills, *It Didn't Happen The Way You Think* (1994); Betty J. Ownsbey, *Alias 'Paine': Lewis Thornton Powell, The Mystery Man of the Lincoln Conspiracy* (1993); Sandy Prindle, *Booth's Confederate Connections* (2019); Edward H. Ripley, *The Capture and Occupation of Richmond*, April 3, 1865 (2007); *Duane Schultz, The Dahlgren Affair* (1998); Barry Sheehy, *Montreal, City of Secrets: Confederate Operations in Montreal During the American Civil War* (2017); Jane Singer, *The Confederate Dirty War: Arson, Bombings, Assassination and Plots for Chemical and Germ Attacks on the Union* (2005); Edward Steers, Jnr, ed., *The Trial: The Assassination of President Lincoln and the Trial of the Conspirators* (2003); William A. Tidwell, *April '65: Confederate Covert Action in the American Civil War* (1995); William A. Tidwell, James O. Hall and David Gaddy, *Come Retribution: The Confederate Secret Service and the Assassination of Abraham Lincoln* (1988); Louis J. Weichmann and Floyd E. Risvold, *A True History of the Assassination of Abraham Lincoln and the Conspiracy of 1865* (1975); and H. Donald Winkler, *Lincoln and Booth: More Light on the Conspiracy (*2003).

I cannot forget the contributions of friends. Friendship, it is said, is the most valuable thing in the world – well, maybe right after the health, safety and welfare of your loved ones, but a close second. Joan Chaconas of the Surratt Society, who discovered George Atzerodt's Lost Confession of 1 May 1865 – to historians, a priceless find – was not only a great help, but an inspiration too. As was Laurie Verge of the Surratt Society. She must have liked me, because she opened doors and gave me opportunities that I'm not sure I deserved, but accepted graciously anyway. Sadly, she is no longer with us – a major loss to the Civil War community and especially to assassination buffs. She was the mother hen of the James O. Hall Research Center of the Surratt Society in Clinton, Maryland, which is a treasure trove of material on the assassination. I thank her and the Center for all their help. And then there are the usual suspects, including Roger Norton, everyone's favourite assassination wonk, who created and maintains at least three websites on the assassination; Dave Taylor, creator of the website known as Boothiebarn; and fellow authors Lawrence Abel, Terry Alford, Kathryn Canahan, David Goetz, Frederick Hatch, Michael Kauffman, James M. McPherson, Fred J. Martin, Jnr, Betty Ownsbey, Sandy Prindle, Barry Sheehy, Jane Singer and Edward Steers, Jnr, all of whom either helped, inspired, or both.

Lastly, let me say a word of thanks to those research facilities that exist, ultimately, only to help others, including the National Archives and Records Administration; the Library of Congress; the Lehrman Institute and the Lincoln Institute; the Georgetown University Special Collections Research Center of the Georgetown University Library; the Western Reserve Historical Society Research Library; the Cleveland Public Library; the Akron-Summit County Public Library; and the Kent State University Library.

Foreword

Smoking Guns

It is said that nothing is certain in life except death and taxes. Well, we all know that many people do not pay taxes, because of either legal avoidance or illegal evasion and fraud. So that leaves death as the only certainty, consistent with the well-known syllogism that begins with the premise that all men are mortal. In truth, however, we really don't know, with 100 per cent certainty, that the premise is true, because the last man or woman hasn't died, and when he or she does, assuming he or she does, there will be no one to record the death, so the premise that all men are mortal will always be an unknown.

The point is that nothing can be completely known with 100 per cent certainty, and this is especially true when we factor in antecedent determinants. A man standing over a dead body with a gun in his hand, which still has smoke coming out of its barrel, and the bullets in which match the bullet that killed the victim, appears to be as guilty of the crime as it is possible to be. Until, that is, it is shown that he happened onto the scene very soon after the killing and picked up the gun after the real killer departed and left it behind.

So, because nothing can be completely known with 100 per cent certainty, the law has evolved standards of proof and rules as to who carries the burden of the same and when it is to be carried, so that verdicts can be reached and judgments made despite the fact that some doubt, even a scintilla of it, remains.

In civil litigation (non-criminal litigation), in Anglo-American jurisprudence, there are two standards of proof. The most prevalent is the 'proof by a preponderance of the evidence' standard, i.e. whoever has more and/or better evidence, and can thus convince the trier of fact (the judge or the jury) that there is a greater than 50 per cent chance that his or her claim or defence is true, prevails. The second is the 'proof by clear and convincing evidence' standard. This is a somewhat more difficult burden to carry than the preponderance of the evidence standard, because it means that the party carrying the burden must establish that the evidence presented during a trial is highly and substantially more likely to be true than not and the trier of fact has a firm belief or conviction of it. US states vary as to which standard of proof they require, but generally speaking, claims that involve fraud, wills, withdrawing of life support, civil liberty issues and equitable remedies will require clear and convincing evidence for a party to prevail.

In criminal litigation, the standard is 'proof beyond a reasonable doubt'. That is to say that to convict a defendant, the prosecution must establish, to the satisfaction of the trier of fact, that the defendant is guilty of the offence or offences charged to a degree that admits of no reasonable doubt. This burden of proof is obviously more difficult to carry than the burden under the two civil litigation standards, which is as it should be inasmuch as the issues in civil litigation relate to one's property, money, rights, privileges and prerogatives, whereas the issues in criminal litigation relate not only to money (fines), but also to one's liberty and even one's life.

And then there is a relic known as the 'scintilla of evidence rule' or just 'the scintilla rule'. Very little is heard about it these days, because it has been largely abandoned. It provides that a motion to remove the decision in a case from the trier of fact (summary judgment or directed verdict) will not be granted if there exists even the slightest amount of relevant evidence (a hint, a spark, a glimmer, a gleam, a trace) in favour of the non-moving party. Federal courts and almost all state courts have abandoned this rule in favour of the 'substantial evidence rule', which requires a party to provide adequate relevant evidence to support a claim, i.e. evidence that a reasonable person will consider adequate for supporting a conclusion. Some courts have gone as far as to say that a scintilla of evidence is no evidence at all. Let me say, in passing, and parenthetically, that despite its poor repute, the application of the scintilla rule to the death penalty makes eminently good sense to me. That is to say that no man or woman should be executed if there is a scintilla of evidence in favour of his or her innocence. The application of this rule in these circumstances would reduce the execution of innocents to near zero, which is disturbingly far from the case in American history.

Needless to say, all the standards of proof referred to above are highly subjective, i.e. exactly what do 'preponderance', 'clear and convincing', 'reasonable', 'scintilla' and 'substantial' really mean? The answer is that they don't 'really' mean anything; they mean what someone says they mean. In the immortal words of Lewis Carroll, in *Through the Looking Glass*, the sequel to *Alice in Wonderland*:

> 'When I use a word,' Humpty Dumpty said, in rather a scornful tone, 'it means just what I choose it to mean – neither more nor less.'
>
> 'The question is,' said Alice, 'whether you can make words mean so many different things.'
>
> 'The question is,' said Humpty Dumpty, 'which is to be master – that's all.'

Well, Alice had a master. And the law has masters too. They are triers of fact, i.e. judges, juries and appellate courts. They tell us what the words mean.

The standard of proof that applies to the criminal wrongdoing that is the subject of this book is, as previously said with respect to criminal litigation in general, 'proof beyond a reasonable doubt', which I have chosen to otherwise express as a 'smoking gun'. But let us be clear about what we mean when we speak of a smoking gun, because it is an ill-defined term. It is generally defined as a piece of incriminating evidence that is deemed to be 'incontrovertible'. That will not do, because, as we have seen above, even a smoking gun is controvertible. It has also been defined as an object or fact that is conclusive evidence of a crime or other wrongdoing. Again, 'conclusive' is too strong; it means that the case is closed, because the issue of guilt or innocence has been decided. But that is not true either, because even smoking gun evidence does not end a case; there is still rebuttal and the possibility, however remote, of neutralising the evidence. It has also been defined as 'unshakeable' evidence, which is again too strong; examples of 'unshakeable' evidence that has been shaken to its core are legion and superfluous. It has also been defined as the strongest kind of circumstantial evidence (evidence that implies that a person committed a crime) as opposed to direct evidence (evidence that directly links a person to a crime without the need for any inference). That seems to be true, but being the strongest kind of circumstantial evidence does not make it 'incontrovertible', 'conclusive' or 'unshakeable'.

Permit me to digress for a minute and say something about circumstantial evidence. It gets a bad rap. It is routinely denigrated as an inferior species of evidence, usually by placing an adjective, such as 'merely', 'only' or 'just' before it. It shouldn't be. Persons charged and tried for criminal wrongdoing are convicted on the basis of it every day, and there's nothing wrong with that. Though, as said, it is not incontrovertible, not conclusive and not unshakeable, the fact is that it is very strong evidence. For that reason, many, perhaps most, prosecutors prefer it to eyewitness evidence and material evidence, which are more easily impeached. Much of the evidence of Confederate complicity in the events of 14 April 1865, presented in this book, is, of necessity, circumstantial, because a writing in which a Confederate leader orders or directs someone to assassinate someone will never be found, for the very good reason that it never existed. No such order would ever have been committed to writing, even in code; it would have been given only verbally, directly to the operative or by courier, just as the orders to James P. Holcombe, Jacob Thompson, Clement C. Clay, Dr Luke P. Blackburn, Thomas Henry Hines and Thomas F. Harney were given, as we shall see. Accordingly, let us consider circumstantial evidence on its merits and not be led astray by a preconceived and erroneous notion of its inferiority.

It is also a fact that there is a well-known species of evidence that is stronger than a smoking gun, which is '*in flagrante delicto*', which means to be caught in the act of committing a crime. Being inferior to '*in flagrante delicto*' must mean that smoking gun evidence has a deficiency, that for all its strength, it is not flawless.

This book is intended to shed light on the issue of ultimate responsibility for the events of 14 April 1865, i.e. the assassination of President Abraham Lincoln and the attempted assassinations of Vice President Andrew Johnson, Secretary of State William H. Seward, Secretary of War Edwin M. Stanton, Lieutenant General Ulysses S. Grant and perhaps as many as ten other federal office holders. More specifically, it is intended to make a case against Confederate leaders for complicity in murder and attempted murder, and though we are not in a court of law, we must and we will apply a standard of proof to give the conclusions credibility.

The term 'Confederate leaders' contemplates, principally, President Jefferson Davis, Secretary of State Judah P. Benjamin, head of the Canadian Cabinet Jacob Thompson and his successor General Edwin G. Lee and most likely other members of the Canadian Cabinet, especially Charles Dunham (alias Sanford Conover), George N. Sanders, James Holcombe, Clement C. Clay and Dr Luke P. Blackburn. (The Canadian Cabinet is the casual name that was given to the contingent of the Confederate Secret Service that was headquartered in Canada, safely away from federal jurisdiction and, it was hoped, Union security and intelligence services.) These are the men sought to be found complicit in the events of 14 April 1865. In the trial of the conspirators, in addition to the eight defendants who were indicted (David E. Herold, George A. Atzerodt, Lewis Payne (Lewis Powell), Michael O'Laughlen, Edmund Spangler, Samuel Arnold, Mary E. Surratt and Samuel A. Mudd), the following persons were named as unindicted co-conspirators: Jefferson Davis, George N. Sanders, Beverly Tucker, Jacob Thompson, William C. Cleary, Clement C. Clay, George Harper, George Young and others unknown. Of these, all but the first were members of the Canadian Cabinet. (Note the absence of any reference to Judah Benjamin; he had fled to England, never to return to the United States.) There was obviously a need for the tightest secrecy, so it is entirely possible that no other government officials were involved. James Seddon, the Secretary of War, retired from public life on 1 January 1865, so he was not in office during the period that the plot ripened. His successor, John C. Breckinridge, is on record as decrying the assassination and telling Davis that he thought it would hurt the South. Vice President Alexander Stephens, never an enthusiastic Confederate (he opposed secession), was an incessant critic of Davis and for that reason was nearly always on bad terms with him. Furthermore, he and Lincoln had been close Whig allies when they were in Congress together in the 1840s. We may safely exclude all three of these men from complicity.

So let us proceed with the case against the Confederate leadership, conscious at all times that the purported smoking guns must establish guilt beyond a reasonable doubt, failing which the case is simply not made, and conscious, too, that though smoking guns do not preclude all doubt, the doubt, by definition, must be reasonable; a hint, a spark, a glimmer, a gleam or a trace, i.e. a scintilla of doubt, will not do.

John C. Fazio
Fairlawn, Ohio
1 June 2022

Preface

The Assassination of Abraham Lincoln

Abraham Lincoln, the 16th President of the United States and, in the view of most American historians, the greatest president in American history (a strong minority favours Washington), was a marked man from the moment he received the Republican Party's nomination for the US presidency on 18 May 1860. Food he received in celebration of his nomination was all found to be poisoned. Horace Greeley, editor and founder of the *New York Tribune*, the highest circulation daily in the United States at that time, estimated that Lincoln received 10,000 death threats during the period he was in office (one term and about six weeks). Most of these were discarded immediately by one or more of Lincoln's three secretaries – William O. Stoddard, John G. Nicolay and John Hay – who deemed them to be trash, unworthy of serious consideration. But about eighty of them were deemed to be realistic threats to the President and were therefore kept in an envelope, labelled 'Assassinations', in Lincoln's desk in the Executive Mansion (the White House).

Consistent with the foregoing, there were many attempts on Lincoln's life after his election. Perhaps as many as four occurred on his trip from Springfield, Illinois, his home, to Washington, DC, for the Inauguration, scheduled for 4 March 1861, a trip by rail that took about thirteen days. One of them, the so-called Baltimore Plot, organised by one Cipriano Ferrandini and a gang known as the National Volunteers, was frustrated by the Chicago Detective Agency, which was led by the great Alan Pinkerton (who would soon lend his talents as a detective, an investigator and a master of intelligence to the war cause) with help from the New York Police Department and Frederick Seward, son of Secretary of State William H. Seward, and others. This episode has been written about extensively, most recently in fine works by Suzanne

Jurmain, *Murder on the Baltimore Express: The Plot to Keep Abraham From Becoming President* (2021); Brad Meltzer and Jon Mensch, *The Lincoln Conspiracy: The Secret Plot to Kill America's 16th President – and Why it Failed* (2020); Ted Widmer, *Lincoln on the Verge: Thirteen Days to Washington* (2020); Daniel Stashower, *The Hour of Peril: The Secret Plot to Murder Lincoln Before the Civil War* (2013); and Michael J. Kline, *The Baltimore Plot: The First Conspiracy to Assassinate Abraham Lincoln* (2008).

That was only the beginning.

The conventional wisdom is that Lincoln, being fatalistically resigned to the ultimate success of anyone truly determined to kill him, took the matter of his assassination, if not casually, at least not as seriously as he could have, and for that reason did not go to extraordinary lengths to protect himself, and, further, that those who were charged with the responsibility of protecting him were similarly careless. The conventional wisdom is wrong again, as it is about so many things concerning Lincoln. Yes, he had an appreciation of the fact that there are many ways for a man to get at another man to kill him if the killer's determination to do so is exceeded only by his ability to do so. But that recognition did not preclude him from taking precautions against perceived threats to his safety, nor did it preclude his protectors from exercising their duties with great diligence and dedication. Ward Hill Lamon, Lincoln's best friend and self-appointed bodyguard (chief among many), put the matter this way:

> there never was a moment from the day he crossed the Maryland line, up to the time of his assassination, that he was not in danger of death by violence, and his life was spared until the night of the 14th of April, 1865, only through the ceaseless and watchful care of the guards thrown around him.[1]

Here are examples of the 'ceaseless and watchful care of the guards' that preserved Lincoln's life until 14 April 1865.

A body of cavalry was detailed by General James S. Wadsworth, Military Governor of Washington, to protect Lincoln when he made his way to and from the Soldiers' Home, which he did in the summer to escape the heat and humidity for which the Southern city of Washington is known. The

Soldiers' Home is a home for retired and disabled veterans of the United States Army. It is a Gothic Revival country 'cottage', which is located on a hill about 3 miles from the White House on approximately 250 acres of land. The Lincolns spent June to November there in 1862, 1863 and 1864. The body of cavalry detailed by Wadsworth was replaced in the summer of 1863 by a 100-man company of Ohioans, which was augmented by an infantry company from Pennsylvania, known as 'Bucktails'.

Beginning in October 1864, four members of the Washington Metropolitan Police were assigned to White House duty as plainclothes bodyguards, to be replaced from time to time, so that by the time of Lincoln's death, eleven had so served. They were armed with .38 calibre pistols. Their assignment was almost certainly related to the fact that the assassination threats against Lincoln had reached thousands in number, with a good number taken seriously by Lincoln's secretaries and by the President himself. It was also related to the fact that many incidents of a suspicious nature had occurred during Lincoln's period in office, incidents that were thought to have a good possibility of being assassination attempts and which showed signs of being something more than rogue operations. These included:

1. Information that came to the New York City Police Department that an attempt would be made on Lincoln's life at the Academy of Music on 20 February 1861, which information led to Lincoln's early departure from the Academy;
2. A carriage accident on 2 July 1863, attributed to a possibly sabotaged chassis, which accident seriously injured Mary Todd Lincoln, the First Lady;
3. Sudden illness in the Lincoln family on 19 November 1863, in Gettysburg, diagnosed as possibly a poisoning;
4. A fire in the White House stables on the night of 10 February 1864, in which all the animals stabled there perished;
5. Delivery to the White House, in early 1864, of shirts that were supposed to have been 'infected' with yellow fever, as a gift from an anonymous benefactor;
6. A shot that was taken at Lincoln as he rode alone towards the Soldiers' Home in August, 1864;

7. A possible poisoning of Lincoln by a drug prescribed for him and prepared by a pharmacy in the city that employed David Herold, one of John Wilkes Booth's co-conspirators;
8. Discovery of a letter in November 1864, on a New York City streetcar, which letter spoke of the assassination of Lincoln and of the failure of prior efforts to accomplish the deed;
9. An attempt by a poorly dressed and unclean man to access Lincoln aboard the *River Queen* at City Point, Virginia, in March 1865; and
10. An attempt by Booth to access and possibly assassinate Lincoln at the Inauguration on 4 March 1865.

On the last day of his life, especially, Lincoln went out of his way to secure protection. He surely sensed that with the war now over, his life was in greater danger than ever before, because of the hatred for him that he knew burned in the breast of many, North and South, a hatred unfulfilled and unresolved as long as the 6' 4" rail splitter and Great Emancipator continued to stride the earth. That Lincoln was in great fear for his life on the night of 14 April 1865 is supported by overwhelming evidence, including:

1. His hesitation to go to the theatre that night, indeed his expressed wish not to go, a position he changed only because he did not wish to disappoint the people, his attendance having been advertised, and because he believed that it was his wife's wish to go;
2. A recurring dream that portended his destruction;
3. Another dream that he had had some days previously that portended his assassination;
4. An illusion that portended a successful first term in office, but a premature termination of the second;
5. The eighty or so assassination threats that he and his secretaries took seriously enough to keep in an envelope in his desk;
6. His remarks to his bodyguard, William Henry Crook, in the afternoon of 14 April, which spoke of the reality of assassination and the impossibility of total defence against it; and
7. His farewell to Crook that day, namely 'Goodbye, Crook', as opposed to his usual 'Good night, Crook'.

Thus it was that Lincoln sought the protection that night of none other than the Lieutenant General of the Armies, Ulysses S. Grant, whom he knew, of course, would be accompanied by an all-but-impregnable retinue of guards. At a cabinet meeting on the 14th, Lincoln invited Grant and his wife Julia to accompany him and Mary Todd to the play. Grant initially accepted, but later declined when he received word from Julia that she preferred to visit family in Burlington, New Jersey. Julia's real reason was that she disliked Mary Todd, had recently been witness to one of her famous outbursts and therefore had no wish to spend an evening with her in a theatre box. Julia was only one of many who disliked the President's wife. Lincoln's secretaries, Nicolay and Hay, did not call her 'the Hellcat' for nothing. In any case, Grant declined the invitation. This caused Lincoln to seek the protection of another powerhouse, namely Major Thomas Eckert, the Assistant Secretary of War under Edwin M. Stanton. In asking Stanton for the loan of his subordinate that night, Lincoln told the Secretary that he had seen Eckert break five pokers over his arm, a demonstration of his physical capabilities, exactly the kind that Lincoln was looking for that night. Stanton, not wishing to encourage Lincoln, whom he had already tried to persuade to avoid the theatre that night, turned him down. But Lincoln wasn't finished. He went directly to Eckert with his plea for company. Not wishing to disappoint the Secretary, Eckert politely declined. That left only Major Henry Rathbone and his fiancée, Clara Harris, as company for the Lincolns that night. Ms Harris was the daughter of a United States Senator from New York, Ira Harris. The Major and Ms Harris had already been invited. Rathbone, who was a formidable soldier with an excellent war record, came within an inch of changing the course of history, but he could not give the same protection to Lincoln that night that either Grant or Eckert could have or would have.

Obviously, Lincoln wanted very much to be guarded that night, and carefully and competently. One has the impression that he sensed a gathering of circumstances that were not favourable to him, as most of us do from time to time, which circumstances did not auger well for his immediate future. He had somehow survived more than four years of war, interminable political strife and an unknown and unknowable number of attempts on his life. Despite every setback, disappointment and personal loss, he had finally been crowned with success. The Union would indeed be preserved, slavery would be dead and peace would come to the land. More than 600,000, perhaps as many as 750,000, in a population of fewer than 32 million, including almost 4 million slaves, had given the last full measure of devotion to assure these results. There appeared, however, to be one piece of the puzzle that wasn't quite in place yet. Lincoln certainly did not want to die, not consciously in any case, as evidenced by the fact that he sought the best protection he could get. And yet, there appeared to be a kind of rough justice to it if he did die. Why, after all, should 600,000 to 750,000 Americans pay the ultimate price while he toured Jerusalem with Mary Todd, which was a desire he expressed to his wife on their carriage ride earlier that day. One of Lincoln's bodyguards, William Henry Crook, put the matter this way:

> President Lincoln believed that it was probable that he would be assassinated. … On that last evening he … said with conviction that he believed that the men who wanted to take his life would do it. … More than this, I believe that he had some vague sort of warning that the attempt would be made on the night of the 14th. … To me it all means that he had, with his waking on that day, a strong prescience of coming change. As the day wore on the feeling darkened into an impression of coming evil.[2]

The ultimate failure of Lincoln's protection had less to do with the efficiency of that protection and his protectors than it had to do with the laws of probability, which is to say that if one takes enough shots at a target, sheer chance will almost guarantee that one of them will hit it. In addition to the attempts on Lincoln's life that took place before he became President, there were about a dozen known attempts during the period he was in office. The frequency of these attempts appeared to increase after the Wistar and Dahlgren-Kilpatrick raids against Richmond in early 1864 and the perceived licence granted by those raids, inasmuch as Wistar's orders provided for the capture of Confederate leaders (Jefferson Davis and his cabinet) and Dahlgren's orders provided for killing them. More will be said later about these raids and their consequences.

But there was another element that assured the success of the enterprise, namely pure chance. Unlike the experience of his co-conspirators, for whom almost everything that could go wrong that night went wrong, almost everything went right for John Wilkes Booth (from his perspective, of course), who reserved the principal target for himself. Part of his success, it must be said, was attributable to careful planning, as he himself later said, but part was simply good luck for him. Rathbone later said that he grasped the bottom of Booth's jacket as he went over the railing (the 'balustrade') of the box after the shooting, but couldn't hold it against Booth's momentum. Though Rathbone was nobody's plaything, a stronger man or a stronger grip could have made all the difference. Booth could have broken his tibia, the weight-carrying bone of the leg, instead of his fibula, in which case he would have been finished, because one cannot walk with a broken tibia. John F. Parker or another guard might have been in the passageway between the outer and inner doors of the box, where a bodyguard was supposed to be, but no one was there. Charles Forbes, who carried various titles of a subordinate nature, and who was guarding the outer door to the box, might simply have refused to grant Booth entry to the passageway that led to the box, but did not. Rathbone's shout – 'Stop that man!' – might have had a positive response, but did not. Booth's horse, held in the alley for him by 'Peanuts' John Burroughs, might simply not have been there, the highly-strung Bay mare being a bit too much for little John Burroughs to hold, but he held it there. Mounted pursuers might have overtaken Booth, but none even tried. And the guard at the Navy Yard Bridge, Silas Cobb, might simply have refused to allow Booth and Herold to cross, inasmuch as their request to do so was made after hours, but did not. Any of these possibilities might have caused the failure of Booth's assignment. Some would even have prevented the assassination, thereby changing the history of the world. But they did not.

In any case, the President's coachman, Francis P. Burke, picked up Major Rathbone and Ms Harris at Rathbone's residence and drove them to the White House in the White House carriage. The President and Mrs Lincoln then boarded the carriage and Burke then proceeded to drive the party to Ford's Theatre, less than a mile distant. John F. Parker, the President's armed guard that night, walked to the theatre and was there before the presidential party arrived at about 8:30. The play, *Our American Cousin*, a light British comedy, was in progress. When the presidential party entered the theatre, after being helped from the carriage to the pavement by Burke, it was escorted into the lobby by Parker and by John Buckingham, the doorkeeper. The party was then escorted to their seats in a dress circle box (off the first balcony, which was known as the dress circle) by Parker, by the President's footman and servant Charles Forbes and by James O'Brien, a theatre usher. As the party and their escorts were crossing the rear of the balcony to access the box, or, more accurately, the passageway that led from the outer door to the inner doors of the box, they were noticed by the audience. The play, naturally, was put on hold for a brief period, and the party was then treated to thunderous cheers and applause and the rising of almost all in the audience, as a gesture of profound respect for the President and his party and a recognition of the President's enormous accomplishments in the previous four years. When the party took their seats in the box, the cheering and applause subsided and the play resumed.

And so we come to Booth himself, the triggerman, the pawn, and his Great Crime.

Booth knew he had his hands full with his assignment. So real was the possibility of failure, that he provided for it. He gave his friend and fellow actor John Mathews, whom he met on Pennsylvania Avenue on the 14th, a letter that revealed his plans for the night, that justified them and that even named some of his co-conspirators (George Atzerodt, David Herold and Lewis Powell). He asked Mathews to deliver the letter to the *National Intelligencer*, a Washington tri-weekly, before 10:00 am the following day unless he made contact with him before that hour.

Further, in the period leading up to the assassination, Booth consumed copious amounts of alcohol, obviously needing a courage booster and something to settle him inasmuch as he was said to appear to be very stressed and even a bit unhinged, according to those who had occasion to observe him at the time. John Deery, who owned a billiard saloon above the lobby of Grover Theatre, later wrote that:

> For a period of about ten days before the assassination, he visited my place every day, sometimes in the afternoons,

> sometimes in the evenings. … During that last week at Washington he sometimes drank at my bar as much as a quart of brandy in the space of less than two hours. … I believe Booth was as much crazed by the liquor he drank that week as by any motive when he shot Lincoln.[3]

But Booth wasn't done drinking. He would continue to consume the stuff right up to his moment of truth. That his brain was addled is proved by his felt need to inquire of the office clerk at the National Hotel (where he always stayed when he was in Washington), in the morning of the 14th, as to what year it was. The clerk later said that Booth was troubled and agitated and looked unusually pale. Julia Grant said he had a wild look when she encountered him during the lunch hour at Willard's Hotel that day. Booth had another bottle of brandy as late as 4:00 pm on the 14th at Deery's. That afternoon, he encountered a journalist friend on Pennsylvania Avenue and engaged him in conversation. The friend later said that Booth's arms and body twitched and he appeared to be preoccupied. Later that day, Booth met an old schoolmate at Pumphrey's Stable. After the schoolmate listened to Booth for a while, he concluded that Booth was drunk. When he was at Ford's Theatre, he flitted in and out of Taltavul's Star Saloon, next door, still drinking as late as eight to ten minutes before the assassination. Jeannie Gourlay, an actress, observed Booth in the theatre and later said that he was so pale she thought he was sick. Others who observed him in the theatre described him as appearing to be drunk, having a peculiar glare in his eyes, having a hideous and fiendish expression, appearing to be crazy, looking terrible, with his eyes seeming to bulge from their sockets and his hair standing on end, and glaring like a wild beast.

We may safely conclude that Booth felt he needed a good lift to his courage, and found it, or thought he did, in that old standby known as John Barleycorn. It profoundly affected his brain and his comportment. It was in this state of mind and this condition that he descended upon Ford's Theatre on the night of 14 April 1865, as did President and Mrs Lincoln, all of whom kept their rendezvous with destiny and, incidentally, radically changed the course of American history.

The notion that Booth learned for the first time, at about midday, of the Lincolns' planned attendance at Ford's on the night of the 14th, when he went to the theatre to pick up his mail, and was so advised at that time by Henry Clay Ford, aka Harry Ford, and that all the preparations he made at the theatre that day were in consequence of receipt of that information, is puerile nonsense. Harry Ford was the Treasurer of Ford's Theatre and the man who arranged the presidential box, combining separate boxes 7 and 8 into one box for the presidential party. The truth is that Booth already knew with near certainty that the Lincolns would be at Ford's that night. His assignment was planned well in advance of its execution and part of the planning involved assuring that the President would be there at that time. Booth was very much a part of the Confederate Secret Service and therefore had his sources of information, only a part of which – as much as he thought they needed – reached his immediate action team (John Surratt, Lewis Powell, Samuel Arnold, Michael O'Laughlen, David Herold, George Atzerodt and the enablers, Dr Samuel Mudd and Mrs Mary Surratt, John's mother – a hodge-podge characterised by ill-will, incompetence, stupidity and incredibly bad judgment).

Picking up his mail was incidental to his true purpose of visiting the theatre in the afternoon. He waited until then, that is to say almost to the last minute, to make his final inspection of whatever changes may have been made to accommodate the presidential party and to make whatever preparations he felt were necessary to facilitate his purpose, because if he had made them sooner he risked seeing them undone, in whole or in part, by theatre carpenters or other personnel, or discovered to his detriment. Being very well known to just about everyone at the theatre who mattered, Booth had the run of the place and could therefore do just about anything he wanted to do there at just about any time. In any case, he found time that afternoon – probably less than half an hour, according to testimony given at the trial of the conspirators in 1865 and at the trial of John Surratt two years later – to do three things. The first was to fashion a 3½-foot long bar or brace from a hastily made music stand. The second was to cut, carve or gouge a hole in the wall, called a mortise, opposite the inside of the outer door to the passageway. He would later use these two feats of carpentry for the purpose of anchoring one end of the brace to the wall while the other end was jammed into the corner of the panel of the door itself, thereby making it nearly impossible for anyone to open the door from the outside to access the passageway, which is to say to interfere with his escape after the shooting. His third feat of carpentry was to make a hole, big enough to see through and therefore referred to as a 'peephole', in door No. 7, which opened into the presidential box and which was the door nearest the outer door. He did it with a gimlet and a knife or other sharp object.

Booth spent the greater part of the rest of the day drinking, renting a horse that he would need for the night, meeting with some of his co-conspirators, composing a letter to the editor of the *National Intelligencer*, chatting with fellow actor John Mathews and other friends and acquaintances, and even harassing the Grants, upon having his attention drawn to their carriage by Mathews during their chat on Pennsylvania Avenue. They were then being driven to the train depot from Willard's Hotel for the trip to New Jersey. He galloped past their carriage, stared into the same menacingly, and then doubled back and galloped past the carriage a second time, again staring menacingly at the occupants and putting a good fright into Julia especially. At about 6:00 pm, he had a drink or two with some of Ford's employees at Taltavul's. One of these was Ned Spangler, a scene shifter, said by many to have been a co-conspirator, but who in fact was guilty of nothing more than idolisation of a seriously warped actor. Spangler preferred fishing, crabbing and drinking to conspiracy. After the drinks, Booth made a final check of the theatre and then returned to the National Hotel for rest and dinner.

While at the National, he dressed for the evening. His dress included riding boots, spurs, a black frock coat, black pants and a black slouch hat. He carried his diary and he armed himself with a .44 calibre derringer, a single-shot pistol, which he loaded with a lead ball. He also carried a long hunting knife. He may have carried other arms, but we have no knowledge of them. He left the National, for the last time, near 8:00 pm.

Booth concluded his day, except for the finale at Ford's, by having a meeting with co-conspirators Powell, Herold and Atzerodt, and possibly John Surratt, at the Herndon House, where Powell had been staying. It was then and there that he allegedly made his final assignments, though we may be sure that Powell, dispatched to Booth from Mosby's Rangers some months earlier, already knew what was expected of him. (Mosby's

Rangers was a regimental-sized unit of partisan rangers, officially designated as 43rd Battalion, 1st Virginia Cavalry, which operated in northern Virginia.) Booth reserved Lincoln for himself. Powell, he said, would kill Seward. Atzerodt and Herold would put an end to Johnson. Atzerodt balked, which is why Booth double-teamed him with Herold. Grant would be murdered by an assassin who was aboard the train to Burlington, New Jersey. His identity is unknown to this day. John Surratt has been offered as a possibility, but the evidence does not favour that conclusion. Stanton would be murdered at his home by other agents. Their identities are also unknown. Michael O'Laughlen is suspected by some, but, again, the evidence is against it. Other federal officeholders may also have been targeted, but the evidence for such attempts is weak. The attacks were coordinated to take place at about 10:15 pm. Booth, Herold and Atzerodt would then meet in Maryland after crossing the Navy Yard Bridge, a rendezvous that would not be kept by Atzerodt, who chose, instead, to abandon Booth and Herold and retreat to a cousin's farm near Baltimore. The three would then ride to Surrattsville (about 10 miles from Washington), where they would pick up carbines and binoculars previously deposited there for them, and then make their escape, possibly even leaving the country. Powell would make his way to Baltimore and the safety of friends and supporters there.

Booth arrived at the rear of Ford's at about 9:30 pm, with his sprightly Bay mare. She was too restless to be tied up, so Booth summoned his good friend Ned Spangler and asked him to hold her until he came for her. Spangler, who couldn't do enough for his hero, accepted the assignment, but then, because of his responsibilities associated with the show, quickly sub-delegated it to little John C. Burroughs, who was known as 'Peanuts' and who agreed to help Ned. Booth then made his way through the theatre, using an underground passageway inasmuch as the show was on, and emerged near Taltavul's, where he stopped for some more courage-builder and nerve-settler. He was so rattled by the task that lay before him that he simply could not, or in any case he did not, sit still somewhere and then make his way to the President's box at the appointed time to fulfill his mission and then make his escape. Instead, he walked in and out of the theatre five or six times, each time looking around furtively, presumably to determine if anything unexpected, and therefore a possible stumbling block, was in evidence, or, conversely, if everything planned and arranged for was in place.

Despite all his planning, and the planning of those who controlled him, there remained great unknowns to Booth, unknowns that had to be known with certainty, or near certainty, to assure the success of his mission. The unknowns all had to do with the state of affairs in the passageway that lay between the outer door and the doors that led into the presidential box and the state of affairs in the box itself. There might be a security person in the passageway whom Booth was not aware of; the doors to the box might not be unlocked; the peephole he had drilled might have been noticed and repaired; the brace that he had placed in the passageway to keep the outer door closed against pursuers might not be where he left it; and, of course, the position of the occupants in the box had to be known exactly. To remove all doubt with respect to these unknowns, he would have to make a dry run, if he could. And he could. So he did. Here is Clara Harris's statement, given immediately after the assassination:

> Nearly one hour before the commission of the deed the assassin came to the door of the box, and looked in to take a survey of the position of its occupants. It was supposed at the time that it was either a mistake or the exercise of an impertinent curiosity. The circumstance attracted no particular attention at the time. Upon his entering the box again Major Rathbone arose and asked the intruder his business. He rushed past the Major without making a reply, and … fired.[4]

The unknowns were now known to Booth and he was thus ready to strike. He made a final pass or two in and out of the theatre and took his final libations at Taltavul's before entering the lobby for the last time shortly after 10:00 pm. From there he climbed the great staircase to the dress circle (the first balcony). He made his way along the rear of the balcony, incommoding several patrons (who later commented on his diabolical appearance), arriving at the outer door, which led to the passageway to the presidential box. There he encountered Charles

Forbes, the President's footman, messenger and personal attendant (in other words, a servant), who stopped him and engaged him in conversation, which was later described by observers as somewhat contentious. Booth was prepared for the obstruction. He gave Forbes a writing, which he supposed, correctly, would persuade Forbes to allow him to pass. No one knows exactly what Booth showed Forbes, but the evidence suggests strongly that it was an authorisation card of a kind frequently used during the period as a means of communication, inasmuch as there were no electronic means available, apart from the telegraph, which has no relevance here. Lincoln used these cards very often and so did everyone else in a position of authority. In fact, he had just made use of one earlier in the evening before departing for the theatre ('Allow Mr Ashmun and friend to come in at 9-AM tomorrow. A. Lincoln April 14, 1865'). Possibly Booth himself, or more likely the Confederate Secret Service, must have prepared such a card, which read more or less as follows: 'Allow Mr John Wilkes Booth to join me in the presidential box this evening.' It was known that Lincoln loved the theatre and valued his friendship with performers. A visit from a famous actor to Lincoln's box, therefore, would not have raised eyebrows, nor would it have compromised Booth's identity inasmuch as he considered his name his 'passport' and used no other name the entire evening, nor did he attempt to conceal his identity, as evidenced by his appearance on stage after the shooting, recognised by all. In any case, after some conversation between Booth and Forbes, the latter allowed Booth to pass into the passageway. With the outer door closed behind him, his heart, especially with all the alcohol coursing through his blood vessels, must have been beating like a locomotive. He nevertheless had the presence of mind to set the brace between the mortise and the inside panel of the outer door, thereby assuring that would-be pursuers would not be able to interfere with him when he made his escape.

His next step, after, perhaps, a peek through the peephole to make sure of Lincoln's position, was to gently push open door No. 8 to the box, which door was partially ajar, and step into the box with a loaded and fully cocked derringer and a big knife, variously described. The President was seated only a few feet from him now. Booth did not tarry. He took a step or two towards the President, levelled his single-shot derringer at the President's head at very close range, uttered at least one justification for his deed, most likely '*Sic semper tyrannis*' ('Thus always with tyrants'), possibly two justifications ('The South shall be free'), and fired. The lead ball struck the lower left side of Lincoln's head and penetrated through his brain before it came to rest just outside his right eye. The direction of the ball suggests that Lincoln may have been turning his head slightly to the left in response to a sense of Booth's presence. The wound was mortal. Most in the audience, by far, had no idea what was happening. Many deemed the report of the pistol to be part of the play. Needless to say, there was an uproar in the box, with all of its occupants, save the one who was mortally wounded, in various stages of consternation and disbelief. Most significantly, Rathbone attempted to subdue Booth, who struck him with the knife in an attempt to kill him. Rathbone parried the thrust with his left arm, which Booth's knife laid open between the elbow and the shoulder with a gash that was several inches deep, nearly causing Rathbone to bleed to death. Booth then climbed over the railing of the box, uttered another '*Sic semper tyrannis*', this time shouting it for the benefit of the entire audience, pulled himself free from Rathbone's grasp of the bottom of his frock coat and then clambered down to the stage, making use of the flagstaff to ease the final drop, but getting his spurs caught in the decorative flags of the box, so that he landed on the stage awkwardly, breaking the fibula of his left leg. He made another declamation upon his landing, probably, 'The South shall be free.' He then hobbled across the stage, made at least two more declamations ('*Sic semper tyrannis*' and something about revenge) and concluded his passage, before making his way to the back door, his horse and escape, by saying, almost to himself, 'I have done it.'

Pandemonium reigned in the theatre, of course. Several doctors made their way to the President's side, did what they could, which wasn't much, and then assisted in moving the President out of the box, down the stairs, through the lobby and into the street. They were looking for a good place for the President to spend his final hours, believing that a carriage ride to the White House would have been fatal. The owner of a boarding house that was almost directly across the street from the theatre (the Petersen House) appeared on the steps of the house and signalled its availability for Lincoln, and so he was brought there. He was placed at an angle on an undersized bed (most beds of the time were too small for the 6' 4" President) and attended by several doctors and visited by dozens of dignitaries through the night. At 7:22 the following morning, the President breathed his last, and history, once again, took a violent turn. When the President's death was clear to all, Secretary of War Stanton, who had largely taken command of the government since he was notified of the tragedy and summoned to the Petersen House, with tears flowing down his cheeks, uttered his immortal: 'Now he belongs to the ages.' Outdoors, a torrential rain had slowed to a drizzle. It was as if the grief of the heavens themselves had been spent and the period of acceptance of the awful reality was at hand.

The President of the United States was now dead. The rest is anticlimax and I will therefore not dwell upon it. Countless sources are available for descriptions of the aftermath, including Booth's escape, capture after twelve days as a fugitive, and killing by Boston Corbett, a Union soldier; the trial of the conspirators (i.e. Booth's immediate action team, including Dr Mudd and Mrs Surratt), and one innocent man (Spangler), and their disposition, including four executions (Powell, Mrs Surratt, Herold and Atzerodt); the attempted assassination of at least four and perhaps as many as fourteen other federal officeholders on the same night that Lincoln was assassinated; the breadth of the conspiracy; the ascension of Andrew Johnson to the presidency; the eleven years of Reconstruction that followed (1865–76); and last, but certainly not least, the fate of Mary Todd Lincoln. The poor woman had lost her beloved son Eddie, at the age of 3, to tuberculosis, her beloved son Willie, at the age of 11, to typhoid, her beloved husband, at the age of 56, to an assassin, and her beloved son Tad, at the age of 18, to pneumonia. Finally, she lost her mind. Who could blame her? She died of a stroke at age 63.

Introduction

The Confederate Government, the Confederate Secret Service and John Wilkes Booth

Another book on the assassination of Lincoln? Well, why not? It was one of the most profound events of the nineteenth century, some would say *the* most profound event that involved an individual rather than mass killing, and undoubtedly changed the course of history. Its effects are still being felt and no doubt will continue to be felt for the foreseeable future. Further, though much has been said and written about it, much remains to be, because it is a fascinating subject, even if a morbid one, with endlessly opening doors and therefore much controversy. This shouldn't surprise anyone; there is nothing more pervasive in all of human history than polarisation and conflict. It is what we do, and we do it because there is much more to it than facts and truth; in fact, nothing less than our very survival is involved, though we are not even aware of it.

There are many theories, of course, as to who was ultimately responsible for the assassination and the attempted assassinations that occurred on the night of 14 April 1865, in Washington. In addition to the simple conspiracy theory (John Wilkes Booth and his action team only), the following theories have found favour with historians and others at one time or another:

1. Vice President Andrew Johnson was complicit;
2. Secretary of War Edwin Stanton was complicit;
3. International bankers (e.g. the Rothschilds) were complicit;
4. The Roman Catholic Church was complicit;
5. Disaffected Northerners (Radical Republicans, Copperheads (aka Peace Democrats) and secret societies (e.g. the Knights of the

Golden Circle, later known as the Order of American Knights and the Order of the Sons of Liberty)) were complicit;

6. Lafayette Baker (head of the National Detective Police, aka the United States Secret Service) was complicit; and
7. The Confederate government and its Secret Service were complicit.

The list is by no means exhaustive, but the other theories are truly bizarre and therefore not worth discussing. All but the last of the seven theories listed have been largely discredited, though one can always find someone, even historians, who will embrace one or more of them and entertain the complicity of just about anyone, even Mary Todd Lincoln! But even the theory of Confederate complicity is having a hard time gaining footing. There are many historians, including Civil War and assassination historians, some of whom are prominent and accomplished, who have not been won over, who remain unconvinced by the theory or who maintain a more or less neutral position, saying that it is, after all, only a theory, unproven. Well, that introduces an interesting question, namely, at what point does an accumulation of facts cease to be a theory and become 'proven'? There are, be it noted, Holocaust deniers, even though the Holocaust is an absolute certainty. It is not a theory. It has never been a theory. It never will be a theory. To say that it is only that, therefore, is to say nothing. Similarly, there are climate change deniers, in the face of the fact that 97 to 98 per cent of climate scientists are on record as saying that climate change is a reality and that global warming is man-made. Similarly, there are substantial numbers of people who deny evolution, despite the fact that 97 per cent of the scientific community affirms it. Anyone can believe anything, or at least say they do, for reasons that have less to do with truth and more to do with bias, prejudice and self-preservation. There is a distinction to be made between belief – genuine belief or conviction – and the desirability of professing belief, for reasons most often not known even to oneself.

Immediately after the assassination of Lincoln and the near assassination of Seward, there was almost no doubt among Union leaders that Confederate leaders had planned both events and arranged for them to be carried out. Secretary of War Edwin M. Stanton, especially, and the War Department in general, were absolutely certain of it and strained every nerve to bring the supposed malefactors to justice. That certainty faded when the case against Confederate President Jefferson Davis and other unindicted co-conspirators collapsed at the trial of the conspirators. The trial was held in May and June 1865, in Washington, and resulted in the conviction of all eight defendants (Samuel Arnold, George Atzerodt, David Herold, Dr Samuel Mudd, Michael O'Laughlen, Lewis Powell, Edman Spangler and Mary Surratt) and the sentencing of four of them to death (Atzerodt, Herold, Powell and Mrs Surratt) and the other four to a penitentiary in Albany, New York, until Stanton changed his mind and sent them to Fort Jefferson in the Dry Tortugas, i.e. hell on earth. The case against the Confederate leaders collapsed because of perjury that was mixed with truth to deodorise it and then deliberately planted in the fertile minds of the military commissioners by three of the government's star witnesses (Richard Montgomery, Charles Dunham (who used the alias Sanford Conover) and James B. Merritt), which perjury was later exposed, as intended, thereby causing inculpatory evidence to be minimised and ultimately ignored. It was a brilliant and incredibly effective scheme masterminded by Dunham and George N. Sanders, another member of the Canadian Cabinet. Some may recall that the ploy was used with the same effect by Agatha Christie in her masterpiece *Witness for the Prosecution*.

The belief in Confederate complicity hibernated for about 123 years, with all the other theories displacing it. The simple conspiracy theory was easily the most popular and still is with a substantial number of those who contemplate such things: a half-mad actor (Booth) hated Lincoln so much, and was so distraught by the South's loss of the war, that he murdered him, at about the same time that one of his co-conspirators, Lewis Powell (aka Lewis Payne and many other aliases) almost succeeded in murdering Secretary of State Seward, and at about the same time that another of his co-conspirators, George Atzerodt, got cold feet and failed to even attempt to kill his target, who was Vice President Andrew Johnson. Then, in 1988, the lid was blown off the simple conspiracy theory by three dogged historians: William A. Tidwell, who had spent his entire adult life in government intelligence; James O. Hall, recognised among aficionados as the dean of assassination historians; and David Gaddy, a Senior Executive in the Department of Defense. The fruit of their labour, which is to say of their extensive and intensive research, was published under the title *Come Retribution*, a masterful and seminal work that concluded that Confederate leaders at the highest level had, in fact, been complicit in the assassination of Lincoln and the attempted assassinations of Seward and Johnson and that the initial certitude that Stanton and other Union leaders had had was justified after all. The authors did not, however, make a case for complicity in attempts to assassinate Stanton and Grant, apparently believing that fixing Confederate responsibility for those attempts was a bridge too far at the time. That deficiency was, it is believed, corrected in my earlier work, *Decapitating the Union: Jefferson Davis, Judah Benjamin and the Plot to Assassinate Lincoln*, a correction that continues, it is believed, in this work.

In 1994, Tidwell followed *Come Retribution* with a solo titled *April '65: Confederate Covert Action in the American Civil War.* He came to the same conclusions he did with his co-authors in 1988 and, in fact, strengthened them, again with a diligent pursuit of, and a love of, truth.

The number of historians who have affirmed Tidwell, Hall and Gaddy's findings and conclusions is increasing.

William Hanchett, a prominent Civil War historian, wrote that *Come Retribution* 'is based upon far more substantial and imaginative research than any previous work on the assassination'. He also wrote that *April '65* 'powerfully supplemented *Come Retribution*'.[1]

Further, Richard N. Current, a well-known Lincoln scholar, wrote, in his review of *Come Retribution*, that the authors' conclusion is made 'with justification'.[2]

Still further, Stephen W. Sears, another leading Civil War historian, wrote, in his review, that 'it is hard to put this book down without acknowledging that this is the way it must have happened'.[3]

And still further, H. Donald Winkler joined Hanchett, Current and Sears in their support of Tidwell, Hall and Gaddy when he wrote that:

> Sanders went on to expose Dunham/Conover, Merritt and Montgomery as liars, thereby discrediting the efforts of

> Stanton, Holt and Johnson to blame the Confederacy for the assassination. … Sanders's propaganda effort paid off. By exposing the chief Union witnesses as liars, the government's case collapsed, even though credible witnesses had indeed submitted untainted affidavits implicating the Southern President and the Confederates in Canada. … Since Dunham/Conover, Merritt and Montgomery were all disgraced as witnesses, Finnegass's [*sic*] testimony and that of other reliable witnesses was not taken seriously. The credibility of all the government witnesses was marred by the fabrications of the three. … For his [Davis's] freedom, he owed a tremendous thank you to the covert operations of George N. Sanders and Charles Dunham. … Thanks to the work of these two men, Clement C. Clay was also released from prison [in April 1866] and returned to his home in Alabama.[4]

It is the purpose of this book to follow in the footsteps of Tidwell, Hall, Gaddy, Hanchett, Current, Sears and Winkler, and others unnamed, by proving, beyond a reasonable doubt, and perhaps even beyond a scintilla of doubt, by the use of clear and convincing evidence, which I have denominated 'smoking guns', that the Confederate government and its Secret Service were complicit in the assassination of Abraham Lincoln and, in fact, complicit in an all-out effort to decapitate Union leadership in the closing days of the Civil War. It should be added that the acceptance of that conclusion does not preclude the acceptance of one or more of the other theories mentioned above. The Confederacy, after all, had many friends in the North. Jefferson Davis himself said, in 1862, that if it were necessary, he (or we) had friends enough in the North to destroy the President and every head of the departments.[5] And Jacob Thompson, head of the Canadian Cabinet until he was replaced near the end of the war, wrote to Judah Benjamin, in December 1864, writing, *inter alia*, that, 'Indeed, I have so many papers in my possession, which in the hands of the enemy would utterly ruin and destroy very many of the prominent men in the North, that a due sense of my obligation to them will force on me the extremist caution in my movements.'[6] Many of these friends of the Confederacy in the North, and I have barely scratched the surface as to their number and influence, could have contributed, and most likely did contribute, in some degree and in some way, to the events of 14 April 1865.

There were at least a dozen assassination attempts against Lincoln from the date of his election (6 November 1860) to the date of his second Inauguration (4 March 1865). It cannot be said, obviously, that the Confederate Secret Service was behind all of them, but it is probable that it had a hand in at least some of them. When we stop to think about it, it is really quite simple. What happened in our Civil War is what happens in virtually all wars: the Black Flag rules. It begins with the first atrocity, which initiates a cycle of violence that doesn't end until the war does, and sometimes not even then. When the cycle begins, man's inhumanity to man is without limit. The pages of our war, indeed of virtually all wars, are soaked with the blood and littered with the bones of the victims of the Black Flag, and if the pages could speak, they would assail our ears with the victims' screams. And let there be no mistake: both sides were guilty. Yes, the Confederacy carried out a year of terror plots against the North (spring 1864 to spring 1865), including an attempt to spread pestilence and the assassination of Union leaders. But, yes, the Union raped the Shenandoah Valley, burned Atlanta, pillaged and plundered Georgia and burned Columbia, South Carolina. For every wanton killing of Union prisoners of war, there was the same for Confederate prisoners, such as the twenty-three Confederate soldiers who were shot to death, in cold blood, by a Wisconsin unit after the battle of Resaca.[7] And for every Andersonville, there was an Elmira ('Hellmira', the prisoners called it). Obviously, one could go on and on in this vein, but the point has been made.

The Confederacy's back was to the wall. The catastrophe that Southerners had fought for four years to prevent was now upon them: the loss of their political independence; the loss of their property and wealth; the loss of their lifestyle and culture; the 'nightmare' of integrating almost 4 million suddenly free slaves into a society of 5½ million whites; and the possible 'mongrelisation' of their race. Their armies were melting away, with massive and irreplaceable battlefield losses and losses due to desertion. Their treasury was all but empty and their resources all but depleted. In these circumstances, it was perfectly predictable – and Seward, in fact, did predict it – that Southern leaders would resort to the most extreme measures, including multiple assassinations, if such measures offered any hope at all of averting the catastrophe. Had the Union been in such dire straits, it is all but certain that Northern leaders would have done the same.

Let us manfully face and accept the truth, with all its grit, grime and gore. A painful truth is better than a soothing lie any day. The truth is that we are all the same animal and have the same nature, which means that we are all capable of good and evil, Davis and Lincoln no less than the rest of us. The truth, further, is that the likelihood of recourse to unconventional warfare is directly proportional to the degree to which we feel that our survival is threatened. Davis proved both truths by approving a policy of summary execution of black prisoners of war, later modified to provide for turning them over to state courts for trial and hanging;[8] by authorising, with Benjamin, a year of 'dirty war', i.e. terror, against the North; and by ordering his Secret Service to play its last card, namely the decapitation of the United States government by multiple assassinations. Lincoln proved the truths by ignoring the Constitution when it suited him, suspending the writ of habeas corpus without authority, closing newspapers, abrogating free speech, incarcerating or exiling his political enemies, including entire legislative bodies, without trial, and, with Stanton, ordering the capture or killing of Davis and his cabinet by raiders against the Confederate capital, which we will cover in some detail in Chapter One.

In making the case for Confederate complicity, there is a common and essential thread that runs through all four of the smoking guns that follow this introduction. If it is true, then everything else falls into place like the pieces of a jigsaw puzzle. If it is not true, then the case is not made, despite the fact that the facts presented are just that – facts, not suppositions, not surmises, not guesswork and not theories, unless expressly identified as such. I speak of the relationship between Booth and the Confederate government and its Secret Service. I contend that Booth was an agent of the Secret Service, by which I mean that he worked for, under authority of, and pursuant to orders from, that Service and/or its superiors in the Confederate government, principally Davis,

Benjamin and, while he was in office, James Seddon, the Secretary of War. As such, he was at all times, since early 1864 if not earlier, known to the government and the Service and maintained a close relationship with both in Richmond and in Canada. He was never a rogue agent. It is not prerequisite to his agency that he took an oath or underwent an initiation rite, though he might have. The formalities of becoming an agent are not important; the substance of being an agent is important. If he worked for, accepted the authority of, and followed the orders of the Secret Service and/or its superiors, then he was an 'agent' of that Service, irrespective of how that status may be technically defined. In this connection, here are eighteen facts that support the thesis just stated:

1. John Surratt, Jnr, was a Secret Service agent from 16 May 1863,[9] if not earlier. He worked closely with Booth from 23 December 1864,[10] if not earlier, and was, in fact, Booth's right hand. He was also Confederate Secretary of State Judah Benjamin's most trusted courier,[11] meeting with Benjamin in Richmond almost weekly[12] and, the evidence suggests, with Jefferson Davis occasionally as well.[13] It is likely that Benjamin chose Surratt to be his courier so that he could monitor Booth and his action team; it is most unlikely that Benjamin was ignorant of Surratt's work with Booth when he chose him to be his courier. It is all but impossible to believe that in all the meetings between Surratt and Benjamin and Davis, Surratt never mentioned Booth and his team. Benjamin and Davis, therefore, had to know from this source about Booth and his team and what they were doing and what they were not doing.
2. Top Secret Service agent Thomas Harbin was close to Booth. They met for the first time on 18 December 1864, in Bryantown, Maryland, if not earlier. The meeting was arranged by Dr Samuel Mudd.[14] Harbin met with Booth again before the assassination and he met with him after the assassination when Booth was a fugitive. Harbin was identified by Atzerodt, in his 1 May 1865 confession, as being a participant in Booth's conspiracy. After the assassination, Harbin left the country for an indeterminate period, possibly as long as five years.[15] Later, when it was safe to do so,

he spoke about his activities as a Secret Service agent and, among other things, said that he reported directly to Davis.[16] Davis and therefore Benjamin had to know about Booth and his team from this source, in addition to what they learned from John Surratt.

3. Samuel Arnold, a member of Booth's action team, wrote, in his memoirs, that, 'There were occasions before I had become acquainted with the fact that others than Surratt and ourselves … were connected in the enterprise.'[17] This statement shows clearly that Booth was working with others besides his action team. We may surmise that they were also Secret Service agents.
4. Lewis Powell said to his interrogator, Assistant Secretary of War Thomas T. Eckert, that it was his impression that arrangements had been made with others for the same disposition of other federal office holders as he was to make of Seward,[18] thus demonstrating the participation of other agents, known to Booth, in the events of 14 April. Powell also told Eckert that federal prosecutors 'did not have the one-half of them',[19] i.e. conspirators, again demonstrating the breadth of the conspiracy and the participation of agents known to Booth who were not of his action team. To his spiritual counsellor, Rev Dr Abram Dunn Gillette, Powell said that he thought others involved had not been apprehended[20] and that he did not know the names of the principal men collaborating with Booth,[21] all of which, again, attests to the breadth of the conspiracy and to Booth's conspiring with other Confederate agents.
5. Booth was in New Orleans for about three weeks in early 1864. While there, he met with Confederate agents George Miller and Hiram Martin. Both names sound like aliases. One or both of these agents may have recruited him and possibly even given him some training. Miller was known to have ties to high-ranking Confederate officials. He is also known to have corresponded for some time with Booth after he left New Orleans. Martin was a blockade runner. By the end of the summer, Booth was in regular contact with Confederate agents and was familiar with their cipher system.[22]
6. Booth was in Montreal for ten days in October 1864 (18 to 27), where he met and hobnobbed with many Secret Service agents,

all members of the Canadian Cabinet, including such prominent figures as Jacob Thompson, George N. Sanders and Patrick Martin. There is some evidence that Booth made more than one trip to Canada in 1864, but it is weak.[23]

7. Booth met with four Secret Service agents at the Parker House in Boston on 26 July 1864. Three were from Canada, one from Baltimore. Shortly thereafter, in early August, he began gathering a team whose purpose he represented to be the kidnapping of Lincoln, which, he said, was perfectly legitimate under the laws of war.[24]
8. Booth spent much time at Mary Surratt's boarding house in Washington when he was in that city, meeting often with Mrs Surratt, her son John and other members of his action team. The boarding house was a safe house for Confederate operatives of every variety – spies, blockade runners, couriers, etc., who came and went at all hours of the day and night. Known visitors included Confederate agents Augustus Howell, Sarah Slater, Thomas Nelson Conrad and Benjamin Franklin Stringfellow. Booth was thus exposed to substantial numbers of the Confederate underground, and they to him.
9. Booth spent much time in New York, meeting with agents and Copperheads (Peace Democrats) there and with sources of funds. In November 1864, he met with five of the richest and most powerful men in the country – all anti-Lincoln – at August Belmont's Fifth Avenue mansion. They were Belmont, General George McClellan, Fernando Wood, Mayor of New York, Charles A. Haswell, a ship designer and secessionist, and Jerimiah Larocque, senior partner of a prominent Copperhead law firm in New York. By meeting with such as these, Booth demonstrated that he was well known not only to lower and middle level agents in the Secret Service, but also to those who had their hands on the levers of power and the bank accounts to make things happen. Atzerodt, in one of his confessions, made reference to Booth's meeting with 'the New York crowd'. And Louis Weichmann, a boarder in Mrs Surratt's boarding house and a key witness in the trial of the conspirators in 1865 and the trial of John Surratt in 1867, stated, in the latter trial, that Booth had mentioned being

entertained in New York at 'an elegant mansion'. David Black, one of Belmont's biographers, who was originally skeptical of the report of Booth's presence at the meeting, has reversed himself and now believes that the evidence of it is clear and convincing.[25]

10. Booth's sister, Asia Booth Clarke, wrote memoirs. She spoke at length about her brother. Among other things, she said he told her that he was in the underground and that the work required travel. She spoke of his unexplained trips, of strange visitors at all hours, and of his calloused hands 'from nights of rowing'. She wrote:

> He often slept in his clothes on the couch downstairs, having on his long riding boots. Strange men called at late hours, some whose voices I knew, but who would not answer to their names; and others who were perfectly strange to me. They never came farther than the inner sill, and spoke in whispers.[26]

11. Booth's fellow actor from New York, Samuel Knapp Chester, whom Booth tried, but failed, to recruit into his conspiracy, testified at the trial of the conspirators. Among other things, he said he met Booth in New York in the latter part of December 1864, or early January, and that Booth:

> said everything was in readiness, and that there were parties on the other side ready to co-operate with them. By these parties I understood him to mean the rebel authorities and others opposed to our Government. He said there were between 50 and 100 persons engaged in the conspiracy.[27]

Let us grant that 50 to 100 is too high; secrecy would have been impossible with such a number. Booth was obviously laying it on thick to induce his friend to sign on. Let us, rather, pay greater attention to what Chester understood Booth to mean by 'parties on the other side' and exactly what that means as far as Booth's connection to 'rebel authorities and others opposed to our Government' is concerned.

12. A letter dated 10 May 1865 was sent from Paris by a Union agent to another Union agent in the States. In it, he spoke of having

read a 'note' from a Confederate agent who said he had been watching Grant for two days, which is further indication of the scope of the conspiracy. He also said he arrived in Washington at 5.00 p.m. on the day of the assassination and within half an hour knew that an attack was going to be made that night. He left the following morning, he said, for Richmond, from where he wrote and sent his note to another Confederate agent in Paris. The Union agent said the Confederate agent identified himself as 'Johnston', which is probably an alias. In addition to what he said about Grant and about his arrival in Washington and when he knew an attack would be made that night, 'Johnston' said, 'Booth will never be taken. He will bullet himself first.' This sentence is quite telling inasmuch as it demonstrates that Booth was well known to the Confederate underground. 'Johnston' also said that if everything had gone according to plan on 14 April, fifteen Yankees would be dead, not one, which is still further indication of the breadth of the conspiracy and the number of agents involved.[28]

13. A letter dated 10 April, but postmarked 17 April, was sent to Booth at the National Hotel in Washington. It read, in pertinent part, as follows:

> I have sent word to Harry to be on the watch for Seward. … You watch the box book at Ford's Theatre. Laura Keene being a great favorite there, there is no doubt but the President and acquaintances will wish to see her performance. … George has the plan fixed for the Secretary and for Stanton. If the four are assassinated our wrongs are avenged. I am all right about my victim. I could have killed him a week ago, but I am waiting for yours. We had a meeting the other night. I was elected Captain of the gang. There is one man to everyone in the Cabinet. …We are all armed. Yours Truly, T.I.O.S.[29]

The letter tells us a great deal about the degree to which Booth worked with others besides his team to decapitate the government, which fits with the attempts on the lives of Stanton and Grant, to say nothing of the other ten who were to have been assassinated according to 'Johnston' in the 10 May 1865 letter quoted above.

14. A letter addressed to Booth by Sam Arnold and found in Booth's hotel room after the assassination reads, in pertinent part, as follows:

    > I was one with you. Time more propitious will arrive yet. Do not act rashly or in haste. I would prefer your first query, 'go and see how it will be taken at R______d' (i.e. Richmond), and ere long I shall be better prepared to again be with you.

    Also found in Booth's hotel room was a Confederate cipher key that was identical to one found in Secretary of State Judah Benjamin's office in Richmond after he evacuated the city on 2 April 1865. The letter and the cipher key demonstrate, rather plainly, that Booth's conspiracy was directly connected to, and subordinate to, the government in Richmond.[30]

15. Booth met Dr Samuel Mudd for the first time on 12 or 13 November 1864, in Bryantown, Maryland.[31] They met again on 18 and 23 December, at least.[32] They were therefore quite well known to each other by the spring of 1865. Dr Mudd was one of many prominent men and women in lower Maryland who were part of what was known as 'the mail line', i.e. individuals who, as the name suggests, carried written and verbal communications between Richmond and Washington and other Northern cities and even to Canada. These men and women now became known to Booth as well. Dr Mudd's home was another Confederate safe house, heavily trafficked by operatives of every stripe. He was therefore a well-known figure in the Confederate underground and hence well known to Confederate leaders. An entirely new door to the underground was thus opened to Booth. We gain some idea of the opening and its potential for Booth from a witness at the trial, namely Mary Simms, one of Dr Mudd's slaves. In speaking of Surratt, she said that in the summer of 1864, 'He came often. He was there almost every Saturday night to Monday night, and when he would go to Virginia and come back he would

stop there.' She went on to say that other Confederate visitors all slept in the woods, but came into the house to eat. She added, 'I have seen Surratt in the house, up stairs and in the parlor with Dr Mudd. They never talked much in the presence of the family; they always went off by themselves up stairs ....'[33] Clearly, Dr Mudd was very much a part of the Confederate underground and involved in clandestine operations for the Confederacy. And so was Surratt. And so, therefore, was Booth.

16. Henry Finegas testified for the prosecution at the trial. He was a commissioned officer of the United States. Unlike other prosecution witnesses Richard Montgomery, Charles Dunham (Sanford Conover) and James B. Merritt, no accusation of perjury was made against him. He said that on 14 or 15 February 1865, he overheard a conversation at the St Lawrence Hall in Montreal, the headquarters of the Secret Service in Canada, between Canadian Cabinet members George N. Sanders and William Cleary, which he described as follows:

    Cleary: I suppose they are getting ready for the Inauguration of Lincoln next month.

    Sanders: Yes, if the boys only have luck, Lincoln won't trouble them much longer.

    Cleary: Is everything well?

    Sanders: O, yes; Booth is bossing the job.[34]

    No comment is necessary.

17. Thomas A. Jones was the Chief Agent of the Confederate Secret Service in Maryland. In 1893, when it was safe to do so, he wrote and published a book of his exploits as a Secret Service agent and, among other things, said that he knew all about Booth and his conspiracy. Needless to say, if *he* knew, how could his superiors in Richmond not know?[35]

18. Beware the premature disclaimer. Beware of volunteered exculpatory statements. In late November 1864, Booth stopped in Philadelphia to see his sister, Asia. Before leaving, he gave her

a packet and asked her to open it, alone, if she did not see him again. After the assassination, she opened it. Among other things it contained a letter addressed 'To Whom It May Concern', which was apparently meant for his brother-in-law, Asia's husband, John Sleeper Clarke. In pertinent part, this is what it said:

> Right or wrong, God judge me, not man … This country was formed for the *white*, not for the black man. And looking upon *African slavery* from the same standpoint held by those noble framers of our Constitution, I for one have ever considered it one of the greatest blessings (both for themselves and us) that God ever bestowed upon a favored nation. … Alas … day by day has she (the American flag) been draged [*sic*] deeper and deeper into cruelty and oppression. … A Confederate, at present (deleted in the original by Booth) doing duty *upon his own responsibility*.[36]

Need it be said that Booth's completely voluntary exculpation of Confederate complicity in his conspiracy is proof positive of it? And why did he delete 'at present'? Had it ceased to be true?

Now, having established beyond a reasonable doubt, and perhaps even beyond a scintilla of doubt, that Booth was, at all times relevant to the assassination of Lincoln, a Confederate agent and very much a part of the Confederate underground, and that, conversely, he was never a rogue agent, we may move on. I ask that the reader keep this fact uppermost and at all times in mind as we consider the smoking guns that prove, again beyond a reasonable doubt, and perhaps even beyond a scintilla of doubt, that Booth was a Confederate pawn, albeit an important and valuable one, who died in the effort, that four of his grunts and hatchet men went to the gallows and the other four to the Dry Tortugas (Fort Jefferson), and that the masterminds walked.

Chapter One

The First Smoking Gun: Godfrey Joseph Hyams and His Counsellors

Black Flag warfare is defined, generally, as warfare without law or convention, in which, therefore, no holds are barred, no quarter is asked for or given, no prisoners are taken and no atrocity is unacceptable. Such warfare was very much a part of the American Civil War from its inception, indeed even of the preliminary hostilities that preceded the opening guns, i.e. 'Bleeding Kansas' and the Missouri-Kansas Border War. Nevertheless, in early 1864, two incidents occurred, both of the same species, that kicked the conflict up to a new level of war without conscience, a level in which even insurrections, multiple assassinations of political leaders, biological and chemical warfare, poisoning of water supplies, burning of metropolises, rapacious raiding of helpless towns, and sabotaging anything, even if it meant killing vast numbers of innocents without tactical purpose, were planned for and in some cases carried out. The incidents were raids, or, more accurately, attempted raids, by Union cavalry on Richmond. They are identified by the names of their commanders.

The Wistar Raid

The first such raid, the Wistar Raid, was under the command of Brigadier General Isaac J. Wistar and took place on 6 and 7 February 1864. Wistar was under the command of Major General Benjamin F. Butler, the infamous 'Beast' Butler of New Orleans fame, also known as 'Spoons' Butler because of his habit of purloining silverware from the homes of wealthy Southerners. The genesis of this raid actually went back to May 1863. In that month and year, paroled Union officers, who had been imprisoned in Richmond, reported to their superiors that, in fact, the Confederate capital was poorly defended. One such officer was General August Willich, who met with President Lincoln on 8 May and gave him that message. In response, Lincoln sent General Joseph Hooker a telegram advising him that, based on this information, it was his judgment that Richmond could be burned and Confederate President Jefferson Davis captured.[1]

For the first time, therefore, the thought of burning Richmond and capturing Davis had apparently found favour with Lincoln. The thought might have died there but for another happening, namely the fact that Lincoln was made aware of the dreadful condition of Union prisoners of war in Confederate prisons in Richmond (Libby and Belle Isle). He was made aware, too, by Elizabeth Van Lew, a Union spy in Richmond, whose dispatch was directed to Butler that because of overcrowding, and to make their rescue by Union forces less likely, the Confederates planned to ship prisoners from the Richmond prisons to a new prison in a remote area of the Confederacy.[2] This was the infamous Andersonville, in Georgia. For these reasons, Lincoln came under great pressure to do something about the prisoners before they were beyond anyone's reach. Believing, as said, that Richmond was lightly defended, per the reports of the paroled Union officers, and that the beleaguered prisoners were in desperate and immediate need of help, the idea of a raid appeared to make good sense to him. Accordingly, he and Secretary of War Stanton gave Butler the green light. But no one, it appears, gave sufficient attention to Van Lew's admonition that Confederate strength and desperation should not be underestimated and that the attempt to liberate the prisoners should not be made 'with less than 30,000 cavalry, and from 10,000 to 15,000 infantry to support them, amounting in all to 40,000 to 45,000 troops'.[3] Despite this intelligence, Butler proposed to make the raid with 6,200 men. Their purposes would be to: 1) Liberate as many prisoners as possible from Confederate prisons; 2) Destroy public buildings, other public property, commissary stocks and communications, cut wires, etc., and blow up the Tredegar Iron Works; and 3) Capture President Davis and his cabinet.[4]

Butler's man for the job was Wistar, who agreed with Butler's view that the three objectives of the raid could be realised with relative ease. Diversionary demonstrations were ordered and carried out at Raccoon's Ford and Morton's Ford on the Rapidan River. Despite these demonstrations, the raid failed, principally because the Confederates had enough advance notice of it (at least sixteen hours) to be ready and waiting for the raiders at the key crossing points on the Chickahominy River, but also because Butler had disregarded Van Lew's admonition as to the number of troops required and as to the direction of the attack.[5] In any case, when Wistar realised that the element of surprise was gone, he abandoned the effort and retreated, pursuant to his orders.[6]

The failure of the raid had unintended consequences that were relevant to the events of 14 April 1865, i.e. the attempt to decapitate the United States government by assassinating Lincoln, Stanton, Johnson, Seward and Grant, at least. Wistar's orders to capture 'the leaders of the rebellion' were published in the Richmond newspapers, which, not surprisingly, put a more sinister twist to them than they deserved, bad as they were. The claim was made that the raid was intended to free prisoners, which was true, but also to assassinate President Davis, which was not.[7]

Confederate leaders and the Southern press were convinced that Wistar's raid was personally approved by Lincoln. It was inconceivable to them that Lafayette C. Baker, head of the National Detective Police (the Union Secret Service), whose District of Columbia cavalry unit was part of Wistar's force, could have been involved without Lincoln's knowledge. Later, the similarity of Wistar's orders and those of Colonel Ulric Dahlgren confirmed that judgment. Once again, perception was more important than reality, and the perception was that the Chief Magistrate of the United States had ordered the death of the Chief Magistrate of the Confederate States. That perception signalled an entirely new perspective of the war from the Confederate side. As Davis saw it, a backwoods buffoon in Washington was making war on sovereign states sooner than allow those states to exercise their sovereign right of secession from his Union. Further, he, Davis, had nevertheless asserted his common humanity with the teller of ribald and salacious jokes and stories by sending him and his wife, Mary Todd Lincoln, condolences on the loss of their son, Willie, in February 1862. And further still, the buffoon's response to that gesture was not to reciprocate with a humane gesture of his own, but to carry on the war, destroy the engine that drove the Southern economy by emancipating the slaves, score major victories in the field in 1863 (Gettysburg and Vicksburg) and then order the death of his political counterpart in 1864. We may safely credit all of these convictions except the last.

Matters might not have deteriorated further if the idea of raiding Richmond had been abandoned, but it wasn't. The reason for Wistar's raid – the condition of Union prisoners of war and their impending transfer – had in no way been affected by Wistar's failure. Lincoln remained committed to the idea of rescue and resolved to give it another try.

The Dahlgren-Kilpatrick Raid

Unlike the Wistar Raid, this second raid, named for Colonel Ulric 'Ully' Dahlgren and Brigadier General H. Judson Kilpatrick, who led it, ran into opposition from the leadership of the Army of the Potomac. And with good reason: because it was as poorly conceived as the Wistar Raid. It was the brainchild of Kilpatrick, called 'Kill-cavalry' because of his reputation for bravery and recklessness. Having made a name for himself by his participation in General George Stoneman's raid on Richmond in May 1863, which had some success on the outskirts of the city, Kilpatrick thought himself qualified to address Lincoln directly as to his plans, and so he did. Being eager and under pressure to do something about the men languishing in Richmond's prisons, and equally eager to disseminate his December 1863 offer of amnesty to Southerners who would repudiate secession and declare their allegiance to the Union, Lincoln was disposed to accept Kilpatrick's proposal, and so he authorised him to proceed. General George Gordon Meade, who commanded the Army of the Potomac at the time, officially endorsed the plan, because he felt that something had to be done about the prisoners, but he thought it was ill conceived and had scant hope of success and therefore disassociated himself from it.[8]

As a condition of Lincoln's approval, Kilpatrick would be joined in the effort by Colonel Dahlgren, who was all of 21 years old and the son of Rear Admiral John A. Dahlgren, who commanded part of the federal blockade and for whom the famous 11-inch naval cannon was named. Ully was also personally known to and well liked by the President. These facts were well known by the Confederate government and had much to do with that government's conviction that the raid was personally approved by Lincoln.

With a force of between 3,000 and 4,000 cavalry (woefully fewer than the number recommended by Van Lew), including men under both Kilpatrick's and Dahlgren's commands who were known as 'pioneers' and who were armed with turpentine, oakum and torpedoes for the purpose of burning the city, the attack began on 28 February 1864. As with the Wistar Raid, the attack was aided by diversionary demonstrations against Confederate forces who were not in the immediate vicinity of Richmond. This included a raid by Brigadier General George Armstrong Custer into Albemarle County. Despite this, the raid was doomed before it began, because the Confederacy had ears all over Washington and Union tongues were wagging all over town about the raid, particularly after Ully Dahlgren got into it and especially in Willard's Hotel.[9]

Virtually everything that could have gone wrong with the raid did. The weather was terrible, with heavy rains, sleet and ice, and Dahlgren's black guide could not find a place to cross the James River, which was swollen because of the rain. During the night of 2/3 March, Dahlgren's force was ambushed, most of the men under his command were captured and he was killed. The raid was a complete failure, due to lack of surprise, lack of enough men, lack of decent weather and lack of drive to carry it to a satisfactory conclusion.

This second raid within less than a thirty-day period might have been little more than a footnote in the history of the war, but for the fact that papers were found on Dahlgren's corpse that ignited a firestorm of rage and controversy that has not abated to this day. The papers were found by a 13-year-old boy, one William Littlepage, who was rifling the Union dead for valuables, a common practice on both sides. The papers eventually made their way into the hands of President Davis, who happened to be in conference with Secretary of State Benjamin when they were delivered. The Confederate leadership, realising the propaganda value of the papers, promptly made photographic copies of the same to prove they were authentic and then delivered them to the press. That, at least, is the official story.[10]

The Richmond dailies began covering the story on 5 March, alleging that the 'Dahlgren papers', as they were now known, comprised 'undisputable evidence of the diabolical designs of the enemy'.[11] What did the papers say? One document was an address on the stationery of the 'Headquarters Third Division, Cavalry Corps', signed by Dahlgren and written in his hand, which read:

> We hope to release the prisoners from Belle Island [*sic*] first, and having them well started, we will cross the James River into Richmond, destroying the bridges after us and exhorting the prisoners to destroy and burn the hateful city; and do not allow the rebel leader Davis and his traitorous crew to escape.

A second, unsigned document, but also written in Dahlgren's hand, was a special order reading:

> The men must keep together and well in hand, and once in the city, it must be destroyed and Jeff Davis and Cabinet killed. Pioneers will go along with combustible material.

In addition, there was a set of notations that referred to planning for the raid and detailing its execution, including the incredible direction that 'Jeff Davis and Cabinet must be killed on the spot'. It should be said, however, that this third incriminating order does not appear in most accounts of the contents of the papers.[12]

Incendiary! Absolutely incendiary! These papers confirmed the worst fears of the Confederate high command, namely that the federal government had resolved upon attacking the Confederate leadership, not merely its armies. Ordering the killing of President Davis and his cabinet was murder, pure and simple.

Though they were distressed by the knowledge that they were now targeted for death, Confederate leaders were delighted to have been handed the materials for a second major propaganda offensive. The press immediately called for retribution in kind. In an editorial, the *Richmond Examiner*, already critical of what it called Davis's 'milk and water spirit in which this war has hither to been conducted', said:

> What then, would we practically suggest? First, to put to death all 'raiders' caught in the fact; secondly, to insist upon the most scrupulous carrying out of retaliation for murders, robberies, and other outrages, with the most punctual exactitude.[13]

The *Richmond Sentinel* was even more pointed as to a proper response to 'Lincoln's orders':

> Let Lincoln and Kilpatrick remember that they have bidden their subordinates give no quarter to the Confederate chiefs. Perhaps even a Scotch cap and a military cloak will not prevent a just and stern vengeance from overtaking them.[14]

The reference to the Scotch cap and military cloak was to garments Lincoln was alleged (falsely) to have worn on his trip to Washington for his first Inauguration, which were said to have foiled would-be assassins. The *Sentinel*, therefore, which was surely read by the Confederate leadership, *was calling for the President's assassination*.

The drumbeat of newspaper coverage, especially the editorials, had their intended effect: Southerners, especially the citizens of Richmond, were beside themselves with rage. Many visited the prisoners captured during the raid for the express purpose of venting their spleen. The wife of Secretary of War James Seddon was among them. Ironically, Dahlgren's father, John, had at one time been her beau, a happenstance, however, that did not keep some of Dahlgren's men from burning part of her estate.[15] She called the captives 'Thieves, Murderers, Fiends, Hell Monsters, Assassins …' and threatened to use all her influence to have them all hanged or put into a dungeon and starved to death. Some in the press called for them to be blown from cannon, burned with turpentine and oakum and otherwise summarily dispatched.[16]

General Braxton Bragg, Seddon and many others were in favour of executing the Union soldiers who had been captured, but General Robert

E. Lee's wiser counsel prevailed. He argued that it would be wrong to visit Dahlgren's barbarous intentions upon the captives and that hanging prisoners was a bad precedent.[17]

But were the documents really genuine or were they forged, in whole or in part? And if all the orders were genuine, did they originate with Lincoln or with Stanton, Kilpatrick or Dahlgren himself, with or without Lincoln's approval?

In the last century and a half, much has been said and written about the authenticity of the Dahlgren papers and the author of the despicable orders. In more recent times, the issues have been studied in depth and addressed by assassination scholars Stephen Sears, Edward Steers, Jnr, Eric Wittenberg, William A. Tidwell, James O. Hall, David Gaddy, Duane Schultz, James M. McPherson and others.

Of course, all the palaver about the authenticity of the papers was then and still is a matter of only academic interest, because, once again, it was perception rather than reality that counted. And the perception was that the documents were genuine, that the Yankees were barbarians and that their agenda, which originated with the tyrant, Lincoln, included decapitation of the Confederate government by wholesale assassinations. The Confederate high command and the Southern press would not let a major propaganda victory be so easily turned aside. As far as they were concerned, they had the goods and they had photographic reproductions of the same to prove it, which they circulated throughout the country and made available to foreign governments.

Whatever lingering doubt the Confederate leadership may have had about the authenticity of the papers – and there was virtually none – was dispelled by the fact that the Dahlgren orders were so similar to Wistar's orders. The conclusion to be derived from this, it seemed obvious, was that Lincoln, impatient to end the war on his terms, had decided to target not only Confederate armies, but its political leaders as well.[18]

We may be certain that Butler issued Wistar's orders to capture, but as to who issued Dahlgren's orders to kill, assuming they are authentic, there is no agreement. Lincoln, Stanton, Kilpatrick and Dahlgren himself are all candidates, with the higher criticism favouring Stanton. The originals no longer exist. When the Confederate Archives – what was left of them – were secured by Union forces after they occupied

Richmond on 3 April 1865, Stanton ordered that the Dahlgren papers be brought to him. They were, and they are believed to have warmed the Secretary as they were consumed by the flames in his fireplace.

In these circumstances, we would expect the Confederate leadership, keenly sensitive to the demands of the hot-breathed Southern press and knowing full well that they were losing the war, would spend a great deal of time discussing the issue. And they did. In the weeks following the raids, i.e. in March and into April 1864, Davis and the political and military elite of the Confederacy spent much time in conference considering appropriate countermeasures to the raids.[19] Minutes of the meetings, assuming they were taken, have apparently not survived. It is entirely reasonable to suppose, given the nature of the countermeasures proposed, discussed and decided upon, that the usual practice of recording meetings was suspended. Subsequent events, however, give us a fair idea of the decisions Confederate leaders made, including attempts to instigate a revolt against Washington in the Northwest (today's Midwest), making use of Copperheads and other anti-Lincoln elements; raids on Northern prisons for the purpose of freeing Confederate prisoners; and possibly the capture of Lincoln for confrontation with the 'victims' of his policies, but more likely well-placed assassinations of those who, in the leaders' unanimous judgment, had ordered their own. As Davis later wrote, 'The enormity of his [Dahlgren's] offenses was not forgotten.'[20]

It is clear enough from what followed the high-level meetings that Confederate leaders saw in the raids, especially the orders to the leaders of the raids to either capture or assassinate Davis and his cabinet, licence to respond in kind. Whatever reservation they may have had about doing so was most likely removed by what was known as the doctrine of military necessity, which justified a direct attack upon an enemy's civilian leadership. Indeed, Columbia University law and political science professor Francis Lieber's rules of civilised warfare for Union forces (General Orders, No. 100 – Instructions for the Government of Armies of the United States in the Field), which became effective on 24 April 1863, condoned the necessity of those measures which are indispensable for securing the ends of the war. It follows that removing Lincoln and other prominent federal office holders was a military necessity for Confederate leaders and would be no worse than what they believed Lincoln had ordered for them. Significantly, however, Confederate Secretary of War Seddon expressly rejected the Lieber Code. Confederate leaders had thus forfeited any justification for the attack on Union leadership that may have accrued to them from those of its provisions that related to military necessity (Section I, paragraphs 14–16), and this despite the fact that Section IX of the Code 'abhors' the 'outrage' of assassination and might, for that reason, be interpreted to override the provisions relating to military necessity. Section IX, however, appears to apply only to proclamations of outlawry and assassinations carried out pursuant thereto, so there is ambiguity as to the true meaning of the Code. The Code defined 'military necessity' as the necessity of those measures that are indispensable for securing the ends of the war. The war had not ended. About 150,000 Confederate troops were still in the field in Virginia, the Carolinas, Alabama and the Trans-Mississippi. They had not surrendered and they and many others in the South did not view General Robert E. Lee's surrender of the Army of Northern Virginia to Lieutenant General Grant at Appomattox on 9 April 1865, as the end of the war. The Confederacy, therefore, may have derived some benefit from the Code if its leaders had approved and adopted it, depending on the interpretation of the relevant provisions and a determination of their application to the attack on Union leadership, which would have been matters for the courts to decide.

In truth and in fact, however, Confederate leaders did not feel the need for justification for a lethal attack on Union leadership. As far as they were concerned, Lincoln had ordered the same fate for them with the raids on Richmond. Action against Union leadership was therefore not a matter of the Lieber Code, but a matter of far older laws, namely the law of 'an eye for an eye' and *lex talionis*.

To accomplish the 'appropriate' countermeasures to the raids, decided upon in the high-level meetings of Confederate political and military leaders, it would be necessary to strengthen Secret Service operations in Canada. Montreal and Toronto had been centres of Confederate espionage, plotting and terror from a very early date, because the operatives there were beyond the reach of federal authority. But in February 1864, Davis sent James P. Holcombe, a former professor of law at the University of Virginia, to carry out, among other things, 'duties already entrusted', but not specified in writing. In April, Davis sent Jacob Thompson of Mississippi, Secretary of the Interior in President James Buchanan's cabinet, and Clement C. Clay, a Confederate States Senator and once a United States Senator from Alabama, to carry out in Canada 'such instructions as you have received from me verbally, in such manner as shall seem most likely to conduce the furtherance of the interests of the Confederate States of America'. It does not require a particularly vivid imagination to understand why the orders and instructions to Holcombe, Thompson and Clay could not be in writing, not even in code. They must have been odious in the extreme, the kind that provided for terror plots, assassinations and the killing of vast numbers of people, which, we know from subsequent events, they were, all justified as retribution in kind. They must therefore never see the light of day, and they never have. They died with their bearers, though their fruits soon became painfully obvious to everyone and found their way into the pages of history.

Holcombe, Thompson and Clay brought with them drafts for $1 million in gold (about $2.2 million in United States greenbacks) to carry out their work. Already in Canada were Beverly Tucker of Virginia, the notorious George N. Sanders of Kentucky, who openly advocated assassination as an instrument of national policy, and William C. Cleary of Kentucky. It would be the purpose of these operatives, who, together with other agents too numerous to mention, came to be known as the Canadian Cabinet, to coordinate the exploitation of what Davis, Benjamin and Seddon believed was peace sentiment in the North, particularly in the north-western states and the border states of Kentucky and Missouri; to coordinate terror attacks in the North, for the purpose of weakening the morale of the Northern people; and, most importantly, to lure the United States into a war with Great Britain by provoking Union border crossings into Canada in pursuit of Confederate raiders. It would not be long before the Canadian Cabinet had enough operatives to carry on their work not only in Montreal and Toronto, but in St Catherines, Hamilton and Windsor as well.

We gain some idea of the machinations of the Confederate government in the weeks following the raids, and the super-secrecy of the same and of the decisions that were made incident thereto, from a letter sent by Secretary of State Benjamin to the Honorable H.H. (Sandy) Stuart (full name: Alexander Hugh Homes Stuart) at Staunton, Virginia, dated 25 March 1864:

> Would it be in your power to come to Richmond as promptly as possible on a matter of great public interest? The President and myself are desirous of conferring with you in person, as the subject is too delicate for correspondence. I need scarcely say that it should not be known that you come on any but your own private business.[21]

The establishment of the Canadian Cabinet could not have been 'a subject … too delicate for correspondence', because it wasn't anything that could be kept secret; federal detectives were soon all over it. What, then, could have been a subject so delicate that it could not even be committed to paper, even in code? We may safely conclude that it was a matter totally consistent with the verbal orders and instructions given to Holcombe, Thompson and Clay and most likely of a piece with the same, a conclusion corroborated by the fact that the letter was written at about the same time that the orders and instructions were given.

Clearly, retribution was in high gear with the Confederate leadership, though the leap from previous warfare without law or convention to warfare carried out pursuant to orders and instructions that could not be given otherwise than verbally, was not difficult to make. As early as May 1862, Confederate General Daniel Harvey Hill, brother-in-law of General Stonewall Jackson and a major figure in the war until he fell out of favour with Generals Robert E. Lee and Braxton Bragg and therefore Jefferson Davis, gave it as his opinion that 'all means of destroying our brutal enemies are lawful and proper'. This opinion must have carried substantial weight with the Confederate leadership as the war continued and prospects for victory grew dimmer and dimmer. Further, as we have already seen, and more significantly, in June 1863, Confederate Secretary of War Seddon rejected Francis Lieber's rules of civilised warfare for Union forces (General Orders, No. 100). Seddon said the Order was a hypocrisy, a whitewash of past Union excesses that was written to give the federal government a moral high ground to commit atrocities.

In any case, what followed the numerous and secret conferences at the highest level in Richmond, in the immediate aftermath of the failed raids on that city and the augmentation of the Canadian Cabinet, was a level of Black Flag warfare still higher than that which had already been waged. This higher level included at least the following events and activities that were initiated, coordinated or controlled by Davis's men in Canada:

1. From Toronto, Jacob Thompson orchestrated an attempt to foment a second civil war in the North and thereby split the East from the West by establishing a Northwest Confederacy. This Confederacy would comprise the states of Ohio, Indiana, Illinois, Kentucky and Missouri. The effort was financed by Confederate gold. Major players were Captain Thomas Henry Hines, John B. Castleman, George Nicholas Sanders, Clement Vallandigham and his Sons of Liberty, and, it was hoped, Confederate prisoners of war freed from Camp Douglas in Chicago, Camp Morton in Indianapolis, Camp Chase in Columbus and Johnson's Island in Sandusky Bay, near Sandusky, Ohio. Secretary of War Seddon's letter to Hines, dated shortly after the failed Dahlgren-Kilpatrick Raid (16 March 1864), was explicit as to the organisation of Copperheads for armed rebellion. Equally explicit was Hines's reply, in which he spoke of the assassination of the executive heads of Indiana, Ohio and Illinois.[22]
2. In July 1864, some twenty to thirty Confederates from Canada planned a raid on Calais, Maine, just south of the Canadian border, for the purpose of robbing the bank there and, possibly, to provoke an incident between the United States and Great Britain. Somehow (probably a spy among the raiders), the US consul in St Johns, New Brunswick, got wind of the plot and notified the cashier of the bank. The bank and the town were thus alerted in time to thwart the raiders' designs. One of the captured raiders, Francis X. Jones, decided to cooperate with his captors. The raid, he said, was part of a plan to capture the entire state of Maine, which was to have been accomplished by landings of Confederate troops, assisted by the CSS *Tallahassee*, whose purpose was to

paralyse local shipping. All this activity, said Jones, was part of the scheme to establish the Northwest Confederacy previously described.

3. On 19 October 1864, Bennett H. Young, a 21-year-old cavalryman from John Hunt Morgan's command, led a twenty-man force in a raid on St Albans, Vermont, about 15 miles south of the Canadian border. Arriving the previous evening and staying in the various hotels, they took control of the town at 3.00 p.m. on the 19th, rounded up the townspeople, set fire to the hotels and other buildings, stole horses and robbed three banks of about $200,000. Some of the citizens resisted. One was killed and others wounded. Young and his men beat a hasty retreat and made it across the border, where Young and thirteen others were arrested and imprisoned. About $90,000 of the loot was recovered. Ultimately, all the raiders were freed and the money that had been confiscated from them by the Canadians was returned to them. But the raid did not succeed in creating war between the United States and Great Britain, which was its principal purpose.[23] The fact that Lincoln revoked an order to invade Canada to pursue the raiders doubtless had much to do with that result.[24] One war was enough for Lincoln.
4. Jacob Thompson proposed that John Yeats Beall organise and lead a raid on Johnson's Island for the purpose of freeing 3,000 Confederate prisoners of war. On 19 September 1864, Beall and nineteen men disguised as civilians seized the ferry *Philo Parsons* off nearby Kelleys Island, together with another ship (the *Island Queen*), which they scuttled. They planned to use the ferry to capture the only Union gunboat on Lake Erie, the USS *Michigan*, which they would then use to assault the prison on Johnson's Island. Co-conspirators aboard the USS *Michigan* were to signal them with rockets at a given time. The signal never came because Union intelligence uncovered the entire plot. The absence of the signal was reason enough for Beall's crew to demand that he abort the operation. Beall agreed. They sailed back to their point of embarkation, near present-day Windsor, Ontario, scuttled the ferry and escaped, except for one crewman.

Beall then joined a band of daredevils, organised by Jacob Thompson, that attempted to derail a train carrying seven Confederate general officers from Johnson's Island to Fort Lafayette in New York. They failed. Beall and a companion, George S. Anderson, were arrested in Niagara Falls en route to Canada and safety. Anderson turned state's evidence. Beall was tried, convicted and, on 8 February 1865, sentenced to be hanged. Because he was from a prominent Virginia family, many in high places, including six United States Senators and ninety-one members of Congress, petitioned President Lincoln for a pardon. Letters, too, were sent to Lincoln and to Stanton on behalf of Beall. Lincoln was prepared to spare him, but Stanton and Seward persuaded him that it would establish a bad precedent. Beall was executed on 24 February 1865.[25]

Beall's execution left a very bitter taste in the mouths of all Confederates. Davis's and Benjamin's knowledge that this prominent Virginian went to his death in their service and following their orders brought their anger against Lincoln to a fever pitch.

5. An event that was far removed geographically, but was nevertheless intended to coordinate with the Confederate conspiracy to establish a Northwest Confederacy, was the voyage of the Confederate raider CSS *Tallahassee*. Under the command of John Taylor Wood, a grandson of President Zachary Taylor and a nephew of Jefferson Davis, she sailed from Wilmington, North Carolina, on 6 August 1864, through the blockade, to Halifax, Nova Scotia, returning safely to Wilmington on 26 August. En route, she captured thirty-five ships, mostly merchantmen, burned at least twenty-six of them and released or bonded the rest. It was Wood's plan to take his ship into New York harbour, set fire to the shipping there, bombard the Brooklyn Navy Yard and then make his way up the East River, through Hell Gate, into Long Island Sound and out to sea again. His ultimate goal was nothing less than the seizure of the state of Maine, coordinating with the Confederate raider CSS *Florida* and making use of troops from John Hunt Morgan's, Joe Wheeler's and J.E.B. Stuart's commands

who would be brought there by blockade runners and who would be joined by troops from Canada. The 16 July raid on the border town of Calais, Maine, may have been carried out as part of this scheme. It must be said that the Confederates were nothing if not daring and ambitious. The plot failed, of course, being far beyond Confederate capabilities at the time, though CSS *Tallahassee* did create a major stir in New York and New England before reaching Halifax.[26]

6. Blowing up things, especially steamboats and other craft on the Mississippi and other inland waterways, was a favourite activity of the Confederate Secret Service's Torpedo Bureau, headed by General Gabriel James Rains. Their operations had actually begun in late 1863, but they were accelerated the following year after the failed raids on Richmond. During the war, more than seventy Union steamboats were destroyed by a division of the Secret Service known as the Boat-Burners, sometimes referred to as the 'Steam-boat Burners', which was led by one Joseph W. Tucker of South Carolina, a one-time minister, and a fellow with the odd name of Minor Major. The Boat-Burners cost the Union hundreds, maybe thousands, of lives and millions of dollars.

   Blowing-up steamboats was relatively easy to do. The favoured method was the use of coal and log bombs. The first was a bomb fashioned to look like a lump of coal, which was placed in a tender or other supply of coal intended to service a ship. When the coal was shovelled into a boiler, the explosion resulted in either great damage to the craft or its sinking, with much loss of life. The second was simply a log hollowed out and filled with gunpowder, which was used in the same way as the coal bomb and with the same effect.[27] Interestingly, a coal bomb, presumably defused, was found on Jefferson Davis's desk in the Confederate White House when Union troops occupied Richmond on 3 April 1865.[28]

7. On 9 August 1864, John Maxwell and R.K. Dillard, Confederate Secret Service agents, succeeded in destroying the Union ammunition depot at City Point, Virginia, using a horological torpedo, i.e. a time bomb. The explosion was so great that Dillard, who was sitting on a nearby hill with Maxwell to watch

the fireworks, lost his hearing completely and permanently. The official death toll was fifty-eight, including a party of women, with another 126 maimed, though some estimates put the human toll much higher than that. Property loss was put at between $2 million and $4 million, an astronomical sum in those days. It was said that the explosion almost killed Grant, Meade and their headquarters staff.[29]

8. On the night of 25 November 1864, Robert Cobb Kennedy, a prisoner of war who had escaped from Johnson's Island, together with seven other conspirators, set fire to dozens of hotels, theatres and museums along Broadway and to shipping facilities along the Hudson River in New York City. They used an incendiary known as 'Greek Fire', which did not work as well as they supposed it would. Kennedy and his fellow arsonists were under the command of Lieutenant Colonel Robert M. Martin, Tenth Kentucky Cavalry, another operative who had been sent to Canada by Davis and Benjamin for the purpose of planning military raids and terrorist attacks that could be directed against the North. According to Charles A. Dunham, alias Sanford Conover, allegedly a Confederate agent, but possibly a double or even a triple agent, even the destruction of New York's water supply by blowing up the Croton Dam was considered, as was the poisoning of the water supply with strychnine, arsenic, prussic acid and other poisons. It must be said, however, that either or both of these plots may be fiction, because Dunham, who may have had as many as twenty aliases and who is surely one of the strangest characters in history, was a chronic liar. Kennedy was caught and hanged on 25 March 1865. Martin was pardoned by President Andrew Johnson in 1866 without being tried.[30]
9. On 27 November 1864, a coal bomb destroyed General Benjamin F. Butler's luxurious steamer, *Greyhound*, again coming within a hair of killing major Union military figures, in this case Butler, Admiral David Dixon Porter and Major General Robert C. Schenck. Butler had been a prime target of the Confederate high command ever since Jefferson Davis, on 23 December 1862, formally proclaimed him to be an outlaw subject to peremptory

execution upon capture. Davis made the proclamation because Butler had hanged William B. Mumford for pulling down an American flag in New Orleans prior to its occupation by Union troops. That, at least, was the official reason given.[31]

10. Dr Luke P. Blackburn of Kentucky thought it a good idea to spread pestilence, principally yellow fever, in the North by means of 'infected' clothing. Testimony was introduced at the trial of the conspirators to the effect that, at Blackburn's direction, Confederate agents had tried to spread yellow fever and smallpox throughout the North, including the White House, by distributing 'infected' clothing that Blackburn had gathered from victims of the diseases in Bermuda and sent to various garment distributors in the United States. The scheme involved assassinating Lincoln by 'infecting' him with yellow fever. This was to be accomplished by sending him 'infected' shirts as a gift from an anonymous benefactor. Blackburn, despite being a physician, did not know that yellow fever could not be contracted by contact with clothing. Few, if any, did know it, until Dr Walter Reed discovered, in 1900, that the disease was spread by the bite of mosquitoes, not by clothing.[32]

Needless to say, the foregoing ten examples of Confederate activities that occurred or accelerated in the wake in the failed raids on Richmond tell only a small part of the story. A massive web of intrigue and skullduggery was controlled and coordinated by Richmond and Canada, but was worldwide in its scope. Operatives at all levels were in every major Northern and Southern city and well represented in London, Paris and other European cities too. Major ports of call for naval operations were Halifax, Nova Scotia, Bermuda and the Azores, all of which hummed with Confederate comings, goings and scheming. Nothing even close to the full story will ever be known, because all the participants, their children and grandchildren are dead and because virtually all their doings were super-secret, with communications often made orally by courier, so sensitive was their content, or by coded or invisible ink messages that were destroyed as soon as they were digested or that perished in the intentional burnings of records and correspondence that were carried out, when defeat was at the doorstep, by those who stood to lose greatly by their exposure. Nevertheless, quantitative and qualitative differences are discernible in the activities that followed the raids compared to those that preceded them. These were attributable to a lust for revenge for the perceived Union attempts to burn the Confederate capital and murder Confederate leaders, as well as for the destruction of so much of the South by Union armies, and to an awareness that, in fact, the Confederacy was losing the war and that only the most extreme measures had any chance at all of preventing the coming disaster.

It sometimes happens that compelling evidence for a postulate is in front of our eyes, and has always been in front of our eyes, but is nevertheless overlooked or ignored. The postulate, of course, is that the Confederate government and its Secret Service were complicit in the assassination of Lincoln and the attempted assassinations of other federal office holders, namely Vice President Johnson, Secretary of State Seward, Secretary of War Stanton and Lieutenant General Grant, at least. The evidence I refer to is in the transcripts of the trial of the conspirators, coupled with knowledge we have of the Confederate response to the Wistar and Dahlgren-Kilpatrick raids against Richmond. Here is the evidence, which, in my judgment, rises to the level of proof that Confederate leaders would not shrink from diabolical deeds, including regicide, if they offered them any chance of winning the war.

We must bear in mind that the three men whom Confederate leaders sent to Canada in February and April 1864, in the wake of the failed raids on Richmond – James P. Holcombe, Jacob Thompson and Clement C. Clay – were the leaders' men. They were the leaders' appointees. They were sent to Montreal by the leaders. They were following verbal orders and instructions given to them by the leaders. They were financed by the leaders. And they were subject to recall by the leaders. Everything they did, therefore, must have been known to Davis and Benjamin, at least, and must have been approved by them. It is inconceivable that the appointees would have carried out activities that had not been approved by the leaders, that were unknown to them or that were contrary to their wishes.

With all that in mind, consider the testimony of Godfrey Joseph Hyams, who testified, under oath, at the trial of the conspirators, that he had been hired by Dr Luke Pryor Blackburn, another member of the Canadian Cabinet, for the purpose of 'disposing' (i.e. selling) of clothing that had been 'infected' with yellow fever, smallpox and perhaps other contagious diseases, throughout the North, for the purpose of spreading pestilence in the North. Part of the scheme involved sending 'infected' shirts to the White House, intended for President Lincoln as a gift from an anonymous benefactor. The clothing had been obtained by Blackburn from Bermuda, where there had been a yellow fever epidemic, and had been transported to the United States and was being stored in trunks. Most significantly, Hyams testified that he not only met repeatedly with Blackburn, for the purpose, but also with Holcombe, Clay and Thompson. Blackburn promised him at least $100,000 for his services, and possibly 'ten times that amount'. Holcombe and Clay buttered him up a bit more by telling him that in addition to the compensation promised by Blackburn, another reward for his services would be that he would become a 'gentleman for the future instead of a working-man and a mechanic'. (Hyams said he also met with Bennett H. Young, leader of the Confederate raid on St Albans, but this is not relevant.) According to Hyams, the men 'seemed perfectly to understand the business in which I had been engaged'.

It was Thompson who paid him (though not much) and it was Thompson who told him that he had met with Blackburn, that he had discussed the matter with him and that he had received his authority to pay Hyams. Hyams also stated that Blackburn and Holcombe had told him that the Confederate government had appropriated $200,000 for the purpose of carrying out the scheme. Needless to say, Hyams never received more than a small percentage of the compensation that had been promised him, despite having distributed some of the clothing, though he did say that he had a further meeting with Holcombe and Clay before he put the matter behind him. Hyams adds that he afterwards heard that the valise that contained the 'infected' shirts intended for Lincoln 'had been sent to the President'. Hyams's testimony was never impeached. Hyams's testimony appears below in full.[33]

That Davis, and therefore Benjamin, knew about this plot to spread pestilence in the North and to assassinate Lincoln by infecting him with yellow fever was proved by a letter written to Davis by Kensey

Johns Stewart, an Episcopalian minister turned Confederate agent and a member of the Canadian Cabinet, who implored Davis to call it off on the grounds that it could not possibly find favour with God. The letter, sent in December 1864, expressly mentions Hyams, thus corroborating his testimony at the trial. The letter was found by James O. Hall, the dean of assassination historians, among the few Confederate records that hadn't been burned. This letter, it should not go unnoticed, demonstrates Davis's willingness to assassinate the President of the United States with infected shirts after he was convinced that Lincoln had ordered his death at least once (the Dahlgren-Kilpatrick Raid) if not twice (the Wistar Raid). In any case, Stewart's plea fell on deaf ears, because four months after his letter, the trunks were still full of 'infected' clothing and the plan was still on, according to Hyams.[34] Stewart's letter to Davis appears below in full.

So what does the foregoing prove, if anything? It proves that as early as the summer of 1864, if not earlier, the Confederate government and its Secret Service were actively plotting the murder of Abraham Lincoln. This was no doubt something they wished for from the moment he was nominated by his party as their candidate for president and may be something they previously attempted inasmuch as there were numerous attempts to assassinate Lincoln that antedated the failed raids on Richmond. The failed raids, however, undoubtedly gave Confederate leaders a new impetus and a greater resolve, because they were seen as furnishing licence to respond in kind.

The foregoing is also most probative of the conclusion that all the attempts on Lincoln's life that occurred subsequent to the raids were related to them, including the shot at Lincoln when he was riding alone towards the Soldiers' Home in August, 1864, and including, of course, the attempt that succeeded in April 1865. It also proves that Confederate leaders were quite willing to even the score with Union leaders for all the death and destruction they had visited upon the South in three years of war, by spreading pestilence in the North, which, for all they knew, might have resulted in the deaths of tens of thousands of innocents, if it would further the cause of Southern independence and stave off what by this time appeared to them to be imminent catastrophe, namely, the loss of their political independence, the loss of their lifestyle and culture, the loss of their wealth and property, the social upheaval attendant to the integration of almost 4 million suddenly free slaves into a society of 5½ million whites, and the possible 'mongrelisation' of their race.

Now let us ask ourselves: If the principal players in the Confederate government and its Secret Service were trying to assassinate Lincoln in the summer of 1864 (and clearly they were, per the testimony of Hyams and the letter from Stewart to Davis), a time when they were still in the game, albeit not by much after major Confederate losses in the Wilderness and at Spotsylvania (May 1864), is it reasonable to suppose that they changed their collective minds in the spring of 1865, when their backs were to the wall, when their resources were all but depleted, and with the Southern press fairly baying for the blood of federal leaders? In the same vein, would these principal players, who had signed on to the assassination of the Governors of Indiana (Oliver P. Morton), Ohio (John Brough) and Illinois (Richard Yates), to facilitate the establishment of the Northwest Confederacy – three men whose contribution to their losses was relatively modest,[35] hesitate for even a heartbeat to order the assassination of men whose contribution to their losses was major, namely Lincoln, Johnson, Seward, Stanton and Grant, at least? In these circumstances, would these principal players accept their defeat graciously, call off the assassins and spare the author of all their grief and all their losses, actual and impending? Clearly, no, because doing so would have been totally inconsistent with virtually everything they had previously done to gain Southern independence and totally inconsistent, too, with human nature, revenge being the strongest human motivator. For these reasons, we must regard Hyams's testimony and Stewart's letter, together, as a smoking gun.

Here, in full, is Benn Pitman's account of Hyams's testimony. Italicised material represents my emphasis.

> INTRODUCTION OF PESTILENCE
> GODFREY JOSEPH HYAMS
> For the Prosecution – 29 May
>
> I am a native of London, England, but have lived South nine or ten years. During the past year I have resided in Toronto, Canada. *About the middle of December, 1863, I made the acquaintance of Dr Blackburn*; I was introduced to him by

the Rev. Stewart Robinson, at the Queen's Hotel, in Toronto. I knew him by sight previously, but before that had no conversation with him. I knew that he was a Confederate, and was working for the rebellion. Dr Blackburn was then about to take South some men who had escaped from the Federal service, and I asked to go with him.

He asked me if I wanted to go South and serve the Confederacy. I said I went (did). He then told me to come up stairs; he wanted to speak to me. He took me up stairs to a private room, and pledged his word, as a Freemason, and offered his hand in friendship, that he would never deceive me; he said he wanted to confide to me an expedition. I told him I would not care if I did. *He said I would make an independent fortune by it, at least $100,000, and get more honor and glory to my name than General Lee, and be of more assistance to the Confederate Government, than if I was to take one hundred thousand soldiers to reinforce General Lee.* I pledged my word that I would go, if I could do any good. *He then told me he wanted me to take a certain quantity of clothing, consisting of shirts, coats, and underclothing into the States, and dispose of them by auction. I was to take them to Washington City, to Norfolk, and as far South as I could possibly go, where the Federal government held possession and had the most troops, and to sell them on a hot day or of a night; that it did not matter what money I got for the clothes, I had just to dispose of them in the best market, where there were most troops, and where they would be most effective, and then come away.*

He told me I should have $100,000 for my services; $60,000 of it directly after I returned to Toronto. He said that would not be a circumstance to what I should get. He said I might make ten times $100,000.

I was to stay in Toronto, and go on with my legitimate business, until I heard from him. He told me to keep quiet, and if I moved anywhere, I was to inform Dr Stuart Robinson where I went to, and he would telegraph for me, or write to me through him. Some time in the month of May, 1864, I went to my work, and worked on until the 8th day of June, 1864; it was on a Saturday night; I had been out to take a pair of boots home to a customer of mine; and when I returned home, my wife had a letter for me from Dr Blackburn, which Dr Stuart Robinson had left in passing there. I read the letter, and went out to see Dr Robinson. I asked him what I was to do about it; he said he did not know any thing at all about it; that he did not want to furnish any means to commit an overt act against the United States government. He advised me to borrow from Mr Preston, who keeps a tobacco manufactory in Toronto, enough money to take me to Montreal, which I did. I went down to Montreal and there got money from Mr Slaughter, according to the directions contained in the letter. The letter instructed me to proceed from Montreal to Halifax to meet Dr Blackburn; it was dated 'Havana, May 10th, 1864'. I went to Halifax, to a gentleman by the name of Alexander H. Keith, jr., and remained under his care until Dr Blackburn arrived in the steamer *Alphia*, on the 12th of July, 1864. When Dr Blackburn arrived, he sent to the Farmer's Hotel, where I was staying, for me. I went to see him, and he told me that *the goods were on board the steamer* Alphia, *and that the second officer on the steamer would go with me and get the goods off, as they had been smuggled in from Bermuda*. Mr Hill, the second officer, told me to get an express wagon and take it down to Cunard's steamboat wharf; I did so, and there got *eight trunks and a valise*. I was directed to take them to my hotel, and put them in a private room. I put them in Mr Doran's private sitting-room.

I then went around to Dr Blackburn and told him I had got the goods off the steamer. He told me that the five trunks tied up with ropes were the ones for me to take, and *asked me if I would take the valise into the States, and send it by express, with an accompanying letter, as a donation to President Lincoln.* I objected to taking it, and refused to do it. I then took three of the trunks and the valise around to his hotel. He was then staying at the Halifax Hotel. The trunks had Spanish marks upon them, and he told me to scrape them off; and that Mr Hill would go with me the next morning, and make arrangements with some captain of a vessel to take them. There were two vessels there running to Boston, and I was to make an arrangement with either of them to smuggle the trunks into Boston. The next morning I went down with Mr Hill to the vessels.

Mr Hill had a private conversation with Captain McGregor, the captain of the first vessel to whom we applied, and he refused to take the goods. We then went to see Captain John O'Brien of the bark *Halifax*. Hill told him that I had some presents in my trunks, consisting of silks, satin dresses, etc., that I wanted to take to my friends. The Captain and Mr Hill had a private conversation, and when the Captain came out, he consented to take them. I was to give him a twenty-dollar gold piece for smuggling them in. I put them on board the vessel that day, and he stowed them away. The vessel laid five days at Boston before he could get a chance to get them off, but he finally succeeded in getting them off, and expressed them to Philadelphia, where I received them, and brought them to Baltimore. I then took out the goods, which were very much rumpled, smoothed them out, and arranged them, bought some new trunks, and repacked them, and brought them to this city.

Dr Blackburn, by way of caution, asked me before leaving if I had had the yellow fever; and on my saying 'No,' he said, 'You must have a preventive against catching it. You must get some camphor and chew it, and get some strong cigars, the strongest you can get; and be sure to keep gloves on when handling the things.' He gave me some cigars that he said he had brought from Havana, which he said were strong enough for any thing.

When I arrived in this city, I turned over five of the trunks to Messrs. W.L. Wall & Co., commission merchants in this city, and four to a man by the name of Myers from

Boston, a sutler in Sigel's or Weitzel's division. He said he had some goods which he was going to take to Newberne, North Carolina, and I told him that I had a lot of goods that I wanted to sell, and to make the best market I could for them, I would turn them over to him on commission. I also told him I would shortly have more, and mentioned that I had disposed of some to Wall & Co., of this city. Dr Blackburn told me, when I was making arrangements, that I should let the parties to whom I disposed my goods know that I would have a big lot to sell, *as it was in contemplation to get together about a million dollars' worth of goods and dispose of them in this way.*

Dr Blackburn stated that his object in having these goods disposed of in different cities, was to destroy the armies, or anybody that they came in contact with. All these goods, he told me, had been carefully infected in Bermuda with yellow fever, small-pox, and other contagious diseases. The goods in the valise, which were intended for President Lincoln, I understood him to say, had been infected both with yellow fever and small-pox. This valise I declined taking charge of, and turned it over to him at Halifax Hotel, and I afterward heard that it had been sent to the President.

On the five trunks that I turned over to W.L. Wall & Co., I got an advance of $100. *Among these five trunks there was one that was always spoken of by Blackburn to me as 'Big No. 2', which he said I must be sure to have sold in Washington.*

On disposing of the trunks I immediately left Washington, and went straight through until I got to Hamilton, Canada. In the waiting-room there *I met Mr Holcombe and Mr Clement C. Clay. They both rose, shook hands with me, and congratulated me upon my safe return, and upon my making a fortune. They told me I should be a gentleman for the future, instead of a working-man and a mechanic. They seemed perfectly to understand the business in which I had been engaged.* Mr Holcombe told me that Dr Blackburn was at the Donegana Hotel in Montreal, and that I had better telegraph to him, stating that I had returned.

As Dr Blackburn had requested me to telegraph to him, as soon as I got into Canada, I did so; and the next night, between 11 and 12 o'clock, Dr Blackburn came up and knocked at the door of my house. I was in bed at the time. I looked out of the window and saw Dr Blackburn there. Said he, 'Come down, Hyams, and open the door; you're like all damned rascals who have been doing something wrong—you're afraid that the devil is after you.' He was in company with Bennett H. Young. I came down and let him in. *He asked me how I had disposed of the goods, and I told him. 'Well,' said he, 'that is all right, as long as big No. 2 went into Washington; it will kill them at sixty yards distance*.' I then told the Doctor that everything had gone wrong at my home in my absence; that I needed some funds; that my family needed money. *He said he would go to Colonel Jacob Thompson and make arrangements for me to draw upon him for any amount of money* I required. He then said that the British authorities had solicited his services in attending to the yellow fever that was then raging in Bermuda; that he was going on there; and that as soon as he came back he would see me. *I went up to Jacob Thompson the next morning, and told him what Dr Blackburn had said. He said, 'Yes; Dr Blackburn had been there, and had made arrangements for me to draw $100 whenever it was shown that I had made disposition of the goods according to his direction.' I told him I needed money; that I had been so long away from home that every thing I had was gone, and I wanted money to pay my rent, etc. He said, 'I will give you $50 now, but it is against Dr Blackburn's request; when you show me that you have sold the goods, I will give you the balance.' He asked me to give him a receipt, which I did: 'Received of Jacob Thompson the sum of $50 on account of Dr Blackburn.'* That was about the 11th or 12th of August last. The next day I wrote to Messrs. Wall & Co., of Washington, desiring them to send me an account of the sales, and the balance due me. *When I received their answer, I took it up to show to Colonel Thompson. He then said he was perfectly satisfied I had done my part, and gave me a check for $50 on the Ontario Bank. I gave him a receipt: 'Received of Jacob Thompson $100, in full, on account of Dr Luke P. Blackburn.'*

I told Jacob Thompson of the large sum which Dr Blackburn had promised me for my services and that he and Mr Holcombe had both told me that the Confederate Government had appropriated $200,000 dollars for the purpose of carrying it out; but he would not pay me any thing more.

When Dr Blackburn returned from Bermuda, I wrote to him at Montreal, and told him I wanted some money, and that he ought to send me some; but he made no reply to my letter. I was then sent down to Montreal with a commission for Bennett H. Young, to be used in his defence in the St. Albans raid case. I there met Dr Blackburn. He said I had written some hard letters to him, abusing him, and that he had no money to give me. He then got into his carriage at the door, and rode off to some races, I think, and never gave me any more satisfaction. As I wanted money before leaving for the States, I went to the Clifton House, Niagara. *Dr Blackburn told me he had no money with him then, but that he would go to Mr Holcombe and get some, as he had Confederate funds with him. Blackburn said that when I returned he would get the money for the expedition, from either Holcombe or Thompson, it did not matter which. From this, and from Holcombe and Clay both shaking hands with me, and congratulating me at Hamilton upon my safe return, I thought, of course, they knew all about it.*

I do not know that Dr Stuart Robinson knew of the business in which I was engaged, but he took good care of me while

I was at Toronto, in the fall, and until Dr Blackburn wrote for me in the spring; and when he gave me Dr Blackburn's letter, he told me to borrow the money from Mr Preston to take me to Montreal, as he said he did not want to commit an overt act against the United States government himself. Mr Preston lent me $10 to go to Montreal. On arriving at that place, according to the directions in Dr Blackburn's letter, I went to Mr Slaughter to get the means to take me to Halifax. Mr Slaughter was short of funds, and had only $25 that he could give me. *He said that I had better go to Mr Holcombe, who was staying at the Donegana Hotel, and he would give me the balance. I went to the Hotel and sent up my name. Mr Holcombe had heard of my name, and he sent for me to come up.* I told him that I wanted some money to take me to Halifax; he asked me how much I wanted; I told him as much as would make up $40; he said, 'You had better take $50'; but as I did not want that much, I only took enough to make up $40. When I came to Washington to dispose of the goods, which was on the 5th of August, 1864, I put up at the National Hotel, registered my name as J.W. Harris, under which name I did business with Wall & Co.

(*The Assassination of President Lincoln and the Trial of the Conspirators*, compiled and arranged by Benn Pitman, Recorder of the Commission; Moore, Wilstach & Baldwin, Cincinnati and New York, 1865, pp. 54–7.)

Another account of Hyams's testimony, which is presented in question and answer form, rather than narrative, appears in Volume II of *The Conspiracy Trial For The Murder Of The President: And The Attempt To Overthrow The Government By The Assassination Of Its Principal Officers (1865)*, by Benjamin Perley Poore; J.E. Tilton and Company, Boston, 1865, pp. 409–19.

And here is the letter from Kensey Johns Stewart to Jefferson Davis. Italicised material represents my emphasis. Underlining is in the original.

To His Excellency
Jefferson Davis President C.S.A.
Toronto C.W.,
Dec. 12th '64

Dear Sir:
As I conceive that the reasons for fulfilling the work undertaken still exist and are even more cogent, I wish to advise you that notwithstanding the miserable failures of many late enthusiasts, and the vigilance and anxiety occasioned thereby, our own plans can be carried out upon two conditions: 1st sufficient time: 2nd that you will put a stop to all these <u>comparatively</u> useless annoyances which do not produce a desire for peace so much as a thirst for revenge. Your Excellency is aware that when a negro is slightly chastened, he hates you, but a just and thorough whipping humbles him. I am aware that temporary vigilance and consequently diversion of forces from other plans, has been occasioned; but not only is this <u>temporary</u>, but it tends to increase the <u>centralization of power</u> in the hands of our enemy, who thus finds us playing into his hands, indeed, when I have seen the <u>character of agents</u> employed, and the impious nature of their work, I have taken the liberty of saying <u>that you have not ordered, and will not endorse the work of these men</u>. *For I cannot regard you as capable of expecting the blessing of God upon, or being personally associated with instruments & or plans such as I described below. As our country has been and is entirely dependent upon God, we cannot afford to displease him. Therefore, it cannot be our policy to employ wicked men to destroy the persons & property of private citizens, by inhumane & cruel acts. I name only one. $100.00 of public money has been paid here to one 'Hyams', a shoemaker, for services rendered, by conveying & causing to be sold in the city of Washington at auction, boxes of* <u>small-pox clothing</u>. As I mean this not for injury of the well meaning party who planned it, nor of the person who paid the money, I wish no other notice taken of it, than that such things be discouraged.

There can be no doubt of the causes of the failure of such plans. It is only a matter of surprise that, God does not forsake us and our cause when we are associated with such misguided friends.

I regard it as a kind and merciful Providence that has delayed my own actions by causing the check for $120,000 (?) I sent by the signal corps to fall into the enemy's hands, for otherwise I should have been endangered by these abortive attempts of others. Col. F has acquired much information and adopted excellent plans, but God has been against him. Everything has failed by Divine intervention. *If God is against me, I will not succeed.* But until you withdraw from me the confidence you have seen fit to repose in me, or I see some other reasons than such as now exist, for discouragement, I must continue to urge upon you the importance of measures which must induce an early peace, and to promise that by God's help I will do the work thoroughly and as speedily as practicable.

It is impossible for Col. F to sit here in Toronto & manage such difficult things in the states. He has truly said to me nothing is going on__?__. He is a true man, & a shrewd one. But he does not see the cause of these failures. If you can find someone better suited to the work, send him out (?). If not, I will do it by God's help. I enclose my memo, in detail, upon other issues than those agreed on. May God hand down your administration to the future, with its past and present, lights untarnished, as the glory of a noble but suffering people.

Truly yours & c
A true copy)
B. Wells)
A.P. Tasker)

(Marginal note):
Original filed with Jefferson Davis papers and letters from K.J. Stewart
Nov & Dec /68 (?)
rel to____?____from abroad

Chapter Two

The Second Smoking Gun: Lewis Thornton Powell and His Svengali

It is not the purpose of this chapter to discuss in any detail the attempted murder of Secretary of State William H. Seward by Lewis Thornton Powell, aka Lewis Paine, Lewis Payne, Mosby, Wood and many other aliases, on the same night that Lincoln was murdered (14 April 1865). And this despite the fact that it is about as good a story as one can find that exemplifies Scottish poet Robert Burns's famous line that 'The best laid schemes o' mice an' men gang aft agley' (i.e. often go awry, from 'To a Mouse') or Prussian Field Marshall Helmuth von Moltke's famous dictum that 'No battle plan survives first contact with the enemy'. That is to say that, unlike Booth's attempt, where almost everything went right for him, whatever could go wrong for Powell did go wrong.

Seward had had a carriage accident on 5 April and was thus wearing a steel frame that held the broken bones of his face together and also had his back propped up by a steel framework back rest. One or the other or both of these appliances saved his life, because they deflected most of Powell's knife thrusts, which therefore never found Seward's flesh. In fact, it appears that only one did.

Another incredible, indeed all but unbelievable, happenstance was the misfiring of Powell's Whitney Navy revolver when he put it to the head of Frederick Seward, the Secretary's son, who had resisted Powell's entreaties to see the Secretary. The frequency of such a weapon misfiring is given at between one in 100 or one in 500, depending on the type of ammunition used.

Add to these extraordinarily bad strokes of luck for Powell was the fact, per his own statement, that Seward's 20-year-old daughter, Fanny, interposed herself between her prostrate and helpless father and the would-be assassin. Powell later said that her face between his weapon and her father disarmed him; that he did not have the heart to take her life too.[1] Interesting how a touch of humanity is sometimes found in the strangest places and at the strangest times and sometimes has the most profound effect on history.

This kind of detail, while interesting, is not relevant to the purpose of this chapter, which is to show the relationship between Confederate leaders and supporters and the second most important member of Booth's team, after John Surratt – Lewis Thornton Powell.

Powell was tough. He was almost 6 feet, 2 inches tall, about 175 pounds (considered heavy before the twentieth-century diet caused overweight to be the new normal) and well built. Though he had a soft streak, or at least a softer one, when the occasion called for it, as evidenced by his repudiation of Gilmor's Raiders (who, he believed, were too rough a class of men for him),[2] by his rescue of two Union prisoners of war who were about to be killed in cold blood by a Confederate captor who had just killed four of their comrades,[3] and by his known love of animals, he was hard as nails when it came to combat (but not murder in cold blood) and the Confederate cause. When he rode with Gilmor's Raiders and Mosby's Rangers, he was described by the real Lewis Payne, son of Dr Albin S. Payne, with whom Powell resided at the time, as 'the boldest of the bold and the rashest of the reckless' and 'the terrible Lewis Powell'.[4] It was also said that he had killed a lot of men and that when any desperate matter was to be undertaken, he was selected.[5] The real Lewis Payne (Lewis E. Payne) wrote that:

> This strange man rode fast and far to share war's fiercest perils. The people here in Virginia who remember Powell as he appeared twenty years ago, with his pale face, slouch hat and mysterious ways mounted on that Bay mare, dashing and splashing through the woods, across fields, over ditches and fences, by day, at night, and through all kinds of weather, almost believe that he must have been a stray knight from the Black Forest.[6]

Such a man, such a fighter, obviously, would not have been cut loose by his Commander, General John Singleton Mosby, aka the Gray Ghost, for anything other than a very good purpose and pursuant to orders from those who had the authority to give them and who, we must assume, believed they had a very good reason for doing so. All of this attests to the very high regard that Mosby had for Powell as well as the very high regard that the Secret Service and the Confederate leadership had for him too. They would not send a boy to do a man's job. But they *would* weaken one part of their war-making machine to strengthen another part that they deemed even more important. Does that not tell us that they gave Booth's mission the highest priority, higher even than the work of the 43rd Battalion, 1st Virginia Cavalry (Mosby's Rangers), its successes notwithstanding?

It has been alleged that Powell was not dispatched by Mosby, but deserted him, and then joined the Secret Service because he didn't know what to do with himself. Later, it was said, he had an accidental meeting with Booth in front of Barnum's Hotel in Baltimore and the next day joined his conspiracy after taking a 'hard' oath. What utter nonsense. One would have a hard time finding a more ridiculous distortion of history than this. Can we just picture this 'stray knight from the Black Forest', who so impressed everyone who knew him with his fighting qualities, his bravery and daring, and his dedication to the Confederate cause, thumbing his nose at his beloved commander and his comrades-in-arms, leaving them to their peril and furtively slinking away into the night, in favour of a mindless and purposeless life in which 'he didn't know what to do with himself'. Mosby's Rangers were hand-picked by the Gray Ghost himself and considered themselves, and were in fact, an elite force. They loved their commander. Desertion must have been all but unknown to this band of brothers, not so much because it was a capital offence, but because desertion of their commander and their comrades-in-arms in the face of the dangers they faced almost daily was a choice worse than death, because a Ranger valued the lives of his commander and his comrades more than he valued his own. Furthermore, can anything be more unrealistic than a Confederate Secret Service that would accept in its ranks a known deserter who had somehow eluded a Mosby firing squad or noose? The story was obviously put out as a cover for Mosby and Powell and for those who would play a part in the transfer of Powell from Mosby's command to Booth's, a transfer fraught with danger and with momentous political and military implications. It was not the first nor the last time that desertion would be used as a cover for intelligence operations

Powell was not new to Secret Service work when he joined Booth's team, possibly in December 1864, but more likely in early 1865. He had become active in the summer of 1864 while still riding with Mosby, who worked closely with the Secret Service. Richard Montgomery, said to be a Union double agent, though his true loyalties cannot be known with certainty (true loyalties of agents, double agents and triple agents were then and still are a matter of great speculation), testified at the trial of the Lincoln conspirators, in May and June 1865, that he had seen Powell in Canada and Niagara Falls in the summer of 1864.[7] And Powell himself told his spiritual counsellor, Rev Dr Abram Dunn Gillette, that in the months prior to the assassination of Lincoln he had made numerous trips to and from Richmond, Washington and Baltimore, as part of his Secret Service work, that prominent men in the latter city had accommodated him in their palatial homes, treated him royally, encouraged him with promises of rewards, variously described, and kept him in funds with which he had come and gone at their bidding.[8] Powell's Secret Service work is therefore amply attested to and had to be known by Confederate leaders in Richmond and Canada.

Nor was he new to actions against the highest levels of Union leadership. Confederate General Bradley T. Johnson wrote in 1869 that Powell was one of five men dispatched by Mosby for the purpose of participating in actions against Lincoln and his cabinet, an account that was confirmed by Lewis E. Payne in 1882.[9]

So Powell came to Washington, which is to say, he came to Booth. He referred to Booth as 'Captain', one sign of the complete subordination of the brave and daring Mosby Ranger, who put his life on the line in every one of his many encounters with the enemy, who was described as 'the terrible Lewis Powell' and who was said to have killed many men, to the 26-year-old actor who, as far as we know, had never killed anyone in his life, nor, for that matter, put on a uniform and risked his life by exchanging fire or storming cannons. Does more need to be said about the premium the Confederate leadership placed upon Booth's mission even if some of them had misgivings about Booth himself, which many did (Secret Service agent Thomas Harbin called him 'a crazy fellow').[10]

His route to Washington was circuitous: first to Fairfax Court House, Virginia, then to Alexandria, Virginia, then to Baltimore, Maryland, and finally to the nation's capital. While he was in Baltimore, he made at least one trip to Washington, and quite possibly more than one, in January or February 1865, to meet Booth, and then came again on 15 March to meet with Booth's action team at Gautier's Restaurant, spending the night, following the meeting, at Mary Surratt's boarding house. Mary Surratt was the mother of John Harrison Surratt, who was Booth's second in command and right hand. Her boarding house was a safe house for Confederate agents and operatives of every description – spies, couriers, scouts, blockade runners, etc. En route, Powell exchanged his uniform for civilian clothes, received a pass and parole, took the Oath of Allegiance to the United States, roughed up a black servant at the Branson boarding house in Baltimore, where he stayed for a period, and was arrested not for the violence against the servant, but for spying (the servant accused him of being a Confederate spy). He was, however, released when it was determined that there was insufficient evidence to hold him. The final leg of his 15 March trip – Baltimore to Washington – was engineered by John Surratt, with an assist from David Preston Parr, who owned a china shop in Baltimore and, like Powell, Surratt and Booth, was also a Secret Service agent.[11]

At the Gautier's Restaurant meeting of Booth and his team (Surratt, Powell, David Herold, George Atzerodt, Samuel Arnold and Michael O'Laughlen), Powell said little, being new to the team and transfixed, as were the others, by the sparks that were flying between Booth and Arnold over the issue of kidnapping, a tempest in a teapot inasmuch as Booth never really intended to kidnap anyone, as we shall see. Two days later – the 17th – Powell participated in the 'failed kidnapping attempt' at Campbell Hospital (sometimes referred to as the Seventh Street Hospital). After that fiasco, which was likely staged by Booth to give his faltering tribe something to chew on, to get them all nicely committed, and also to retrieve some weapons and tools that he had previously deposited with Arnold and O'Laughlen, he returned to

Baltimore, most likely to confer with agents there, but possibly to see Margaret (Maggie) Branson, possibly both. He had become romantically involved with Maggie since their meeting at West's Buildings Hospital in Baltimore after his wounding at Gettysburg. Indeed, he later told Assistant Secretary of War Major Thomas T. Eckert that he had fallen in love with her.[12] He then went to New York, most likely, again, to confer with agents there, but also to rendezvous with Booth, who arrived soon after he did. He may also have gone to Canada. He returned to Washington on 27 March after stopping once again in Baltimore.

So Powell is now back in Washington and primed, like a loaded gun, to do something momentous. After the Campbell Hospital thing, whatever it really was (the only certainty is that it was *not* a bona fide kidnapping attempt), he had been to Baltimore and most likely met with agents and backers there, even if he did see Maggie Branson. These were the prominent and wealthy men who gave him money and told him that his work would earn him not only personal glory and the eternal gratitude of the Southern people, but also, most likely, financial security for the rest of his days in an independent Confederacy. Is it likely that all this backing and encouragement was given to Powell so that he could kidnap someone – an act that could do the Confederacy no good at all (What would they have done in the face of Northern stonewalling? Pulled out Lincoln's fingernails?), according to Confederate President Jefferson Davis and top Confederate agent Thomas Nelson Conrad?[13] Davis said that only one kidnapping plan was ever presented to him, that of Major Joseph Walker Taylor, in the summer of 1862. It is worth mentioning, in passing, that this statement obviously excludes Booth's plan, for the very good reason that it never existed. It was Taylor's plan to kidnap Lincoln while he was making his way to or from the Soldiers' Home, which Lincoln did with some frequency in the warmer months to escape the city's heat, a fact well known to Confederate intelligence. In response, Davis said:

> I cannot give my authority, Walker … what value would he be to us as a prisoner? … If he were brought to Richmond, what could I do with him? He would have to be treated like the Magistrate of the North, and we have neither the time nor the provision.[14]

Another alleged kidnapping plot was the Captain Thomas Nelson Conrad and Sergeant Daniel Mountjoy Cloud Plot in 1864, which may have been an assassination plot disguised as a kidnapping plot and which apparently never ripened to a degree that would warrant Davis's attention. This is what one of its authors – Conrad – had to say about it:

> Even had we succeeded in capturing Mr Lincoln or any two or three members of his cabinet besides, a child could conclude in the light of subsequent events that the move would have accomplished no tangible good to the Confederacy. … At different times during the war, schemes for capturing Mr Lincoln and taking him to Richmond as a prisoner, had been planned more than once. … But plans invariably miscarried from different causes and an open attempt was never made.[15]

After the assassination, Conrad addressed the issue of a kidnapping plan by Booth in these words:

> the story which gained circulation after Mr Lincoln's death – that Booth and his fellow conspirators were the men at that time [late September 1864] planning a kidnapper's work appears to have as little foundation as a dozen other yarns in the same connection … there is every reason to believe no evidence in that direction was produced simply because there was none.[16]

In his memoirs, Sam Arnold, Booth's co-conspirator, complained of 'most favorable opportunities' (for kidnapping) which were missed. When he told Booth about them, Booth ignored him, saying he was too busy to think about them. Clearly, Booth never intended to kidnap anyone. Arnold also said that:

> Of course I know nothing of the assassination plot. The kidnapping was of such a quixotic nature that there is nothing in it, and with the last no overt act was committed,

> therefore, no proceedings could be established under the law.[17]

Let us remove whatever doubt may remain with respect to this issue by reference to the opinions of three men who probably knew more about the issue than anyone else, namely Judge Advocates Thomas Maley Harris and John Armor Bingham, both members of the Military Commission that tried the conspirators, and Assistant Secretary of War Major Thomas T. Eckert. Harris and Bingham were present every day of the trial and therefore observed and listened to some 371 witnesses. Both concluded that there was absolutely nothing to the kidnapping story, that it was an elaborate ruse to conceal Booth's true purpose, which was always assassination.[18] And Eckert, after a series of interviews with Powell after the assassination, concluded that murder was Booth's objective from as far back as January 1865, and that Powell was as much a part of the plan to accomplish that objective from that date as Booth was.[19] We may be nearly certain that Harris's and Bingham's conclusion is closer to the truth than Eckert's, which was limited by the fact that he was more concerned with Powell and his role than with what Booth intended prior to January 1865. He could speak authoritatively with respect to the former, but not the latter. We may safely conclude that Booth's objective was never kidnapping, that it was always assassination, from the moment he was recruited as an agent by the Confederate Secret Service, probably in early 1864, but it is only peripherally relevant to the issue before us, which is the control exercised by the Confederate leadership over Booth and Powell and their co-conspirators.

It should be noted, in passing, that I have chosen to use the word 'kidnap' and its derivatives to describe the taking of someone against his or her will. The word is used interchangeably in the historical records with the words 'abduction' and 'capture' and their derivatives, but I have chosen to use 'kidnap' because it is the word most often used, despite the fact that 'capture' is the more precise word, because according to the Union's own rules of war (The Lieber Code, General Orders, No. 100), the 'capture' of an enemy military leader was a legitimate act of war. Lincoln, being the Commander and Chief of the United States Army and Navy, under the Constitution, was obviously an 'enemy military leader'.

Shall we assume that the prominent and wealthy men in their palatial Baltimore homes did not have the intelligence of a child, or is it more likely that they were very shrewd operators who knew exactly what they were doing by bankrolling and encouraging Powell? That is to say that Powell's orders, and therefore his purpose and goal, were made clear to him from the beginning, if not directly from the leadership in Richmond, then through intermediaries such as the prominent and wealthy Baltimoreans who treated him royally and financed him, or by Mosby, Surratt, Parr or Booth himself, and that his purpose and goal were as well known to all of these as they were to Powell and Booth. That Powell visited Seward's mansion on Thursday morning (13 April) and again the next morning, came to the window and made inquiries there as to the state of the Secretary's health, supports a conclusion that he knew full well that he would try to murder him on Friday night, the order to do so having already been given to him before the 13th, most likely *well* before the 13th, indeed most likely in January 1865, when he apparently made first contact with Booth, who instructed him at that time to shoot Lincoln as he walked from the Telegraph Office to the White House, as we shall soon see.

When Powell was in New York, following the Campbell Hospital episode, he and Booth doubtless met with agents and supporters there too. What was their game? Listen to conspirator George Atzerodt in his 1 May 1865, confession:

> Booth said he had met a party in N. York who would get the Prest. certain. They were going to mine the end of the pres. House, near the War Dept. They knew an entrance to accomplish it through. Spoke about getting friends of the Presdt. to get up an entertainment & they would mix it in, have a serenade & thus get at the Presdt. & party. These were understood to be projects. Booth said if he did not get him quick the N. York crowd would. Booth knew the New York party apparently by a sign. He saw Booth give some kind of sign to two parties on the Ave. who he said were from New York.[20]

Does anyone suppose that 'get the Prest. certain' referred to kidnapping? Does anyone suppose that 'get him quick' referred to kidnapping?

And who comprised this 'New York crowd' and the 'New York party' anyway? Does anyone suppose that it was a rogue operation? Or is it more reasonable to suppose that it was following orders from Richmond? Clearly, the latter. And if they were under orders from Richmond, is it reasonable to suppose that Booth and his team were not? Clearly, that is *not* a reasonable supposition.

Powell may also have gone to Canada. If he didn't on this occasion (following Campbell Hospital), he did earlier, because Union agent Richard Montgomery testified at the trial of the conspirators that he saw him there and in Niagara Falls in the summer of 1864.[21] The Confederate Secret Service had its headquarters in Canada, nicely out of the jurisdiction of the United States and the effective reach of Lafayette C. Baker's National Detective Police, aka the United States Secret Service. Agents of the Confederate Secret Service were comfortably ensconced at the St Lawrence Hotel in Montreal, but some were in Toronto, Hamilton, St Catherines and Windsor. What was their game? We may judge their intentions from the conversations between agents that were testified to and recorded in the trial of the conspirators, wherein there is one reference to 'capturing' and dozens to assassination. And isn't that exactly what we should expect? The logistics of kidnapping a public figure successfully, especially a very high-ranking public figure and especially from a public place, are all but impossible. Who would seriously undertake such a near-impossibility, especially when there are no real rewards for accomplishing it? In his summation to the Military Commission at the trial of the conspirators, Judge Advocate John A. Bingham mocked and ridiculed all talk of kidnapping as follows:

> Thus it appears by the testimony that the proposition made to Davis was to kill and murder the deadliest enemies of the Confederacy – not to kidnap them, as is now pretended here; that by the declaration of Sanders, Tucker, Thompson, Clay, Cleary, Harper, and Young, the conspirators in Canada, the agreement and combination among them was to kill and murder Abraham Lincoln, William H. Seward, Andrew Johnson, Ulysses S. Grant, Edwin M. Stanton, and others of his advisors, and not to kidnap them; it appears

> from every utterance of John Wilkes Booth … that, as early as November [1864], the proposition with him was to kill and murder – not to kidnap. …
>
> … it was to be done at the theatre by throwing the President out of the box upon the floor of the stage, when the accused was to catch him. The very announcement of this testimony excited derision that such a tragedy meant only to take the President and carry him gently away! This pygmy to catch the giant as the assassins hurled him to the floor from an elevation of twelve feet! … No man can, for a moment, believe that any one of these conspirators hoped or desired, by such a proceeding as that stated by the prisoner, to take the President alive in the presence of thousands assembled in the theatre after he had been thus thrown upon the floor of the stage, much less to carry him through the city, through the lines of your army, and deliver him into the hands of the rebels. No such purpose was expressed or hinted by the conspirators in Canada, who commissioned Booth to let these assassinations on contract. I shall waste not a moment more in combatting such an absurdity.[22]

May we safely conclude that Powell's mission, when he arrived in Washington on 15 March, was assassination and that he and Booth were of one mind on the subject? We may, and for further support of that conclusion, if more is needed, we have the statement by Mortimer Ruggles, who was one of three Confederate soldiers who escorted Booth and Herold to the farm of Richard Garrett, when they were fugitives. Ruggles said that Booth, after the three Confederate soldiers had gained his confidence, told him: 'In the plot to kill, Paine [i.e. Powell] alone was implicated … not even Herold knowing what was to be done. Atzerodt knew nothing of the intended assassination.'[23] The last part of that statement is inconsistent with other evidence we have, but this is not the place to examine it.

Observe Booth's use of the passive voice when he said 'what was to be done'. Not 'what I decided to do', or 'what I was going to do', or 'what I planned to do', or words of a similar kind that would indicate that this was a Booth thing, Booth's idea, something he very recently decided to do, on his own, without input from anyone else, after plotting and scheming for months to kidnap the President, per the conventional wisdom. The passive voice, rather, is indicative of a plan and deed that had long been decided upon by others, relative to whom he was little more than a pawn, an important one, to be sure, in the overall scheme of things, when there was little left to the Confederacy but decapitation of their enemy by multiple assassinations, but still a pawn, following orders from above and giving them below. 'What was to be done.' Does that sound like something Booth decided to do when he found out, about noon on 14 April, when he visited Ford's Theatre, that Lincoln and Grant were going to be at Ford's that night? Does it sound like something Booth decided to do at the 8.00 p.m. Herndon House meeting between him, Powell, Herold, Atzerodt and possibly John Surratt? Does it sound like something he decided to do three nights previously when he heard Lincoln talk about enfranchising blacks in Louisiana? All three of these propositions constitute the conventional wisdom. Or does it sound more like something that was in the works for a long time and that involved more hands than his? 'What was to be done' – the words are enormously telling, pregnant with meaning as to where ultimate responsibility for the great crime lay and as to when the decision was made and the orders given to decapitate the United States government. Once again, the conventional wisdom is wrong.

It was late in the game. Despite the failures of the Wistar, Dahlgren and Kilpatrick raids against Richmond, by May 1864, at the latest (the battle of Spotsylvania), the issues of Union and Emancipation had been decided militarily. Kidnapping of Lincoln, always a bad idea, held no hope at all for saving the Confederacy, but multiple assassinations did. It was a long shot, to be sure, but a long shot is better than no shot at all. And even if, as was likely, Confederate leaders did not get as many as they would like, they might at least get *some*. And even if, as was likely, they did not create the chaos necessary to win the war, or at least to avert total defeat, they might at least deny to *some* the sweetness of their triumph and thereby realise *some* retribution against those who had crushed their dreams of independence, their tormentors, their despoilers and their would-be assassins. Accordingly, after

Wistar-Dahlgren-Kilpatrick, if not before, kidnapping was not an option. All talk of it, therefore, was deception, an attempt to mislead and conceal, a red herring, or the work of amateurs. The real goal was to 'leave the government entirely without a head'.[24] That is what Jacob Thompson, head of the Canadian Cabinet, said, according to Charles Dunham (alias Sanford Conover), a Cabinet member who testified for the prosecution. Thompson added, according to Dunham, that if Lincoln, Johnson, Seward, Stanton, Grant and Chase (Salmon P. Chase, Secretary of the Treasury, later Chief Justice of the Supreme Court) were assassinated, there was no way, under the Constitution, the government could elect another president.[25] The decision to assassinate these men, therefore, was made, and it was most likely made in March or April 1864, in Richmond, after the failed raids. Powell had a role to play in this plot, and he would play it. But before Booth gave him his assignment to murder Seward, he would urge him on at least three occasions to murder the President himself, in Washington, thereby relieving Booth of the very difficult and stressful task of doing so, one for which Powell, having made a career of killing (in combat, but not murder in cold blood), was obviously better suited, or so Booth thought.

The first occasion was on a very wintry night. Booth, in some degree conversant with the President's habits and schedule, most likely through his Secret Service contacts, instructed Powell to lie in wait in bushes and shrubs that lined the footpath between the White House and the War Department. Powell did so, crouching in the bushes in front of the White House Conservatory, armed with a revolver, waiting for Lincoln to return from a visit with Stanton and/or the Telegraph Office. In time, and as foreseen by Booth, Lincoln came Powell's way, but he was not alone. Walking with him, presumably as a bodyguard, was Major Thomas T. Eckert, who, in addition to being the Assistant Secretary of War, was head of the War Department's Telegraph Office. It was a cold and frosty night, with ice on the bushes and on the footpath, the result of a quick freeze of a light rain. Powell heard Lincoln say to Eckert, 'Major, spread out, spread out, or we shall break through the ice.' The two then stopped and Lincoln, characteristically, used the occasion to tell Eckert a story from his youth in Illinois in which a travelling companion uttered the same words when they were crossing a frozen Sangamon Creek. Powell, perhaps disarmed by Lincoln's quaint storytelling, but more likely intimidated by the presence of the bodyguard, left the scene without having accomplished anything and without having made his presence known, making use of the ice-encrusted shrubs to conceal his exit.

This account is corroborated in its entirety by Eckert himself, who interviewed Powell, at length, after the assassination. Recalling the conversation between Lincoln and Eckert, Powell asked Eckert if he was Lincoln's companion that night and was told by Eckert that, in fact, he was. Powell's biographer, Betty J. Ownsbey, places this incident in January 1865, which is consistent with the description of the weather, though there is nothing in the original source establishing the date with certainty. The Naval Observatory record for 21 January 1865 is consistent with the description of the weather that night, so it must be regarded as probable that the incident occurred on that date, though the record for 14 December 1864 is also consistent with the description of the weather, and that date, therefore, is also a possibility, albeit a remote one. It was during this period that Powell was staying at Miller's Hotel and the Branson boarding house in Baltimore, so it must be the case that Powell made at least one trip to Washington from Baltimore, probably more than one, for Booth-related work, before his arrival on 15 March for the main event or events. In this connection, Maggie Branson claimed to remember a night in February when Powell did not return to the boarding house, so a trip to Washington in that month is also a possibility.[26] Booth, of course, was very disappointed by the outcome of his well-laid plan and, if what happened later is an indication, berated Powell for his failure. But Booth had nothing if not singleness of purpose. He wasn't finished and neither was Powell.

On an afternoon in March, Booth took Powell to the White House grounds. If this occurred prior to 15 March, it had to have been incident to another special trip by Powell from Baltimore. It could have been 16 March, the day after the Gautier's Restaurant meeting and the day before the Campbell Hospital episode, or 27 March or thereafter, inasmuch as he returned to Washington that day from Baltimore. In any case, Powell's Svengali again urged him to kill the President, this time by sending a card in to the President, using any name at all, and then, upon being admitted to his presence, shooting him. Booth apparently had a very cavalier view of the President's accessibility. One had only to send his card, with any name on it, and the Chief Magistrate of the United States would find time for him or her, putting aside the business of moving armies and the navy to win a civil war, finding the money to finance the effort, maintaining decent relations with the rest of the world, overseeing domestic policies and programmes, contending with political adversaries and pressure groups all over the landscape and keeping Mary Todd and the rest of his family reasonably happy. Nothing, apparently, was said to Powell about getting past armed guards, Secretaries John Hay and John G. Nicolay, Assistant Secretary William O. Stoddard and any number of other loyalists who served the President one way or another in the White House.

Well, Booth was far from a mental giant. In fact, there is enough evidence to conclude that he was quite stupid. How bright can a man be who believed that slavery was 'one of the greatest blessings ... that God ever bestowed upon a favored nation', who drank excessively, who often scrapped physically with his peers and who hated cats and is said to have killed all those he found on the family farm? His sister, Asia, said he was a slow learner. She described him as 'my slow student' who was 'not quick at acquiring knowledge' and 'found it far from easy to keep up with his classmates'. His brother Edwin, one of the finest actors of his day and a staunch Unionist, said he was a 'rattle-pated fellow, filled with quixotic notions ... a wild-brained boy'. He added: 'All his theatrical friends speak of him as a poor, crazy boy, and such his family think of him.' Recall that Secret Service agent Thomas Harbin used substantially the same term that Edwin did to describe Booth, calling him 'a crazy fellow'. In any case, the order was tall for the recently acquired conspirator, so he declined, despite Booth's goading. Whether he did so because his experience as a killer did not include victims who were high-ranking political figures, or because he was averse to cold-blooded murder, or because he had the good sense to realise that such an effort was almost certain to fail and might get him killed in the bargain, cannot be known. What is known, however, is that Booth again berated him for lack of courage. But, again, Svengali wasn't finished, and neither was his pupil.

In the evening of 11 April, Lincoln addressed a substantial crowd from a window in the north portico of the White House. With Robert

E. Lee having surrendered to Ulysses S. Grant at Appomattox only two days earlier, and with the war clearly nearing a successful conclusion, he was in a celebratory mood and, among other things, spoke about enfranchising blacks in Louisiana. This, of course, infuriated the racist Booth, who was in the crowd with Powell and Herold. Silhouetted against the light, Lincoln appeared to present an easy target for an assassin. Wishing to catch fire with someone else's hands again, Booth urged Powell to take advantage of the opportunity and simply shoot the President then and there. Again, Booth overestimated his powers of persuasion, because, again, Powell refused. Perhaps he was simply awed by the President's august presence. Or perhaps he realised that he would be torn limb from limb by the crowd if he shot the President, even if he only wounded him. Or perhaps it was some of both. In any case, Booth again accused Powell of cowardice, which must surely have disturbed and angered the stray knight from the Black Forest, who had faced more perils in one week in Virginia than Booth had faced in his entire life. Fine fellow this Booth: refuse to catch fire that he could as easily catch and you are a coward. What caused 'the terrible Lewis Powell' to continue with a 26-year-old abusive actor, and in a subservient role no less? The only thing that *could* cause it: He was, by his own admission, a Confederate soldier and he was following orders. At the Gautier's Restaurant meeting, Arnold, furious with Booth because he persisted with his 'kidnapping' plan, despite every good reason to abandon it, had said, 'You [Booth] can be the leader of the party, but not my executioner.' Powell must surely have been thinking the same thing, even if he didn't say it.[27]

What followed, three days later, was Powell's attempt on the life of Seward, some aspects of which we touched upon earlier. Though Seward survived, as previously said, Powell incarnadined the household, seriously wounding five family members and servants before leaving the scene in a frenzy, mounting his one-eyed Bay and galloping away. Frederick Seward, the Secretary's son, was so gravely wounded by the blows rained upon his head by Powell, who used his misfired and broken revolver for the purpose, that he barely survived.

What was not previously said, however, is that the conventional wisdom, accepted by almost all assassination historians, is that Herold accompanied Powell to Seward's home on the fateful night and then waited for him outside, like a dutiful sentry, because Powell was stupid, didn't know his way around the city and would therefore need a guide to help him escape after the bloody deed was done. The conventional wisdom, further, is that Herold panicked and fled on his mount when he heard the cry of 'murder' from William Bell, a 19-year-old black servant who ran down the stairs and out the front door. What we have here, pure and simple, is a case of a statement made thirty years after the fact by someone who was not an eyewitness (Louis Weichmann, a boarder in Mary Surratt's boarding house), that was seized upon by early historians and repeated so often by later historians that it now wears the mantel of truth. And this despite the fact that there is no original source, nor is there a scrap of evidence worthy of the name, to support this scenario and that, conversely, there is abundant evidence to support the opposite conclusion, i.e. that Powell was unaccompanied by Herold or anyone else when he went to the Seward mansion that night. Well, this too, as with the misfortunes that befell Powell during his attempt, previously described, is interesting, but, again, is not relevant to the principal purpose of this chapter, which is to establish that Powell was, directly or indirectly, at all times from the summer of 1864, if not earlier, under the direction and control of the Confederate leadership in Richmond and Canada, principally Davis, Benjamin and Thompson, and Thompson's successor, General Edwin G. Lee. So we will forego further discussion of the issue.

Powell was caught after trying and failing to leave the city and make his way, almost certainly, to Baltimore. He didn't fail to leave the city because he was stupid and didn't know his way around it (he had no problem finding his way to Seward's mansion on the mornings of the 13th and 14th, nor finding his way to Mrs Surratt's boarding house on the night of the 17th); he failed because his horse had an accident and went lame, which forced him to abandon the animal and proceed on foot into and through fields, woods and cemeteries. After three days and nights of a feral existence and desperate for sleep and food, he gambled and lost. He went to the only place in the city where he knew he could get help – the boarding house. He arrived at 11.00 p.m. on the 17th and was greeted not by Mrs Surratt, but by government detectives. His appearance was all they needed to arrest him. His attempt to explain his presence went nowhere.[28]

What followed, including his trial and execution, need not detain us. What will occupy us, however, are conversations he had with Thomas Eckert and Abram Dunn Gillette during the period of his incarceration.

Powell was interviewed extensively after 22 April by Eckert, who was skilled in the art of interrogation. It took him a while to gain Powell's confidence, but he did gain it, to a degree, except that some of the things he said to Eckert were conflicting, and no amount of confidence in Eckert would induce Powell to reveal the names of his contacts other than those of Booth's action team, who were already known to the prosecution.

For obvious reasons, Eckert did not take notes during his sessions with Powell. He said he prepared a 'memorandum', which he planned to use to record Powell's comments about Seward, his intentions, his motives, his regrets, etc., but he apparently lost it, because he never prepared his summary for Seward and he never produced the memorandum, later saying that he wasn't even sure where it was – Washington or New York. There is something disingenuous about this. Perhaps he felt that publicising Powell's comments would be a violation of the trust that Powell had placed in him. It would not be surprising if a bond had developed between them and that Powell had asked for and received from Eckert his word that some of what he told Eckert would remain unsaid to anyone else. In any case, there are no written records of the conversations and we are thus forced to make do with Eckert's recollections. These conversations took place from approximately 22 April until the day preceding Powell's execution (7 July), so there must have been a lot said. But except for a few statements, the contents of the talks are lost to history, which may be what Eckert wanted. Still, what survived and emerged is heavy with significance.[29]

Powell told Eckert that he recognised Booth as his superior officer,[30] from which we may conclude that Powell was never a rogue agent and that Confederate leaders worked through Booth to control him. There is no other reasonable conclusion. Powell was still a Confederate soldier. As such, he followed orders. A subordinate position is not something he would have assumed without being instructed to do so. These were the rules of the game. Booth has a team and a mission. You are to become a member of his team and assist him in his mission. He is the leader and you must accept him as such.

In response to a question about co-conspirators, Powell said that it was his 'impression' that arrangements had been made with others for the same disposition of other federal office holders as he was to make of Seward.[31] It seems likely that Powell was hedging; that he knew full well that such arrangements had been made, but chose to say that it was only an 'impression', thereby making the revelation more tolerable to his conscience and also making follow-up questions relative to the identities of would-be assassins, which he had no wish or intention to answer, less likely. Eckert said repeatedly that Powell was exceedingly careful not to reveal the identities of others whom he knew to be involved in the conspiracy. In any case, can we read in Powell's statement anything but a well-laid plan to decapitate the United States government, or if not a well-laid plan, at least a plan? Clearly, by so saying, he could not have had reference to Booth's immediate action team, who were otherwise occupied on the fateful night. Furthermore, Atzerodt had balked at his assignment that night (Powell would later confirm this) and Herold was said, in the trial of the conspirators, to have the mentality of an 11-year-old[32] – not exactly assassination timber. (On the night of the assassination, Herold was required only to assist Atzerodt and then to wait near the Navy Yard Bridge to assist Booth in his escape.)[33]

Powell's statement exactly dovetails with the 10 May 1865 letter, previously referred to, from a Union agent in Paris to another Union operative in the States, which letter came into the possession of the Bureau of Military Justice after the assassination. In the letter, the Union agent quotes from a note from a Confederate agent, identified as 'Johnston' (probably an alias), that he had partially read. In 'Johnston's' note, he states that if everything had gone according to plan on the 14th, fifteen Yankees would be dead, not one ('had it been carried out as was arranged previously, some 15 of the Yankee leaders would have been now quietly resting where they should have gone 4 years [ago]'). Significantly, 'Johnston' also said that he had followed Grant for two days, thus demonstrating the breadth of the conspiracy. He also said that he arrived in Washington at 5.00 p.m. on the day of the assassination and that within half an hour knew that an 'attack' would be

Right: Asia Booth Clarke, *c*.1850s. She loved her brother, John, and he her. She said he was enigmatic – gentle and romantic, but also dogmatic and fanatical. She and her husband, John Sleeper Clarke, assailed by the assassination and its aftermath, emigrated to England in 1868, where she died in 1888.

Below: Gen. Benjamin F. Butler, *c*.1860s. Never far from controversy, this colourful political general is not noted for any great accomplishment on the battlefield, but for his command of occupied New Orleans and his infamous Order No. 28, which provided that any woman who offended a Union officer would be regarded as a 'woman of the town' plying her trade. For that he was called 'Beast' Butler, and for purloining silverware from Southern homes he was also called 'Spoons' Butler.

Clement C. Clay, Jr., *c.*1860s. He was a United States Senator from Alabama (1853–61) and, together with Jacob Thompson, was sent by Jefferson Davis and Judah Benjamin to Canada in April 1864, with verbal orders only, to organise terror plots against the North. He joined James Holcombe, who had been sent to Canada by Davis and Benjamin in February 1864, also with verbal orders only. *(Courtesy of the Library of Congress)*

Dr Samuel A. Mudd, *c.*1860s. He said that Southerners were more sensitive than Northerners, with a keener sense of honour. Sadly, his post-arrest behaviour did not exemplify that code. He said his Oath of Allegiance to the United States wasn't worth 'a chew of tobacco'. His own counsel, Frederick Stone, later wrote that 'his prevarications were painful … it was a terrible thing to extricate him from the [coils] he had woven about himself.' *(Courtesy of the James O. Hall Research Center, Surratt House Museum/MMCPPC)*

Dr Luke P. Blackburn, *c.*1860. A Kentuckian and supporter of the Southern cause, he acquired a reputation as an expert on the nineteenth-century scourge known as yellow fever. Sadly, he appears to have turned his back on his earlier work fighting the disease and played a major role in an 1864 scheme to spread pestilence in the North, which scheme included an attempt to assassinate Lincoln by infecting him with the disease. The evidence against him is not conclusive, but it is clear and convincing. He rehabilitated himself after the war and was elected Governor of Kentucky from 1879 to 1883.

Gen. Edward H. Ripley, *c.*1860. He was a brigadier general of the 9th Vermont Infantry who commanded the occupying forces in Richmond on and after 2 April 1865. It was to him that William H. Snyder, an enlisted man in Gabriel Rains's Torpedo Bureau, reported the dispatch from the Bureau, on or about 1 April, of a party whose mission he vaguely understood to be the murder of Lincoln and perhaps other federal officeholders. Ripley tried to alert Lincoln to the danger, but the President was utterly exhausted from his labours and therefore not disposed to take the warning seriously.

Francis Lieber, *c*.1865. Despite being from South Carolina, this German-American jurist supported the Union cause and warned his fellow Southerners against secession. He worked with the War Department and President Lincoln in drafting laws of war, the most famous of which was General Orders No. 100, aka the Lieber Code. It governed the Union army, but was expressly rejected by Confederate Secretary of War James Seddon. Despite that rejection, the Confederate army did endorse and apply many of its rules.

Frederick Seward, *c*.1860s. Assistant Secretary of State under his father and later in the Hayes administration, he played a major role in saving Lincoln's life in 1861 (the Baltimore Plot) and his father's in 1865. Because he wisely refused Powell access to the Secretary in his sick bed, he was pistol-whipped by Powell. He survived the beating, though barely, and lived until 1915. *(Courtesy of the Seward House Museum)*

Above left: Gabriel J. Rains, *c*.1865. After being wounded at the battle of Seven Pines (1862), he was placed in command of the Conscription and Torpedo Bureaus at Richmond and acquired a reputation as an explosives wizard. He oversaw the protection of the harbours of Charleston, Savannah, Mobile and other Southern ports, making use of torpedoes, now called mines. He also invented anti-personnel land mines, which became known as 'Rains mines'.

Above right: George N. Sanders, *c*.1860s. He was the wounded grizzly bear in the Canadian Cabinet, because his son had died in Union captivity. He was also an assassin's mentor. He was a very bright fellow, bright enough to devise and then implement a scheme to shift the blame for the assassination away from the Confederate leadership and onto someone who could no longer be punished for it. It worked. *(Courtesy of the Library of Congress)*

H. Judson Kilpatrick, 1863–5. Known as 'Killcavalry' (or 'Kill Cavalry') because of his disregard of casualties in battle, which appeared reckless to some, but aggressive, fearless and ambitious to others. He was as reckless in his personal life as he was in battle, which caused him to be jailed more than once. His most famous exploit was his raid (with Ulric Dahlgren) on Richmond from 28 February to 2 March 1864, which failed, but which ignited a firestorm of controversy about the ultimate purposes of the raid.

Above left: Isaac J. Wistar, *c*.1860. He had a lackluster career in the war, acquiring more fame afterwards as a penologist and prolific writer, which included an autobiography. His most famous exploit was his raid on Richmond, under the direction of Gen. Benjamin Butler, on 6 and 7 February 1864. His purposes were to free Union POWs, wreck public property, including the Tredegar Iron Works, and capture Confederate leaders, including Davis. It failed, but the Southern press had a field day with it, especially the last purpose, which was converted from capture to assassination.

Above right: Jacob Thompson, *c*.1860s. He was the United States Secretary of the Interior under President Buchanan (1857–61). In April 1864, he was sent by Jefferson Davis and Judah Benjamin to Canada, together with Clement Clay, both of whom joined James Holcombe, who had been sent there by Davis in February. Their purpose, contained in verbal orders only, was to organise terror plots against the North, including spreading pestilence and assassination of federal officeholders. *(Courtesy of the Library of Congress)*

James P. Holcombe, *c*.1860. He was a professor of law at the University of Virginia and an author of legal treatises. During the war, he represented his district in the first Confederate Congress. In February 1864, Jefferson Davis sent him to Canada with verbal orders to organise terror and assassination plots against the North. He was soon joined by Jacob Thompson and Clement C. Clay, who also had verbal orders, which included assisting Dr Luke P. Blackburn with a scheme to spread pestilence in the North and to assassinate Lincoln using 'infected' shirts.

Jefferson F. Davis, *c.*1861. He had been a United States Congressman (1845–6), United States Senator (1847–51 and 1857–61) and United States Secretary of War (1853–7) before becoming President of the Confederate States of America (1861–5). Sooner than accept the election of a Republican president, he would 'tear this Constitution to pieces'.

John A. Bingham, *c.*1870. He was a member of the US House of Representatives from Ohio (1855–63 and 1865–73) and the US Ambassador to Japan (1873–85). He was also a very highly regarded lawyer, which is why Lincoln appointed him Judge Advocate of the Union army and why Stanton appointed him to serve as Assistant Judge Advocate General in the trial of the Lincoln conspirators. He was also the author of the 14th Amendment to the Constitution of the United States, which provided for national citizenship, privileges and immunities, due process and equal protection of the laws.

Above left: John H. Surratt, Jnr., *c*.1860s. 'If you knew all the things I have done, it would make you stare (or gape),' he said to Dr Lewis J.A. McMillan, his guardian aboard the *Peruvian* on their trip to Europe in September 1865. 'We have killed Lincoln, the niggers' friend,' he said to Henri Beaumont de Ste. Marie, a former schoolmate and a fellow Papal Zouave in Italy. Sadly, he got away with everything; he was released in 1867 after a trial and a hung jury and he lived until 1916. *(Courtesy of the Library of Congress)*

Above right: John S. Mosby, *c*.1860s. The 'Gray Ghost' hardly needs an introduction. His fighting qualities were unsurpassed and the exploits of his Rangers (43rd Battalion, 1st Virginia Cavalry) are legendary. Regrettably, with respect to the assassination of Lincoln, his hands were not clean. He could not have been ignorant of the Harney mission and its purpose, which, the evidence is persuasive, he facilitated. To three Confederate soldiers who made contact with Booth after the assassination, he said (according to one of them), referring to Booth, 'By God I could take that man in my arms.'

John Wilkes Booth, *c*.1860s. The faces of thousands of women smiled and turned to him 'as the sunflowers turn upon their stalks to follow the beloved sun'. His comeliness, however, concealed a weak mind that would be his undoing and the undoing of many others. His brother, Edwin, described him as 'a rattle-pated fellow, filled with Quixotic notions … a wild-brained boy. … All his theatrical friends speak of him as a poor, crazy boy, and such his family think of him.' Confederate agent Thomas Harbin referred to him as 'a crazy fellow'.

John Yeats Beall, 1865. He was from a prominent Virginia family. Without official authority, he launched two privateers near the confluence of the Potomac River and Chesapeake Bay. He was captured and jailed from November 1863 to 5 May 1864. Upon his release, he tried to free Confederate POWs imprisoned on Johnson's Island, Ohio, and then to derail a train carrying other POWs near Niagara, New York. He was captured, tried, convicted and sentenced to be hanged. Many in high places, North and South, tried to save him, but without success. He was executed on 24 February 1865.

Judah P. Benjamin, *c.*1860s. He was a United States Senator from Louisiana (1853–61) and, successively, Attorney General (1861), Secretary of War (1861–2) and Secretary of State (1862–5) of the Confederate States of America. His smile was said to infuriate his enemies, but give great comfort to President Davis. At the same time, it betrays the temper of a man capable of masterminding terror and assassination plots, which he did. Knowing he would not escape the hangman, at the end of the war, he first destroyed all his records and correspondence and then fled the country. After an incredibly harrowing journey, he made it to England and established an entirely new career and life, dying a natural death in 1884 in Paris, where he is buried. He was 72. *(Courtesy of the Library of Congress)*

Above left: Lewis T. Powell, 1865. He was described as 'the terrible Lewis Powell'. It was written that he 'rode fast and far to share war's fiercest perils … a stray knight from the Black Forest'. He 'had the reputation of having killed a great many men, and when any desperate matter was to be undertaken, he was selected'. *(Courtesy of the Library of Congress)*

Above right: Execution of four Lincoln conspirators. The Military Commission that tried the eight defendants found all of them guilty. It sentenced Edman Spangler to six years in prison. It sentenced Dr Samuel Mudd, Samuel Arnold and Michael O'Laughlen to life in prison. It sentenced Mary Surratt, Lewis Powell, David Herold and George Atzerodt to death by hanging. In this photo by Alexander Gardner, the latter four have begun their eternities. *(Courtesy of the Library of Congress)*

The Lincoln Conspirators. This composite photo identifies John Wilkes Booth, Mary Surratt, Lewis Powell, David Herold, Samuel Arnold, Michael O'Laughlen, Edman Spangler, George Atzerodt and John Surratt as Lincoln conspirators. Inaccuracies are: Spangler was not a conspirator, he was innocent; Booth was a conspirator, of course, but he was dead, having been shot to death on 26 April 1865 by Boston Corbett, one of the troopers who surrounded him in a barn; John Surratt was not tried with the others, because he was a fugitive at the time, but was captured in Egypt and returned for trial by a civil court in 1867; and Dr Samuel Mudd, who almost certainly was a conspirator, and who was convicted as such, is not shown.

Louis Weichmann, *c.*1860s. Together with John Lloyd, the proprietor of Mary Surratt's tavern in Surrattsville (now Clinton), he was the prosecution's star witness at the trial of the conspirators in 1865. Despite Herculean efforts by very competent defence counsel, his testimony was never contradicted. In 1867, he testified in John Surratt's trial, said essentially the same thing he had said in the 1865 trial and then spent the rest of his life in fear. On his deathbed in 1902 he affirmed that he had told nothing but the truth in both trials.

Mary E. Surratt, *c.*1850. Said Louis Weichmann, one of her boarders: 'Here was a woman devoted body and soul to the cause of the South … her meat and drink.' Though there are still some who contend that she was innocent of participation in the conspiracy to murder Lincoln, the great weight of scholarly opinion is that she was in fact guilty, a judgment that finds greater favour with the passage of time and more research. *(Courtesy of the James O. Hall Research Center, Surratt House Museum/MNCPPC)*

Above left: Robert Cobb Kennedy, *c*.1865. Despite a privileged childhood, he had a bad record at West Point, for which he was thrown out. His military service consisted of his fighting at the battle of Shiloh, where he was wounded. He was imprisoned on Johnson's Island, Ohio, but escaped, being one of only a few to succeed in doing that. He went to Canada, where he was recruited by Jacob Thompson to burn New York City. The plot was only partially successful. He was subsequently arrested, tried, convicted and then hanged at Fort Lafayette in New York on 25 March 1865.

Above right: Samuel Knapp Chester, *c*.1860s. He was an actor friend of Booth's from New York City. Booth went there and tried to recruit him in his conspiracy to 'kidnap' Lincoln, telling him that there were between fifty and 100 involved in the conspiracy and promising him that he would never want for money again. Chester was having none of it. He testified at the trial of the conspirators that it was his impression, listening to Booth, that Booth had the support of 'insurgent leaders'.

Thomas Henry Hines, *c*.1860s. This was the man chosen by the Confederate leadership to oversee a plan to initiate a second civil war in the North by splitting the east from the west and creating what was known as the Northwest Confederacy, which would consist of the states of Ohio, Indiana and Illinois. The plan called for the assassination of the governors of all three states, as well as all federal, state and even municipal officials who stood in the way. Hines, who took his orders from Jacob Thompson and James Seddon, who took theirs from Jefferson Davis and Judah Benjamin, demonstrated great personal courage, but the plan failed utterly because Union intelligence quickly learned of it and took appropriate countermeasures.

Thomas T. Eckert, *c.*1860s. An Ohioan by birth, he became an expert telegrapher, putting that skill to use first for General George B. McClellan during the Peninsula Campaign and then in the War Department under Secretary Stanton. He earned the great respect of both Stanton and Lincoln for his skills as a telegrapher, but also for his organisational skills. After the assassination of Lincoln, he was assigned to interrogate conspirator Lewis Powell. He did so at great length and with great skill, which led to a relationship between the two men characterised by trust and a fine rapport. Sadly, most of his notes of the conversations he had with Powell were lost, or so he said.

Thomas A. Jones, *c.*1875. This self-described chief of the Confederate Secret Service in Maryland picked up where Samuel Cox left off. He provided the two fugitives (Booth and Herold) with food and newspapers while they hid in the pine thicket of Cox's property until such time as Jones felt it was safe for them to cross the Potomac River. In 1893, when it was safe, he wrote a little book, telling, if not all, at least more than he had previously told. Among his admissions was the fact that he knew all about Booth and his conspiracy.

Ulric Dahlgren, *c.*1864. He was the son of Admiral John A. Dahlgren and a favourite of Lincoln. The elder Dahlgren commanded part of the federal blockade and invented the famous Dahlgren cannon, used to great effect by Union warships. The younger Dahlgren, together with H. Judson Kilpatrick, led a raid on Richmond from 28 February to 2 March 1864. It failed and he was killed. Papers found on his corpse were said to contain orders to kill Jefferson Davis and his cabinet. Though possibly forged, at least in part, the papers were accepted as genuine by the Confederate leadership and the Southern press and therefore the great majority of Southerners. At least in part, these alleged orders accounted for the Confederate campaign of terror against the North in the last year of the war, including, quite possibly, the assassination of Lincoln.

Ward Hill Lamon, *c.*1860s. He was one of Lincoln's closest friends and his self-appointed bodyguard. During Lincoln's term, Lamon, aware of the constant threat of physical harm to his president, guarded him zealously, frequently walking about the grounds of the White House at night and even wrapping himself in his cloak and lying down to sleep in front of Lincoln's door. Lincoln sent him to Richmond on 14 April 1865, on business. Before leaving, he admonished the President to avoid public outings, especially the theatre. *(Courtesy of the Library of Congress)*

William H. Seward, *c.*1850, before the attack by Lewis T. Powell. He was Governor of New York (1839–42), United States Senator (1849–61) and United States Secretary of State (1861–9). His 'irrepressible conflict' speech, given in 1858 in Rochester, New York, portended a national cataclysm. *(Courtesy of the Seward House Museum)*

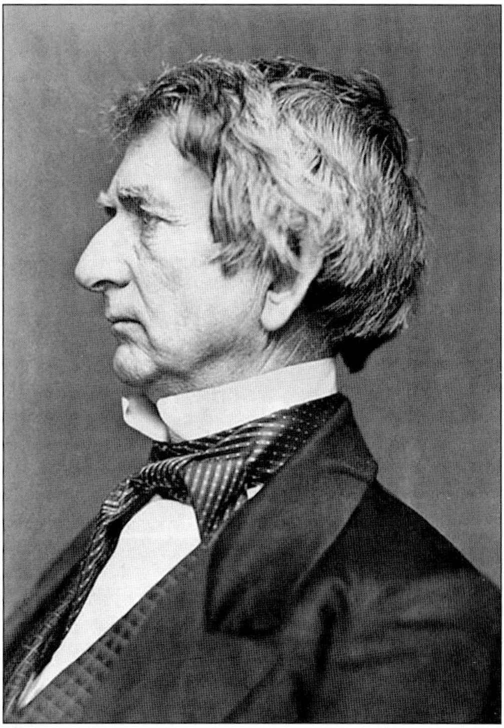

William H. Seward, *c.*1866, after the attack by Lewis T. Powell. *(Courtesy of the Seward House Museum)*

Thomas H. Harbin, *c.*1860s. He was a Confederate spy who participated in Booth's conspiracy despite having a dim view of the actor – referring to him as 'a crazy fellow'. Atzerodt mentions, in one of his many confessions, Harbin's participation. Harbin met with Booth before and after the assassination of Lincoln, facilitating the escape of the two fugitives, Booth and Herold. He then left the country for an indeterminate period, perhaps as long as five years. When he returned, and when it was safe between safe and the comma: to do so, he wrote about his exploits as a Secret Service agent and said, *inter alia*, that he reported directly to Jefferson Davis. That admission speaks volumes about Davis's, and therefore Judah Benjamin's, knowledge of Booth's conspiracy.

Samuel Bland Arnold, 1865. He was a handsome man who revelled in pleasure, but who was 'always hard up for money', which made him easy prey for Booth. Though he exercised incredibly bad judgment, he was fundamentally a decent man: what he supposed would be his last words on earth were of Dash – his dog. When he and his fellow conspirators (Michael O'Laughlen and Dr Samuel Mudd), who were serving their sentences at Ft. Jefferson, were contacted by President Andrew Johnson's enemies, who promised them freedom in return for their implication of Johnson in the assassination of Lincoln, he told them, in so many words, that they were crazy and to go home.

made that night, thus demonstrating knowledge of Booth's plans by the Confederate underground at least three hours before he allegedly made them at the 8.00 p.m. Herndon House meeting. He also said that Booth had said he would never be taken; that he will 'bullet himself first', thus demonstrating that Booth was not only familiar to the Confederate underground, but was a part of it.[34]

We may safely conclude, therefore, that Powell was part of a broad conspiracy to decapitate the United State government, that he took his orders from Booth and that Booth took his orders from those who were higher in the command structure, i.e. Davis and Benjamin or intermediaries whose identity will almost certainly never be known, but whose existence we can be certain of, based upon admissions that were made by John Surratt. In his affidavit of 10 July 1866, addressed to Secretary of State William Seward, Henri Beaumont de Ste Marie, Surratt's fellow Papal Zouave in Italy, stated that in conversations he had had with Surratt, the latter admitted to him that he and Booth had killed Lincoln, adding that 'they had acted under the orders of men who are not yet known, some of whom are still in New York and others in London', and, further, that '[I] had acted under the instructions of persons under (Davis's) immediate orders'.[35] And who, it is fair to ask, gave the orders to these men 'who are not yet known', and who were the men who were 'under Davis's immediate orders', who in turn ordered Booth and Surratt to kill Lincoln and most likely Vice President Johnson, Secretary of State Seward, Secretary of War Stanton and Lieutenant General Grant and perhaps others? The answer is obvious and interesting and surely has much to do with the fact that Judah Benjamin fled the country after the fall of Richmond on 2 April 1865, and never returned. Recall that Benjamin's most trusted courier was John Surratt, with whom he met almost weekly, and that top Confederate agent Thomas Harbin, who was close to Booth, meeting with him before and after the assassination, reported directly to Davis, according to his own admission. But there is more.

In response to a question by Eckert as to what other persons were implicated in the plot to assassinate, Powell said, 'All I can say about that is, that you [federal prosecutors] have not got the one-half of them.'[36] Not got the one-half? They had nine (Booth was dead and the other eight were in the dock). Does that mean that at least eighteen were involved in the conspiracy? That is exactly what it means, and almost certainly more than eighteen. Booth told Herold that there were thirty-five involved in the conspiracy.[37] And, as we have already seen, he told Samuel Knapp Chester, his friend and fellow actor, when they met in New York, where Booth tried and failed to recruit him, that there were between fifty and 100 involved in the conspiracy.[38] Let us grant that Booth was laying it on thick with Chester to induce him to join the conspiracy; secrecy would have been impossible with such a number. Let us settle, therefore, on eighteen to thirty-five conspirators. Could such a number have been necessary to assassinate one man? Could such a number and their doings have escaped the attention of Confederate intelligence, and therefore the knowledge of Confederate leaders, in a city saturated with Confederate agents? Clearly no, to both questions. Is such a number consistent with what we know about the participation of others in the conspiracy? Of course. Powell said to Gillette, his spiritual counsellor, that he did not know the names of the principal men collaborating with Booth, clearly revealing that there were such.[39] He obviously did not have Booth's action team in mind, because he knew all of them cold, so the statement tells us clearly that Booth was working with others in addition to his team. That conclusion accords well with Arnold's statement, in his memoirs, that 'There were occasions before I had become acquainted with the fact that others than Surratt and ourselves, already spoken of, were connected in the enterprise.'[40] Might that include the fellow who followed Grant on the train to Burlington, New Jersey, on the night of the assassination, intending to assassinate him, but frustrated by an alert brakeman and a locked car door? And might it include the fellow on Stanton's porch who tried to gain access to his home so that he could assassinate him, stymied by a broken doorbell? Or the fellow who was seen hiding behind a tree box on Stanton's property, who fled when an attempt was made to apprehend him? Might it include riders who, on the night of the assassination, ignored demands for a password and barrelled through Union pickets whose gunfire failed to stop them? How about the blasé horseman and his servant who feigned surprise, mocked news of the assassination and the attempted assassinations to two privates and then rode off to safety just after dawn on the 15th in the vicinity of Glenwood Cemetery? And then there were the many who fired on federal pickets in the vicinity of the capital and who were then not apprehended. And let us not forget the known Confederate operatives who left their homes under suspicious circumstances on the night of the 14th and then returned, also under suspicious circumstances, one announcing that 'we have done the deed'. Nor shall we forget all the major figures who were most likely complicit in the great crime who fled the country after the assassination, including Judah Benjamin (never to return), Jacob Thompson (for four years), George Sanders, a power in the Canadian Cabinet (for seven years) and top Confederate agents Benjamin Franklin Stringfellow (for two years) and Thomas Harbin (for as many as five years).

Further, Powell met with Gillette on the night before his execution, apparently ready to bare his soul (but still not ready, obviously, to name names) knowing that his doom awaited him the next morning. He told Gillette that he thought others involved had not been apprehended, which is telling – further evidence that there was more to Booth's attempt to decapitate the government than his immediate action team.[41] He also told Gillette that he did not know the names of the principal men collaborating with Booth, still further evidence of Booth's network of agents who were not part of his immediate team.[42]

He told him, too, that rebel leaders were responsible for his death.[43] Whom shall we believe he had in mind by the term 'rebel leaders'? Surely not small fry. Most likely not even the intermediaries, though there were plenty of these. Rather, those who lifted this free spirit from a life of 'dashing and splashing through the woods, across fields, over ditches and fences, by day, at night, and through all kinds of weather' and put him under the authority of a 26-year-old, stupid and hare-brained actor, with orders to murder people, even the Chief Magistrate of the United States. Why would he blame 'rebel leaders' if he did not know that it was they, ultimately, who were responsible for his leaving Mosby and joining Booth? He told Colonel Dodd, who had special charge of the prisoners before their execution and who was in constant conversation with Powell, that he was informed and believed that he was acting under an order from 'rebel authorities' and did not, therefore, originally view his act as a murderous one.[44] This is a very telling admission.

He naturally expressed it in terms of a belief, but, truly, who would know better than he whether or not he was acting under an order from 'rebel authorities'? This is not just another agent; this is the Confederate soldier, the Mosby Ranger, the 'boldest of the bold and the rashest of the reckless', the 'terrible Lewis Powell'. Would such a man, esteemed and revered wherever he went, accept an assignment to place himself at the command of a 26-year-old actor and to follow his orders, even orders to murder – not to kill in combat, but to murder in cold blood – if he didn't know who his ultimate authority was? He was 'informed'. Would whoever informed him inform him falsely – say he was acting pursuant to an order of 'rebel authorities' if he wasn't? Clearly no, to both questions. This is one of those admissions against interest that all but nails down the issue of who was in ultimate control of Lewis Powell through the agency of John Wilkes Booth and who, therefore, was ultimately responsible for the orders or urgings by Booth to Powell to kill Lincoln.

He said he was led into the conspiracy by Booth and John Surratt,[45] which may well have been a lie inasmuch as he was conveniently, for him, casting blame on a dead man and a fugitive. But if it was true, he could only have meant that the original initiative to join Booth's team came from those two men or perhaps only one of them, most likely Surratt. They either knew of his fame as a fighter and of his total dedication to their cause and therefore believed he would fill a need they had for muscle, or they let their need be known and relied on others to fill it. In either case, they did what they felt they had to do to bring him aboard. But someone else would have had to meet their need if 'rebel leaders' had not agreed to his transfer from Mosby to Booth, so important to their grand plan was the Booth mission.

Powell expressed regret and remorse for his deed, though he said he thought he was doing right at the time, because he still claimed to be a Confederate soldier.[46] Gillette said he was impressed with Powell's intelligence,[47] which is relevant to the supposed rationale for Herold to accompany him to the Seward mansion and also relevant to the disappointment he must have felt at being subordinated to 'a rattle-pated fellow, filled with quixotic notions … a wild-brained boy … a poor, crazy boy' who was intent on cold-blooded murder.

Further, it was on this occasion (6 July) that Powell told Gillette about his numerous trips to and from Richmond, Washington and Baltimore in the months leading up to the assassination and about how prominent and wealthy men (unnamed of course) in the latter city had accommodated him in their palatial homes, treated him royally, encouraged him with dreams of glory and the lasting gratitude of the Southern people and kept him in funds with which he had come and gone at their bidding.[48] How, it is fair to ask, would these Baltimoreans know what Powell was doing unless it was common knowledge to Confederate intelligence? And if it was common knowledge to Confederate intelligence, how could it not be common knowledge to the Confederate leadership?

Now let us ask and answer a question. Question: Is it even possible that everything described above as having been done by Powell from the summer of 1864, including his trip or trips to Canada and Niagara Falls, where he doubtless met with Secret Service heavy hitters, e.g. Clement C. Clay, with whom he was seen in conversation at the Queen's Hotel in Toronto, Jacob Thompson, Beverly Tucker, George N. Sanders, William C. Cleary, Patrick C. Martin and perhaps even Dr Luke P. Blackburn and James P. Holcombe, who, together with Clay and Thompson, were coordinating an assassination attempt on Lincoln by infecting him with yellow fever; his Secret Service work; his meetings in Baltimore with prominent men who accommodated him, encouraged him, promised him rewards and kept him in funds; his dispatch by Mosby from the Rangers, as one of five men, for the purpose of participating in actions against Lincoln and his cabinet; his acceptance of Booth as his superior; his trip or trips from Baltimore to Washington to meet with Booth, in January or February 1865, at which time he was given an opportunity to assassinate Lincoln, but chose not to do so; his instructions by Booth, on two other occasions, to murder Lincoln, both of which were rebuffed by him; his 15 March trip to Washington, with the help of Secret Service agents John Surratt and David Preston Parr, for the purpose of meeting with Booth's team in Gautier's Restaurant; his spending a night at Mary Surratt's boarding house; his participation in the Campbell Hospital episode; his subsequent trips to Baltimore, New York and possibly Canada; and his attempt on the life of Secretary of State Seward, in the course of which he left a house full of bloodied but living victims; was all carried out as a rogue operation, without the knowledge, approval and direction (generally, not, obviously, of the details) of the highest levels of the Confederate government and its Secret Service, i.e. President Jefferson Davis, Secretary of State Judah Benjamin, head of the Canadian Cabinet Jacob Thompson and his replacement Edwin G. Lee? Answer: no.

It is a flagrant affront to reason to suppose that 'the terrible Lewis Powell', this 'stray knight from the Black Forest', deserted Mosby's Rangers, joined the Secret Service because he didn't know what to do with himself, was accepted by the Secret Service despite his being a deserter, met with prominent and wealthy men in Baltimore who feted him in their palatial homes, encouraged him and financed him because they liked the cut of his jib, casually found Booth by bumping into him in front of Barnum's Hotel in Baltimore and then took a 'hard' oath and casually joined his conspiracy the next day as a subordinate, because he was starving, broke and without purpose, design or destination.

We may conclude by saying that the conspiracy to decapitate the United States government, in the closing days of the Civil War, was very extensive and involved many players and that a conspiracy of such breadth could not possibly have been carried out without the knowledge, approval, direction and control of the Confederate government and its Secret Service. That conclusion is based on the following facts:

1. Powell's statements to Eckert that federal prosecutors did not have one-half of the conspirators and that it was his impression that arrangements had been made with others for the same disposition of other federal office holders as he was to make of Seward;
2. Powell's statements to Gillette that others involved had not been apprehended and that he did not know the names of the principal men collaborating with Booth;
3. Arnold's statement that he became aware of the fact that others, outside of Booth's immediate action team, were connected to the enterprise;
4. Herold's statement that Booth told him there were thirty-five involved in the conspiracy; and
5. Chester's statement that Booth told him there were between fifty and 100 involved the conspiracy.

We may also conclude by saying that the fact that Booth ordered, or at least urged, Powell to murder Lincoln on at least three occasions, one as early as January 1865, proves that Booth's purpose and goal, at least from January, if not earlier, was assassination, as Eckert also concluded and as Bingham and Harris also concluded, except that they took Booth's purpose and goal back to his initial involvement with the Secret Service rather than just to January 1865. Manifestly, Powell took his orders from the Confederate leadership, ultimately, and from Booth more immediately. Equally manifest is the fact that Booth took his orders from the Confederate leadership in Richmond and Canada and that his orders were not to kidnap anyone, but to assassinate as many federal office holders as possible, so as to 'leave the government entirely without a head' and so as to make it impossible, under the Constitution and the Presidential Succession Statute of 1792, which was in effect at the time, for the government to elect another president, thereby providing an opening for Confederate leaders to snatch a sweet and heroic victory from a preening, overbearing and hated enemy.

Chapter Three

The Third Smoking Gun: The Thomas Francis Harney Mission and Plan B

The Thomas Francis Harney mission

Thomas Francis Harney (most often called 'Frank') was a slippery fellow. Not a lot is known about his beginnings and nothing of his endings. During the heart of his career, he was engaged in Confederate Secret Service work, especially with the Torpedo Bureau, one of at least eight arms of the Secret Service, whose business, need it be said, was secret, so it is no surprise that not much is known about him. Surely, he wanted it that way and so did his superiors. Indeed, it has even been suggested that Thomas Francis Harney might not be his real name, but a nom de guerre.

This much is known, or at least strongly believed. He was born in Blair County, Pennsylvania (the central part of the state), probably in 1837. He lived in Harrisonville, Cass County, Missouri (the western part of the state), where he was a schoolteacher. He joined the Missouri State Guard in 1861 and was heavily engaged in the battles of Carthage, on 5 July, Oak Hills (or Wilson's Creek), on 10 August, and Dry Wood Creek (or the battle of the Mules, as it is sometimes called, because the Confederates captured the Union cavalry's mules), all in Missouri. The State Guard was driven out of Missouri and defeated at the battle of Elkhorn Tavern, or Pea Ridge, in north-western Arkansas on 2 March 1862, thereby preserving Missouri for the Union. Harney escaped serious injury in all four encounters. After Elkhorn Tavern, many of the Guardsmen enlisted in the official Confederate army. Harney did so at Corinth, Mississippi, on 1 May 1862, and then fought in the battle of Iuka,

Mississippi, on 19 September, and the battle of Corinth on 3 October. He was seriously wounded in the last encounter and convalesced at Abbeville, Mississippi. Two months later (2 December), he was captured at College Hill, Mississippi, and was sent to Gratiot Street Military Prison in St Louis, a hellhole built for 200 prisoners, but housing 2,000 when Harney arrived. He was held there until 2 June 1863, with intermediate stops at Allen Point, Virginia, and Alton, Illinois. While at Gratiot, he told prison officials that he was born in Blair County, Pennsylvania, that he resided in Harrisonville, Cass County, Missouri, and that he had been a schoolteacher before the war, but no records have been found that confirm any of this. He also refused to take the Oath of Allegiance. On 2 June, he was sent to City Point, Virginia, for exchange.[1]

In July and August 1863, he served on detached service with General James Longstreet and General Joe Johnston, who was blamed by Jefferson Davis for the loss of Vicksburg, Mississippi, on 4 July. The relationship between Davis and Johnston was always difficult, to put it mildly.

Following his service with Longstreet and Johnston, he signed on for service with the Torpedo Bureau, which oversaw the production, testing and use of mines, sub-terra shells, hand grenades, coal bombs, log bombs and just about anything that would explode. The Bureau was then under the command of Brigadier General Gabriel J. Rains, whose commanding officer was Longstreet. Harney was attracted to the wizard war people and they to him, but whether the initiative to join came from Rains or Harney is unclear. In any case, Harney's background suited him for the work of the Bureau and Rains recognised it. Harney continued his Secret Service work until 1 January 1864, sharpening his skills with explosives and explosive devices.[2]

In 1864, he saw service in Charleston, South Carolina, Richmond, Virginia, and Mobile, Alabama, at least.

He may have had a hand in arming the CSS *H.L. Hunley*, a submarine (the first), for her attack on the USS *Housatonic*, a wooden ship, in Charleston harbour on 17 February 1864, inasmuch as he was in Charleston before the mission was undertaken. The attack succeeded in sinking *Housatonic*, with the loss of five Union men, but it was a Pyrrhic victory, because *H.L Hunley* and the eight brave warriors who manned her were lost in the effort. Let us think about how brave one has to be to climb into a small, cigar-shaped vessel, whose technology was in its infancy, knowing that many who had already done so were dead as a result.[3]

In June 1864, Harney was in Richmond mining the James River.

Harney may also have had a hand in the massive explosion caused by John Maxwell and R.K. Dillard of the Secret Service at General Grant's ammunition depot at City Point, Virginia, on 9 August. The explosion and its results are described in some detail in Chapter One.

Harney most certainly did have a hand in the placement of 'torpedoes' (sea mines) in Mobile Bay, which Admiral David G. Farragut famously damned before ordering his flotilla to proceed at full speed past the shore batteries of Fort Gaines and Fort Morgan during the battle there on 5 August 1864.[4]

Harney became so adept at the use of explosives that it was said that wherever he went, he left Union casualties and property loss in his wake.

By early 1865, the fortunes of the Confederacy appeared to be sinking fast. Her armies were melting away as a result of battlefield losses and unprecedented desertions. Her treasury was all but empty and her resources all but depleted, and there did not appear to be any way to replenish either. No foreign power had formally recognised her. She was isolated, alone and devastated by Union armies in her heartland. Her fighting men – those who were still in the field – were ill-equipped, ill-clad and ill-fed, while their enemies had everything they needed to continue the fight, their roads and docks choked with war materiel – weapons, ammunition, clothing, food. Indeed, it is fair to say that Confederate leaders knew they were beaten, but just weren't quite ready to throw in the towel, hoping for some miraculous turn by which they might yet salvage a victory of sorts.

That Confederate leaders knew that the outcome of the war was no longer in doubt, despite the willingness of many to fight on, is attested to by the fact that the Confederate government changed its enciphering key in February 1865 from 'Complete Victory' to 'Come Retribution'. The change tells us not only that government leaders knew there wasn't going to be any victory, but also that they had resolved to have their revenge against those they deemed most responsible for their loss. And isn't that exactly what we would expect? Isn't that perfectly consistent with human nature – to want to cause loss to those who have caused loss to oneself, regardless of consequences? It is not in our nature as humans, when we seek revenge, to not be deterred by the possibility, or even the certainty, of blowback. Revenge is too sweet for that. It is, in fact, the strongest human motivator, stronger, even, than the pursuit of wealth and its preservation and protection once acquired. That is most likely why it is said to be a dish best taken cold. It was well known throughout the South that Lincoln was a kind and magnanimous man, a gentle giant who loved to tell jokes and stories, and that his death, therefore, might be the worst thing that could happen to a defeated and prostrate South. Fine and good, but not enough. He was the author of all their loss and grief and that was enough to justify taking his life. Better a corpse than a Father Abraham.

Defeat meant, of course, what the South feared, indeed dreaded, and what her sons had fought so long, so gallantly and so tenaciously to prevent, and which was now upon them, namely:

1. The loss of their political independence;
2. The loss of their wealth and property;
3. The loss of their lifestyle and culture;
4. The social upheaval attendant to the integration of almost 4 million suddenly free slaves into a society of 5½ million whites; and
5. The 'mongrelisation' of their race.

In these circumstances, the Confederate government did what virtually every belligerent government would do, and what virtually every belligerent government has done, in the same or similar circumstances: it turned to irregular modes of warfare, sometimes called Black Flag warfare or terrorism. General Rains, master of the wizard war, justified the use of concealed explosive devices (later known as 'booby traps') in a message he sent to the War Department in response to Longstreet's objections to some of the means of waging war employed by Rains's Torpedo Bureau, a justification given greater weight by an endorsement from Rains's superior, General Daniel Harvey Hill, who wrote, 'In my opinion all means of destroying our brutal enemies are lawful and proper.'[5] This message was identical to the sentiment expressed by Secretary of War James Seddon in his rejection of Columbia University law and political science professor Francis Lieber's rules of civilised warfare for Union forces (General Orders, No. 100). Seddon said Lieber's rules were hypocritical and were written to deodorise federal government atrocities, an unkind cut for the professor, who had laboured hard and long to bring some degree of civility to a thoroughly uncivilised practice.[6] In point of fact, however, the Confederacy did have what it considered to be a legitimate excuse, namely the Wistar and Dahlgren-Kilpatrick cavalry raids against Richmond in February and March 1864, especially the orders found on Dahlgren's corpse, which provided for the murder of Confederate President Jefferson Davis and his cabinet by the raiders, all of which is described in some detail in Chapter One.

All of this meant, quite plainly, that the gloves were off, though in truth they had never really been on, because the American Civil War was a Black Flag affair from its inception and even before that in 'Bleeding Kansas' and the Kansas-Missouri Border War. The Black Flag meant prisoner of war camps in which the prisoners died like flies from neglect and abuse and the survivors looked like they came out of Auschwitz; summary executions of black prisoners of war; massacres on a grand scale; the depredations of psychopathic killers; the burning of cities; and the wanton and wholesale destruction of non-military property.

The irregular warfare that had characterised the fighting by both sides from the beginning of the war, and which grew hotter after the raids on Richmond, became white hot by the spring of 1865, as Confederate leaders scrambled to avert total disaster and, if possible, snatch some kind of victory from what appeared to be certain and total defeat.

What to do? All attempts to assassinate Lincoln, including the attempt to do so by infecting him with yellow fever, had failed. There were at least a dozen such attempts from the date of his election (6 November 1860) to the date of his second Inauguration (4 March 1865). Assassinations of political figures, who are almost always well guarded, are complicated and difficult affairs, almost always the result of conspiracies, multiple minds and hands, intelligence and coordination; they are almost never accomplished by lone wolves. More importantly, the attempts on

Lincoln's life were motivated by personal animus and/or revenge for the raids on Richmond and, more specifically, Dahlgren's orders; they were not part of a scheme to win the war. Confederate leaders knew full well, at this stage, if they had not always known it, that Lincoln's death, though much desired and highly gratifying, would not affect the war substantially inasmuch as Vice President Andrew Johnson would simply step in, according to the Constitution, and carry on. That they hated Johnson as much or more than they hated Lincoln was immaterial.

Likewise, all the terror plots against the Union, from the spring of 1864 (after the raids) to the spring of 1865, had mostly fizzled or backfired and in any case had not brought victory, had not brought on war between the United States and Great Britain and had not substantially affected Northern morale or the Union war effort. These included Dr Luke Pryor Blackburn's yellow fever plot; Jacob Thompson's and Thomas Henry Hines's Northwest Conspiracy; the raids on Calais, Maine, and St Albans, Vermont; the voyage of the CSS *Tallahassee*; the destruction of the Union ammunition depot at City Point, Virginia; John Yeats Beall's numerous acts of terror in Ohio and New York; and the fires that destroyed or damaged much of New York City. Quite the contrary: the plots gave Northern leaders the fodder they needed to demonise Southern leaders in the court of public opinion, making it easier for the North to continue the war to a successful conclusion. As Lincoln had said, 'In this age, in this country, public sentiment is everything. With it, nothing can fail; against it, nothing can succeed. Whoever molds public sentiment goes deeper than he who enacts statutes, or pronounces judicial decisions.' Assassinating only Lincoln, and carrying out more terror plots of the same kind that had had such disappointing results for the Confederacy, therefore, were obviously not what was called for.

What was called for, rather, was something that would cripple the United States government and make that government's continuation of the war extremely difficult if not impossible. Multiple assassinations of the right people might do that, with an assist from the Presidential Succession Statute of 1792, which was in effect at the time. The statute provided that in the event of a simultaneous vacancy in the offices of President and Vice President, the President Pro Tempore of the Senate would act as an interim president until such time as the Electoral College could elect a new president, a process to be put in motion by the Secretary of State. No provision was made for the replacement of the Secretary of State if that office was vacant at the same time as the vacancies in the offices of President and Vice President. The simultaneous assassination of the President, the Vice President and the Secretary of State, therefore, would create chaos in the government. If the President's cabinet, or a good number of them, could also be assassinated at or about the same time, the chaos would be so great that the wheels of government would quite likely grind to a halt. And if the Secretary of War (Edwin M. Stanton) and the Lieutenant General of the armies (Ulysses S. Grant) and perhaps even the man who had burned Atlanta, laid waste much of Georgia and burned Columbia, South Carolina – William Tecumseh Sherman – were also assassinated, the wheels of the military would also quite likely grind to a halt. Such a scenario offered a good possibility that Generals Robert E. Lee and Joe Johnston could combine their forces, lift the siege of Petersburg and turn the tables on the hated enemy, thereby enabling the Confederate government to negotiate a favourable peace. It was absolutely breathtaking just to contemplate the possibilities, and certainly worth a try, despite the logistical and other difficulties attendant to such a monumental undertaking. What else was left to Confederate leaders? 'Come Retribution'? With her armies melting away, what form could that possibly take but multiple assassinations?

The assassinations could be accomplished by blowing up a gathering of office holders or by individual assassins targeting individual office holders. For the first, an explosives expert was obviously the first priority. Thomas Harney filled the bill admirably. He had a great record and had established a great reputation for leaving a path of death and destruction in his wake, so he was chosen to command the operation. He would be given all the resources and all the help he needed. For the second, there were several action teams, one of which was John Wilkes Booth and his team. They had the great advantage of being in Washington, where they would be needed.

Booth's team was anything but professional, though they weren't as bad as they are frequently made out to be. Surratt was well connected to Confederate leaders in both Richmond (he was Benjamin's 'most trusted courier') and Canada. Powell brought muscle to the operation and experience with Mosby's Rangers. Herold, being a 'passionate' bird shooter, knew the countryside like he knew the back of his hand. Atzerodt was the river rat; he made part of his living shepherding people back and forth across the Potomac and therefore knew the massive artery about as well as anyone knew it. Arnold was quite bright, bright enough to be the only one to challenge Booth and later write memoirs. O'Laughlen was Booth's boyhood friend, as was Arnold, was reasonably intelligent, had served in the Confederate army, and though he had taken the Oath of Allegiance to the United States in 1863, remained dedicated to the Confederate cause. As for the enablers, Mrs Surratt kept safe houses in Surrattsville and Washington and Dr Mudd kept another safe house in Maryland and was a link in the 'mail line' between Richmond and Washington and thus knew all the Confederate operatives in lower Maryland. Everyone had a function, and everyone was pretty good at something. The problem was that they were not of one mind as to their purpose; most continued to labour under the fiction that they were going to kidnap the President and one – Arnold – told Booth and the others that if they hadn't accomplished the kidnapping by a certain date, he was pulling out. But it was late, options were limited, it was a fallback option anyway, and the Confederate government would simply have to make do with what it had.

Furthermore, Booth was well connected with others outside of his action team. Recall that conspirator Lewis Powell had said to Assistant Secretary of War Thomas Eckert that all he could say about others being complicit in the great crime was that federal prosecutors did not have 'the one-half of them' and that it was his impression that arrangements had been made with others for the same disposition of other federal office holders as he was to make of Seward. Recall too that Powell had said to his spiritual adviser, Rev Dr Abram Dunn Gillette, that he thought others involved had not been apprehended and that he did not know the names of the principal men collaborating with Booth. These statements by Powell are corroborated by Sam Arnold's statement in his memoirs that he knew that others besides the action team 'were connected in the enterprise'. Recall too that David Herold had told his interrogator, Judge Advocate General John Bingham, that Booth had told him there were thirty-five involved in his conspiracy, and that Samuel Knapp

Chester, Booth's actor friend from New York, testified at the trial of the conspirators that Booth had told him there were fifty to 100 involved. All of this proves, of course, beyond any doubt, that Booth worked with far more people than his immediate action team to decapitate the United States government on 14 April, or as much of it as he could, which is also probative of the involvement of Confederate leaders in the events of that night, because such a number of conspirators, even if we accept the lower figures rather than the higher, could not possibly have escaped their notice, and therefore their direction and control.

So Harney left for Washington on or about 1 April 1865, his purpose being nothing less than the decapitation of the United States government by killing as many office holders as could be lured into a wing of the White House prior to blowing it up. But before we discuss the mission and its results, it is important to establish that the mission was not a scratch operation that sprang up overnight. On the contrary, a mission fraught with as many difficulties and having as many political and military repercussions as this one must have been in the works a long time, certainly weeks, perhaps a month or more. Success was posited not only on what was done in Richmond, i.e. gathering a team, training it for this particular mission, instructing it as to what was to be done, what was to be expected and what roles were to be played by individual members, and making provision for everything needed, including food, clothing, arms, transportation and so forth, but also what was to be done in Washington, i.e. arranging for as many federal office holders as possible, with special attention to be given to the most influential ones, to be at a certain place, on a certain day and at a certain time. Atzerodt's 1 May 1865 confession, as we have seen, suggested that an 'entertainment' and/or a 'serenade' was to be used as the lure.

With respect to the arrangements in Washington, we may surmise that there was treachery in the White House. It is not the first time we have had circumstantial evidence of it. According to Susannah Hamm, a Richmond resident who claimed to have first-hand knowledge of assassination plans that were made in early March 1865, in that city, 'The plan of inviting Mr Lincoln to the theatre was fixed upon in Richmond,'[7] a statement that accords well with Booth's statement to his fellow actor, Samuel Knapp Chester, at their meeting in New York in late December or early January 1865, that 'the affair [the abduction of the heads of the government] was to take place at Ford's Theater in Washington'.[8] Further, crack Confederate agent Benjamin Franklin Stringfellow said, in an 1880 letter, that he was in Washington in March 1865, on assignment by Jefferson Davis, and that while there he was in constant communication with an officer occupying an important position about Mr Lincoln, an officer to whom he had made a proposition.[9] Further, Robert Lincoln, the President's son, alleged that he had evidence of treason of a member of Lincoln's cabinet.[10] Still further, Jacob Thompson, head of the Canadian Cabinet, refused to write memoirs, he said, because it would destroy someone still in Congress who had the confidence of the federal government at the same time he aided the Confederacy.[11] And still further, there is Thompson's letter of 3 December 1864, to Judah Benjamin, in which he referred to the many papers in his possession 'which in the hands of the enemy would utterly ruin and destroy very many of the prominent men in the North'.[12] We should not be surprised by any of this; men and women on one side of a conflict of arms secretly helping the other side is something that happens in every war, especially civil wars.

So everything is in readiness and Harney knows what he is to do. But he needs a couple of things: he needs a green light and he needs money to finance his operation. Perhaps it would be more accurate to say that his superiors need the green light, i.e. President Jefferson Davis, Secretary of State Judah Benjamin and head of the Torpedo Bureau Gabriel Rains. It would come from the Canadian Cabinet. Though there is no proof, it must be considered likely that agents in Canada had something to do with the arrangements made in Washington to schedule the event that would induce federal office holders to gather at a certain place and at a certain time, thereby maximising Harney's chances of success. Coordination was key: Harney's arrival must be timed to coincide with the time of the gathering. Arriving too late would be fatal. Arriving too early might not be fatal, but would increase the danger substantially. The object was to slip into the city unobtrusively, with help from Mosby men, accomplish the deed quickly and then slip out without fuss or fanfare, to safety, also with help from Mosby men. The critical importance of timing is apparent.

The green light was almost certainly delivered by John Surratt and Sarah Slater. We have already met Surratt and will meet him again in these pages. Slater was another Confederate courier, said to be something of a mystery lady, who was young (about 20), attractive, veiled and fluent in French. It was also said that Atzerodt was smitten with her. (Poor fellow: all he wanted was to be respected and loved. He didn't have a chance. It cost him his life.) Surratt and Slater arrived in Richmond on either 29 or 31 March with dispatches from Jacob Thompson and Edwin G. Lee, who succeeded Thompson as head of the Canadian Cabinet, for Benjamin. (According to the register of the Spotswood House Hotel, Surratt arrived on 29 March and left on 1 April. According to Surratt's 1870 Rockville, Maryland, lecture, he arrived on 'Friday evening before the evacuation of the city', i.e. 31 March. Remember that Surratt was the consummate liar and was nothing if not inconsistent in nearly everything he said. One has to be extremely careful, therefore, in separating truth from fiction with him.) Slater, who left Montreal on 17 March with dispatches for Benjamin, was to have been escorted to Richmond by Augustus Howell, another Secret Service agent, but he was arrested as a spy at the Surratt Tavern in Surrattsville on 24 March, so Surratt either volunteered or was ordered to escort her from Washington to Richmond.[13] Surratt stayed in Richmond long enough to meet with Benjamin and Davis[14] and then left the city with Slater on 1 April, heading for Montreal with dispatches from Benjamin for Thompson and Lee, first stopping at Washington, New York and possibly Newport, Rhode Island.

It is possible that General Mosby was also in Richmond at this time for the purpose of being apprised of the dimensions of the Harney mission and of the role he was to play in the same, namely helping Harney and the men he needed to have with him into the city and their exit therefrom after the deed was done. There is, however, no hard evidence of it, much less proof, merely naked allegations,[15] but we may regard it as not especially important inasmuch as Mosby and Richmond had well-established means of communication by signal system and telegraph. We may be certain that one way or another, Mosby was fully informed of the mission and of the role he was expected to play in it. It must be regarded as quite likely, too, that he knew all about the fallback plan that involved Booth and his team. He was, after all, not new to Booth. It was Mosby who allowed Powell to cut his ties with the Rangers to join Booth's team. Further, there is at least one report of a meeting between Booth and Mosby in August or September 1864, in one of Mosby's northern Virginia hideouts, though it cannot be confirmed.[16] Still further, Mosby felt he had good reason to involve himself and his Rangers in Booth and Herold's escape after the assassination.[17]

Judging from the disposition of Mosby's forces prior to Harney's capture, the help to be given by Mosby most likely included making a diversion to distract Union cavalry in the area, thus making entrance to the city safer, and the establishment of security and reception parties to facilitate the getaway.[18] The fact that Mosby was asked to establish a new company – Company 'H', a fifty-two-man unit – this late in the war, also argues for his knowledge of the ultimate goal of the mission. We may therefore be certain that Mosby knew what Harney's purpose was, which should surprise no one. He was, after all, a major player, the principal Confederate field commander in Virginia, who controlled large swaths of that state and Maryland, and who had the undying loyalty of about 400 tough and battle-hardened fighters. Further, he was being asked to play a major role in what might be the Confederacy's last hope to turn the tables on their enemies. In these circumstances, how could he *not* know of Harney, his mission and his objective? After the war, of course, he denied knowing anything whatsoever about the assassination plot. That is and always will be a possibility, but a very remote one in view of the evidence, admittedly circumstantial, but nevertheless very persuasive. Communications relative to a matter as sensitive as this one would never be committed to paper, even in code, so a writing containing orders that would prove complicity will never be found, because it never existed. Mosby's profession of ignorance is neither more nor less than we should expect him to have said.

As for the money, there were two funds in the Confederate Treasury for Secret Service activities. One was labelled 'Necessities and Exigencies' and was used to finance routine activities of the Service, such as spying. The other was labelled 'Secret Service' and was used to finance the so-called wizard war, i.e. operations that were intended to kill a lot of people with violent action of one kind or another. On 1 April, Benjamin had Davis sign a Treasury Warrant for $1,500 in gold from the Secret Service Fund. In his 1870 Rockville lecture, Surratt said he received $200 in gold to cover the expenses of his return trip to Montreal, which must have come from this warrant, the balance going to Harney for his purposes. Davis surely knew what the money was for. It is altogether unbelievable that Davis, the President of the Confederate States of America, would sign such a warrant, especially at this late date and in the circumstances then existing, without knowing its purpose. Accordingly, we must conclude that the Confederate leadership knew that an attempt was going to be made on the life of Davis's political counterpart in Washington as well as the lives of other federal office holders.[19] And isn't that exactly what we would expect? With the end of four years of titanic struggle and sacrifice in sight, hundreds of thousands of Southern men dead, much of the South laid waste, and the loss of everything they had fought for now staring them in the face, and with no option left to them but multiple assassinations, why *wouldn't* the Confederate leadership order the attack? Few if any national executives would do otherwise in the same or similar circumstances. Those circumstances included the belief of Confederate leaders that Lincoln had issued the same order for them and, what is worse, had done so when circumstances were not at all desperate for the Union cause. In his fine book, *April '65: Confederate Covert Action in the American Civil War*, William A. Tidwell put the matter this way:

> What has been established … is a network of documented facts that logically coincide with the information that would have had to exist if Davis did decide to attack the leaders of the Federal government. One can refute the logic only by a bizarre distortion of reason. The probability that all of these facts were true and that Davis did not make the critical decision is very slight indeed.[20]

On 1 April, or 2 April at the latest (the day Richmond was evacuated), Harney left Richmond for Washington, intending first to rendezvous with Mosby in Fauquier County. In the words of William Tidwell, James O. Hall and David Gaddy, whose book *Come Retribution* must be considered a watershed publication in the field of Lincoln assassination scholarship, 'The connection seems obvious; the word was passed to activate the project mentioned by Atzerodt in his confession.'[21] Recall what Atzerodt had said in his confession of 1 May 1865:

> Booth said he had met a party in N. York who would get the Prest. certain. They were going to mine the end of the pres. House, near the War Dept. They knew an entrance to accomplish it through. Spoke about getting friends of the Presdt. to get up an entertainment & they would mix it in, have a serenade & thus get at the Presdt. & party. These were understood to be projects …

That Booth and Atzerodt were referring to the Harney mission cannot be doubted.

Atzerodt does not indicate when this information came to him from Booth. Inasmuch as Booth is known to have been in New York from 21 to 23 March, returning to Washington on the 25th after a stop in Baltimore, and given the fact that Harney left Richmond not more than one week later, it seems likely that Booth picked up the information during that visit to New York and then passed it on to his team as soon as he returned to Washington, though an earlier date is a distinct possibility inasmuch as New York was practically Booth's second home.

Why did Confederate leaders need direction from Canada before authorising Harney to get underway? Quite likely, as said earlier, because it was Secret Service operatives in Canada who were tasked with making the arrangements in Washington for the gathering of the President and other federal office holders at a time and place certain and also making whatever other arrangements were necessary to accommodate Harney and his men, which included making whatever ordnance they would need available to them. Harney could hardly proceed to enter Washington without these assurances. There is no proof of this, but it seems a likely explanation as to why Confederate leaders did not unleash Harney until they first had approval from Canada to do so.

In any case, Harney left Richmond with a team of demolition specialists and guides of uncertain number and identities. The evidence suggests that he carried with him fuses and timing devices only; the explosives would be supplied later by Mosby or by parties in Washington.

Most likely, it was his intention to use another 'horological torpedo', i.e. a time bomb or bombs, which had worked so well for Maxwell and Dillard at City Point. He went first to Gordonsville by train. There he was met by Major Cornelius Boyle, the Post Commander, who was a key figure in the transfer of agents and communications between Richmond and Washington. Boyle advised Mosby, who was headquartered near Upperville, in Fauquier County, about 75 miles north of Gordonsville, of Harney's arrival. Monitoring Harney's progress was obviously a matter of great importance. Boyle furnished Harney with a horse and a guide – almost certainly Thomas Franklin Summers, a very reliable fellow who knew the territory as well or better than anyone. On 3 or 4 April, Summers took Harney to Mosby, who detached about 150 of his intrepid Rangers to shepherd Harney, Summers, and whomever else Harney thought he would need for the job, across the Potomac at Upperville and into Washington and then out of it safely after accomplishing their purpose. Their purpose, let it not be forgotten, was to leave the White House, or at least a substantial part of it, in shambles and littered with the dead bodies of federal executives, legislators and jurists. The detached Rangers included, for the most part, Company 'D' and newly formed Company 'H', a fifty-two-man unit that Mosby put together at North Fork Church in Loudoun County on 5 April. The entire force was put under the command of 24-year-old Captain George B. Baylor, a Virginian who had established a reputation as a hard fighter. It seems like there were no other kind under the command of the Gray Ghost. That Mosby would assign 150 of such men to the task of getting Harney in and out of Washington is clearly an indication of how critically important he and the Confederate leadership in general deemed the mission.

Well, as we all know, the best laid plans of mice and men go oft awry, and it was as true for Harney and his escorts as it was for Robert Burns's mouse.

The force left Upperville on 8 April and headed for Washington. When they were within 15 miles of the city, at Burke Station in Fairfax County, a detachment from the Eighth Illinois Cavalry, under Colonel Charles Albright, assaulted their rear, causing the Mosby men to do something they were not used to doing – panicking and scattering. The Illinoisans numbered about 250 to about 125 Rangers, so it is no surprise that they scattered. Harney, Summers and two others escaped and made it to the Potomac, but they were spotted and captured by a scouting party of the Eighth Illinois under Colonel William Gamble. Though there is some uncertainty about the date, most sources state that the capture took place on 10 April rather than 9 April. One of Mosby's men described the loss of Harney as 'irretrievable'. We take from that word the meaning that the loss could not be undone, but what the Ranger more likely meant was not so much that it could not be undone, but that Harney could not be replaced, because there was simply no one else who could do what he was going to do. 'Irreplaceable', therefore, would have been a better word choice, but let us not split hairs; the two words are close enough to convey the same meaning: the plot had failed and there wasn't anything that Mosby could do about it.[22]

Harney, Summers and their two comrades were taken first to the Fairfax Court House, then to the Alexandria Slave Pen Guard House, then to the Alexandria Jail, and finally to the Old Capitol Prison in Washington. In the Alexandria Jail, Harney was listed as a 'member of the Engineer (Torpedo) Bureau, Department of Richmond, found with ordnance'. Colonel Albright's report for 10 April indicates that Harney 'brought ordnance to Colonel Mosby and joined his command'. Despite these references to ordnance, the fact was, not surprisingly, that Union authorities had no idea who they really had in custody, because they knew nothing about his mission. Harney had a cover story for the ordnance: He was sent from Richmond to bring it to Mosby. And there the matter stood, right through the assassination and its immediate aftermath, i.e. no suspicion whatsoever, much less a charge of attempted murder or complicity in attempted murder, attached to Harney. He was sent to Elmira Prison in New York State on 1 May 1865, another hellhole that compared well with Andersonville in Georgia for inhumanity (its prisoners called it 'Hellmira'). He remained there until 7 July 1865, the same day that four of the Lincoln conspirators (Mary Surratt, Lewis Powell, David Herold and George Atzerodt) were hanged following their conviction. On that day, he was paroled, took the Oath of Allegiance to the United States, left the prison and then passed out of history. But that is not the end of the story.[23]

While Harney was making his way north towards his fate, a fate that snuffed out what was almost the Confederacy's last hope, but which left a lot of government officials still on their feet, there was an interesting development back in Richmond. On 4 April, about the time that Harney met with Mosby and the same day that Lincoln toured the ravaged and smoldering city with his son, Tad, surrounded by a token guard of sailors and, unbeknownst to him, many plain-clothes detectives, a Confederate soldier made contact with Brigadier General Edward H. Ripley of the 9th Vermont Infantry, who commanded the forces occupying the city. The city was swarming with throngs of whites and freedmen, many of whom trailed Lincoln and some of whom even knelt before their deliverer, who naturally discouraged their doing so, saying they should kneel only before God. In these circumstances, therefore, it was not easy for the soldier to access Ripley, but he managed it and Ripley granted the soldier's request for an interview. The soldier was described by Ripley as a 'more than usually intelligent and fine looking man in uniform'. What Ripley did not say, though he might have, was that the man had a conscience and good sense. The man's name was William H. Snyder, though Ripley always refers to him by his last name only. Ripley published an account of the interview, and of what he did in consequence of it, in 1907, in a booklet he wrote and had published, titled *The Capture and Occupation of Richmond, April 3rd, 1865.* Ripley's account corroborates the account of Harney's mission, as described above, so well that the relevant portions of it deserve to be given here exactly as Ripley wrote them. Here they are:

> [Confederate prisoners] were mostly men who on the abandonment of their capital saw that further fighting was useless and upon the retreat of Ewell's corps quietly stayed behind. One of these came to my quarters on the day of Lincoln's arrival on Admiral Porter's flagship, *Malvern*, April 4, and begged an interview … with me on a very important subject. [He] was a more than usually intelligent and fine-appearing man in uniform, by the name of Snyder.
>
> He began by saying that he was an enlisted man in Rains's torpedo bureau, an organization of the Confederate secret service which had among its duties … all kinds of deviltry and irregular warfare, calculated to create panic or discontent in the rear of the Union armies. …

With the capture of Richmond and the abandonment of the Petersburg lines, he believed the war was hopeless and not another gun should be fired. Indeed his conscience told him every life taken now was in a way a wanton murder, and every right-minded man should strive to avert the shedding of another drop of blood. …

He then said that what he was particularly anxious to tell me was this:

He knew that a party had just been dispatched from Rains's torpedo bureau on a secret mission, which vaguely he understood was aimed at the head of the Yankee government, and he wished to put Mr Lincoln on his guard and have impressed upon him that just at this moment he believed him to be in great danger of violence and he should take the greater care of himself. He could not give names or facts, as the work of his department was secret, and no man knew what his comrade was sent to do, but of this he was convinced, that the President of the United States was in great danger.

Upon expressing willingness to make a statement and swear to it, I called in Captain Staniels, acting assistant adjutant-general, who took down his statement under oath. I then told him I should feel obliged to keep him in custody until I could arrange an interview with President Lincoln. I wrote the President a note and sent it at once aboard the *Malvern*, asking an interview at his earliest leisure on an important matter. It was then about 10 o'clock in the evening. In reply he wrote me a personal note, saying he would see me at 9 o'clock the next morning. I was promptly on hand, taking Snyder and his statement with me.

Admiral Porter's boat was waiting at the dock. The President received me most cordially in the Admiral's cabin, and then sat down … I taking my seat opposite him. … As I progressed in the explanation of my errand, Mr Lincoln let his head droop upon his hands as his elbows rested on the table, his hands supporting his chin and clasping either cheek

> in an expression of the most heart-breaking weariness, his great, melancholy eyes filling the cabin with the mournful light they emitted. I read the paper; I urged upon him the reasonableness of the warning, the good faith and apparent integrity of the man, and to make the impression deeper, if possible, I begged him to let me bring him in and talk with him, but it was all to no purpose. Finally, he lifted his head, and, casting upon me that face above all human faces that of a 'man of sorrows and acquainted with grief', he said: 'No, General Ripley, it is impossible for me to adopt and follow your suggestions. I deeply appreciate the feeling that has led you to urge them on me, – but I must go on as I have begun in the course marked out for me, for I cannot bring myself to believe that any human being lives who would do me any harm.' The interview then ended. He was so worn, emaciated, and pallid that he looked more like a disembodied spirit than the successful leader of a great nation in its hour of supreme triumph. I never saw him again; he left Richmond that afternoon, and City Point for Washington in a few days. My warning to him was on the morning of the 5th of April; on the night of the 15th – a short ten days after – he lay in his blood at Washington, a victim of the wolfish desire for revenge against which Snyder so honestly and prophetically warned him.

We have to ask: Why would Lincoln say that he could not bring himself to believe that any human being lived who would do him any harm? Assassination was always a threat from the day he received gifts of poisoned food, following his nomination by his party and his election in November 1860, to the day of his second Inauguration, 4 March 1865, and no one knew it better than he did. Indeed, he kept an envelope labeled 'Assassination' in his desk in the White House, which contained approximately eighty assassination threats that he or his Secretaries (John Hay, John Nicolay and William Stoddard) took seriously after they read and discarded almost all the other communications they received because they considered them to be trash, unworthy of anyone's time.

Further, at least a dozen attempts had been made on his life from the date of his election and he was quite aware of some of them. Was Lincoln just being sarcastic? It did not appear to be an occasion for sarcasm. Maybe he was just looking for a way out of a difficult situation for him, so he trivialised the warning in his jocular manner as a way to justify his negative response. Either way – sarcasm or trivialising (perhaps it is a distinction without a difference) – Lincoln's statement was an unkind cut, which must surely have hurt Ripley, who had the purest of motives and who thought so highly of the President. Well, it wasn't the first time that Lincoln was not at his best. He was, after all, as Ripley said, weary beyond words. So perhaps we should, for that reason, forgive his misstep.

Can there be any doubt that Harney undertook his mission, a mission whose purpose it was to assassinate the President of the United States and as many other federal office holders as possible, and a mission that was aided at every step by trainmen, post commanders, guides, other agents and the Gray Ghost himself, with the knowledge, approval and direction of Confederate leaders? No.

Plan B

Word of the failure of the Harney mission was communicated to Booth immediately. That much we can be certain of, because from the date of Harney's capture, or at most a day or two after, Booth's plan to murder Lincoln and as many other federal office holders as he could, making use of his team and of agents outside of his team, went into high gear. We don't know, however, how news of the failure came to him. It may have come through the Confederate underground, i.e. word of mouth, as some historians believe, or it may have come from the Confederate signal system and/or the telegraph, which is more likely. The Confederate underground was known to be incredibly efficient, but it would have taken more than incredible efficiency to get word of Harney's capture to Booth, by word of mouth, within a couple of days of its occurrence. It is more likely that the news came very soon after it happened by the only means of communicating something as quickly as that during that period, namely the Confederate signal system and the telegraph. The means of communication, however, is not important; what is important is the fact that the communication was made, because it proves that the option to make use of Booth and his team was a part of the overall plan as it was conceived in Richmond and Canada. If such use had not been foreseen as a possibility and planned for accordingly, no one would have notified Booth of anything. That is to say, that whoever notified Booth of the failure must have known that such notification was the next step of the plan.

In fairness, there are those who contend that Booth was not notified of the failure by any Confederate having anything to do with the mission, but learned of it some other way, such as from newspaper accounts, inasmuch as the encounter at Burke's Station was reported in the Washington newspapers. Booth then, according to those holding this view, decided, entirely on his own, with nary a word, an order, an instruction or a direction from Richmond, from Mosby or from Canada, to approximate the intended results of the Harney mission.[24] A variant of this theory is that Booth never learned of the Harney mission from any source, nor of its failure, and that the decision of the 26-year-old actor, who knew nothing of politics or the military, to decapitate the United States government, with incalculable political and military repercussions, was, again, his alone, with absolutely no input from any outside source, certainly not from Richmond, Mosby or Canada.

The theory and its variant are absurdities. To begin with, how could Booth attempt to approximate the intended results of the Harney mission if he didn't know what those intended results were, which, of course, he would not know if he were not apprised of the mission and its purposes and if he were not informed of its failure? The newspaper accounts said nothing about a mission or its intended purposes, because none of that was known at the time; they merely and matter-of-factly reported a clash of arms at Burke's Station between Union cavalry and Mosby men. The variant theory – that he knew nothing of the mission or its purposes, not even from newspaper accounts (which would have meant nothing to him anyway, even if he had read them) – but, by an extraordinary coincidence, again without any outside input from anyone, decided at that time to decapitate the United States government, is equally absurd.

It is absurd because it presumes that there was no connection whatsoever between the Confederate government, its Secret Service and Booth, despite overwhelming evidence to the contrary; because it presumes that Booth, the Confederate Secret Service agent, would, entirely on his own, without orders, attempt to decapitate the United States government, with incalculable political and military repercussions; and, more specifically, because it presumes that Harney's mission and its failure on 9 or 10 April, and the assassination and attempted assassinations that occurred on the night of 14 April, are totally unrelated. Not reasonable, not sensible and contrary to the evidence.

All of this leads us, inexorably, to the conclusion that Booth most certainly did know of the Harney mission and knew, too, that in the event of its failure, he, his team and those with whom he was connected, but who were not a part of his team, would be called into action, as back-up Plan B, to assassinate as many federal office holders as possible.[25] That could have been as many as fifteen according to the 10 May 1865 letter previously referred to, in which a Union agent in Paris wrote that a Confederate agent ('Johnston') had, in a note that he had partially read, written that if everything had gone according to plan on the 14th, fifteen Yankees would be dead, not one. He also wrote that Booth had said that he will never be taken; that he will 'bullet himself first', thus demonstrating that Booth was not only known to, but was a part of, the Confederate underground.

Mosby must have learned of the failure of the mission and Harney's capture very soon after it happened. It is therefore most likely, though by no means certain, that it was he who initiated the communication of the news to Booth, though he may well have delegated the responsibility to a subordinate. Again, the means of communication is not particularly important; it is the fact of communication that is important.

The first item that leads us to the foregoing conclusions is the fact that Booth communicated with John Surratt, whom he knew was in Montreal, at the beginning of the week of the assassination. There is, however, some uncertainty about the nature of the communication. During the trial of Surratt in 1867, one of the government's star witnesses was Dr Lewis J.A. McMillan. It was he in whose charge Surratt was placed by Catholic clergy aboard the *Peruvian*, in September 1865, on their voyage to England and the Continent. Surratt, travelling under the alias John McCarty, had many conversations with McMillan. Being outside of American jurisdiction, having confidence in his listener and being under the influence of alcohol (he was known to be a pretty good tippler), he spoke to McMillan openly, or as openly as he dared to. On the stand, the following exchange took place between McMillan and lead Prosecutor Edwards Pierrepont:

Q. I will call your attention to the early part of April – the month of the assassination of the President – and ask you what the prisoner told you on the subject of dispatches at that time?

A. All I remember about this is that he said, at the beginning of the week during which the assassination took place, that he was in Montreal; that he had arrived there within a few days, from Richmond, with dispatches …

Q. Did he say what day of the week of the assassination he was there?

A. He told me that he was there at the beginning of the week of the assassination.

Q. Did he tell you what he received and from whom he received it?

A. He stated that he received a letter from John Wilkes Booth, dated 'New York', ordering him immediately to Washington, as it had been necessary to change their plans, and to act promptly.

Q. Did he tell you what he did?

A. He told me that he started immediately on receipt of the letter.

Q. Did he tell you anything that he did on his way to Washington; and if so, what?

A. The first place he named was Elmira, in the State of New York.

Q. Did he state anything that he did there?

A. He told me that he telegraphed to John Wilkes Booth, in New York.
Q. Did he tell you what he learned?
A. He told me that an answer came back that John Wilkes Booth had already started for Washington.[26]

We can see from this exchange that Booth felt the need to contact Surratt at the beginning of assassination week. It is tempting to interpret Booth's use of the word 'letter' to mean a telegram inasmuch as Booth's summoning him to Washington 'immediately' would suggest the necessity of an immediate communication rather than one that would probably take a couple of days to reach the addressee. That would also tie it rather convincingly to the capture of Harney and the consequent failure of his mission. The problem with that interpretation is that McMillan said that Surratt told him the letter was 'dated New York' and it is known that Booth wasn't in New York on 9 or 10 April; he was in Washington on both days. He was, however, in New York on 2, 3 and 7 April. The great likelihood, therefore, is that when Surratt used the word 'letter', he meant a hand-written letter in the usual sense, not a telegram, and that Booth posted it in New York on 7 April, a Friday. Inasmuch as there is no Sunday delivery, it makes sense that Surratt would receive it on Monday, the 10th, which is the beginning of the working week. If the letter was sent on the 7th from New York, then it appears that it was not related to the failure of the Harney mission, which occurred on the 9th or 10th, though it is always possible that Booth wanted Surratt with him in Washington because of the possibility that he would be called upon to implement Plan B, a possibility that Booth was informed of on or about 1 April, when the Harney mission got underway. Another possibility is that 'dated New York' was a Booth stratagem to conceal the true origin of the letter (or telegram) and thereby conceal his whereabouts at the time he sent it, i.e. Washington on the 9th or 10th. Observe, in this connection, that McMillan testified that Surratt had told him that the 'letter' was 'dated New York', not that it was postmarked New York. All of this is conjectural, obviously, but if the communication really did originate from New York on the 7th rather than Washington on the 9th or 10th, one has to ask: What on earth was so momentous on or about the

7th that would change Booth's plans to such a degree that he would feel compelled to summon his co-conspirator to Washington 'immediately' and 'promptly'? It is admittedly an unknown, but there is a strong sense that Booth's communication to Surratt is in some way related to the Harney mission, and perhaps, more specifically, to its failure.

Further, Booth's order to Surratt to return to Washington 'immediately' and to act 'promptly' demonstrates that the 26-year-old actor was still very much in command of the seasoned Secret Service agent who was Judah Benjamin's 'most trusted courier', and that Booth and Surratt were very much a team, just as Surratt had said to McMillan when he told him that he and Booth had spent $10,000 (about $160,000 in 2020 dollars) on their conspiracy to 'abduct' Lincoln,[27] and just as Surratt had said to Henri Beaumont de Ste Marie, his fellow Papal Zouave in Italy, when he told him that 'we have killed Lincoln, the nigger's friend'. Interestingly, Louis J. Weichmann, Mrs Surratt's boarder, who testified at both the trial of the conspirators and the trial of John Surratt, in his book, *A True History of the Assassination of Abraham Lincoln and of the Conspiracy of 1865*, mentions the letter, Surratt's immediate departure for Washington in response thereto, his stop in Elmira, his telegram to Booth and the response to the telegram, namely that Booth had already started for Washington.

So what does the letter tell us? Why was it necessary for Surratt to return to Washington 'immediately' and to act 'promptly' and why did Surratt respond accordingly, but then stop in Elmira? The message Surratt received in response to the telegram he sent Booth in New York from Elmira, that Booth had already left for Washington, fits with what we know of Booth's schedule: we know that he was back in Washington on the 8th and did not leave the city until the night of the assassination.

With respect to the first question, the letter tells us that the great likelihood is that Booth was made aware of the Harney mission, and the contingency plan that he might be ordered to implement, about the time that Harney left Richmond, i.e. on or about 1 April. It makes sense that Confederate leaders would not notify him of the mission and the contingency plan until the mission was actually underway, consistent with the principal of 'need to know'. He would, of course, have been told that he needed to prime his team, and the other agents with whom he remained in contact, to go into action in the event of the failure of the Harney mission and that he needed to do so promptly, rather than wait for word of Harney's success or failure. It seems likely that the Confederate leadership, in the closing days of the war, with their manpower and resources depleted and with enemy cavalry all over the area to be penetrated, especially the heavily fortified city of Washington itself, must have realised that the risks were great and that there was a distinct possibility, therefore, that the mission would fail and that Booth would be called upon as the Confederacy's last hope.

The problem for Booth, as far as contacting Surratt and summoning him to Washington for a role in the contingency plan, was that both men were on the move and communication was thus difficult. On 1 April, Booth was in Baltimore, on the 2nd and 3rd in New York, on the 4th en route to Newport, on the 5th and 6th in Boston, on the 7th in New York again and on the 8th back in Washington.[28] At the same time, Surratt was in Washington on the 3rd, en route to New York on the 4th, in New York on the 5th and in Montreal on the 6th and thereafter until he left for Elmira and Washington pursuant to Booth's letter.[29] It appears, therefore, that though Booth was apprised of the Harney mission about the first of the month, he did not find it convenient to write to Surratt until the 7th, a letter that reached Surratt on the 10th, assuming, as said earlier, that Booth did not intentionally falsify the origin of the communication. His lateness in contacting Surratt, and his uncertainty as to whether or not and when he would be ordered to duplicate Harney's mission, as closely as possible, probably account for his order to Surratt to return to Washington 'immediately' and to act 'promptly'.

As for why Surratt stopped in Elmira and perhaps stayed there until after the assassination, as he claimed, there is a great deal of mystery, which, no doubt, is exactly what he wanted. There are three accounts of what he did after arriving in Montreal on the 6th; they all come from him and they are all very different. The first is contained in the testimony of McMillan in Surratt's trial as to what Surratt told him aboard the *Peruvian*;[30] the second is in Surratt's 1870 Rockville lecture;[31] and the third is contained in an interview he gave to journalist Hanson Hiss, which appeared in the *Washington Post* on 2 April 1898.[32] We will cover these in some detail in Chapter Four, because they are only peripherally relevant to the purpose of this chapter, which is to show that the Confederate government and its Secret Service launched a major attack, led by Thomas Harney, against the leaders of the United States government, with their principal target being President Abraham Lincoln, that they kept Booth and his team and his contacts in the wings, as it were, for action, with or without Surratt, in the event of the failure of the Harney mission, and that, accordingly, they at all times knew about, directed and controlled Booth, who was never a rogue agent.

The postulates, then, are: 1) that Booth was informed of the Harney mission and its purpose and of the possibility that he would be called upon to approximate its results in the event of its failure, about the time that Harney left Richmond, i.e. on or about 1 April; and 2) that Booth was informed of the failure of the mission very soon after it occurred and therefore knew, from that time, that the last hope of saving what he considered his country, the Confederate States of America, was in his hands, i.e. the hands of a 26-year-old actor, 'a crazy fellow' (according to Confederate agent Thomas Harbin) and a 'rattle-pated fellow, filled with quixotic notions … a wild-brained boy', spoken of by all his theatrical friends as 'a poor, crazy boy' (per his brother Edwin). He knew, too, or in any case, he believed, that at a time when he would need professional hitmen, he would be forced to make do with a team that, except for Powell and Surratt, he had little confidence in, a team that lacked cohesion and singleness of purpose. Some of them, according to Booth, didn't even know until 8.00 p.m. Friday night, the 14th, that assassination was on the agenda, being still deluded with the kidnapping fiction. Judging from some of the letters that came into the possession of the Bureau of Military Justice after the assassination, some of the men arrayed against Union leadership on the night of 14 April *were* professional hitmen, but they weren't on Booth's immediate action team.

If the postulates are true and accurate, we should expect that Booth's behaviour between 1 and 14 April – what is known of it – reflected, in some degree, his circumstances. Let us look.

1. On 1 April, or perhaps the day after, he was most likely informed of the Harney mission and of the role he would be expected to play in the event of its failure. He left Washington for Baltimore on the afternoon train.

2. On the 2nd, he was in New York, where he met and chatted with his older brother Junius and with fellow actor John McCullough.
3. On the 4th, he and a female companion took a steamer to Newport.
4. On the 5th, he and his female friend took the 3.00 p.m. train to Boston, saw his brother Edwin play *Hamlet* in Boston and spoke to actress Rachel Noah backstage.
5. On the 6th, he entertained himself at a shooting gallery near the Parker House Hotel, visited his brother Edwin at the theatre and bumped into a friend, Orlando Tompkins, whom he took to a jewellery store. There he bought a ring and had it inscribed: 'J.W.B. to O.T. April 6, 1865'. As he handed it to his friend, he said, 'Here, Doctor, I never gave you anything before and I may never see you again.'
6. On the 7th, he travelled to New York. He was drinking heavily and was loudly drunk when he met with his actor friend, Samuel Knapp Chester. He told Chester that he had had an excellent opportunity to kill Lincoln at his second Inauguration on 4 March.
7. On the 8th, he left New York for Washington. He wrote to Sam Chester, telling him that he would soon be leaving for Oil City, Pennsylvania. Upon his arrival in Washington, he registered at the National Hotel, where he always stayed when he was in Washington.
8. On the 10th, or perhaps the day after, he was informed of the failure of the Harney mission and ordered to activate the contingency plan. He went to Mary Surratt's boarding house and asked Mary about her son, John. He ran into a friend, H.B. Phillips, who invited him to have a drink with him. Booth responded by saying that he would do 'anything to drive away the blues'. He again entertained himself at a shooting gallery. He told Edman Spangler that he was going to leave the city and asked him to sell his horse and buggy.
9. On the 11th, he again made use of a shooting gallery. Spangler advised him that he had not sold his horse and buggy yet. Booth told him to keep trying. That evening, he, with Powell and Herold, saw Lincoln, from a window in the White House, speak to a crowd below him on the lawn. Among other things, Lincoln spoke about

enfranchising newly freed slaves in Louisiana. Booth responded to that by saying, 'That means nigger citizenship. Now, by God, I'll put him through. That is the last speech he will ever make.' Could such certainty of success for Booth have been the product of anything but careful plans that had already been made and that involved multiple hands and minds?

10. On the 12th, he visited the ticket office at Ford's Theatre and spoke ill of blacks. Atzerodt checked out of the Pennsylvania House, saying he would be away for a few days. Atzerodt then visited the Kirkwood House and inquired about Andrew Johnson's room number. A patron showed him the room and pointed out Johnson in the dining room.
11. On the 13th, Booth went to Ford's Theatre in the morning. He later asked the manager of Grover's Theatre if he was going to invite Lincoln to the theatre that evening. Powell was seen at Seward's home, peeking into a window and inquiring about the Secretary's health. Michael O'Laughlen came to Washington from Baltimore and looked for Booth at the National. Booth, Herold, Atzerodt and Powell met in the latter's room at the Herndon House. Booth asked Atzerodt to register at the Kirkwood to justify being there. An intruder at Stanton's home was later identified at the trial as O'Laughlen.
12. On the 14th, Booth wrote to his mother at 2.00 a.m. He had breakfast in his hotel. Powell again went to the Seward home. Atzerodt took possession of his room at the Kirkwood. O'Laughlen looked for Booth. Late in the morning, Booth bumped into Dick Ford, associated with the theatre, who was with John E. Coyle of the *National Intelligencer* and Major Thomas Donoho, a friend of Booth's father. Booth asked them what would happen if Lincoln and his cabinet were swept away? Donoho answered, 'What would be the result of an earthquake?' Coyle added, 'They don't make Brutuses nowadays.'[33] Query? What else besides an order to approximate the results of the Harney mission would cause Booth to ask such a question and to include Lincoln's entire cabinet in it, an objective quite beyond his capabilities and his plans for the evening? Booth went to the boarding house and told

Mary to take his binoculars to the tavern in Surrattsville and to tell the tavern keeper, John Lloyd, to take out the carbines that had been deposited there by Surratt, Herold and Atzerodt, because they would be picked up that night. Again, I ask: How does one account for such certainty of success if one does not accept the fact that plans for multiple assassinations had been long in the works and that they involved the hands and minds of professionals and of those who were high up in the chain of command? Booth went to Ford's at noon and was told that Lincoln and Grant would be there for the evening performance. Booth arranged for the hire of a horse and picked it up. He met fellow actor John Mathews on Pennsylvania Avenue and gave him a letter for delivery to *The National Intelligencer* the next day unless he asked for the return of the letter before 10.00 a.m. the next day. The letter rationalised his intentions and even named Atzerodt, Herold and Powell as co-conspirators. Mathews drew Booth's attention to a carriage riding by with General Grant and his wife in it. Booth galloped past it one way and then doubled back and passed it the other way. Then he went to Willard's Hotel, where he knew the Grants were staying, and inquired as to their destination. He was told they were on their way to the railway station and New Jersey, so Booth knew by late afternoon that Grant would not be at Ford's that night. Booth left a note at the Kirkwood in the mailbox of William A. Browning, Vice President Johnson's private secretary, for the purpose of implicating Johnson in the assassination of Lincoln planned for that evening inasmuch as he was not able to make contact with Johnson on the 14th, though he tried, and therefore believed there was a good chance that the attempt to assassinate him would not succeed. At 8.00 p.m., Booth, Powell, Herold, Atzerodt and possibly John Surratt met at the Herndon House. Booth said that he would kill Lincoln, that Powell would kill Seward and that Atzerodt would kill Johnson. Atzerodt balked, saying he had signed on for kidnapping, but not for killing. Booth assigned Herold to double-team with Atzerodt in the attempt on Johnson and then to meet him on the road to Surrattsville, to help him find his way through the countryside. A 'feverishly excited'

> Mary Surratt warned blockade runner Richard M. Smoot to leave the city. Booth went to the boarding house for a third time that day to talk to Mary. Booth led his horse to the rear door of the theatre, had a drink at Taltavull's Star Saloon, next door, then entered the theatre and assassinated Lincoln. He escaped from the theatre and met Herold on the road to Surrattsville.[34]

To all of the foregoing, we must add the following. In the period leading up to the assassination, four days of which passed with Booth's knowing of the failure of the Harney mission and that the salvation of the Confederacy was now, principally, his responsibility, Booth drank very heavily. We have already seen that he drank heavily on the 7th and was loudly drunk when he met his friend, Sam Chester. In addition, when Booth returned to Washington on the 8th and through the night of the assassination, seven days in all, he drank heavily at John Deery's billiard saloon above the lobby of Grover's Theatre. Deery later wrote a reminiscence in which he said that in the earliest days of spring that year, Booth struck him as very stressed, that he drank much more than usual and sometimes appeared to be losing his sanity. He wrote:

> For a period of about ten days before the assassination, he visited my place every day, sometimes in the afternoon, sometimes in the evening …. During that last week at Washington he sometimes drank as much as a quart of brandy in … less than two hours. … I believe Booth was as much crazed by the liquor he drank that week as by any motive when he shot Lincoln.[35]

Deery's memory was off a little, because Booth wasn't in Washington ten days before the assassination, but he was there seven days before the assassination, and we already know that he was drinking heavily from at least 1 April even when he wasn't in Washington, so his points are well taken despite the error.

Booth continued such excessive drinking, at Deery's and at Taltavull's, next to Ford's Theatre, almost to the moment he shot the President. His brain was so addled that he had to ask the clerk at the National what year it was, and then to assure him that he wasn't joking, that he truly did not know what year it was.[36] He was described by several who had contact with him on the fateful day as 'troubled and agitated', 'entirely at variance with his usual quiet deportment', 'unusually pale', 'having arms and a body that "twitched"', 'preoccupied with his thoughts', 'a man with a wild look', 'drunk', 'pale', having 'a peculiar glare in his eyes', having 'a hideous and fiendish expression' and looking 'terrible. … His eyes seemed starting from their sockets, and his hair stood on end.'[37]

Does all of the foregoing sound like dysfunction that Booth was experiencing due to something he had unilaterally decided to do? Or does it sound like dysfunction that he experienced and endured because he was under great pressure from others, i.e. under orders from superiors, to do something? If the former, he could simply have dropped his plan and put an end to all his misery. But if the latter, he had no choice but to proceed, and thus the mental wreckage.

We can explain much of Booth's behavior in the period leading up to the assassination in terms of what he perceived to be the enormous responsibility that might, and then *did*, fall to him. Yes, he had been a Secret Service agent since, most likely, early 1864, and yes, after his meeting with four Confederate agents at the Parker House in Boston in July 1864, he had gathered a team, clouding their vision with nonsense about kidnapping to induce them to come aboard for possible lethal action against the Confederacy's enemies, and yes, he had worked closely with other agents, including Surratt and Powell, for the purpose, and yes, he had run quinine to the South and all that other stuff, but it was all child's play compared to what he might now be ordered to do, and then *was* ordered to do. It was no longer inchoate; it was now actual, the real thing, and it was here and it was now. He was being ordered to change the course of history by drawing blood. And not just any blood, but the blood of giants, men who strode the corridors of power in one of the four most powerful nations on earth, indeed the blood of the Chief Magistrate of that nation. It had now fallen to him, this not-very-bright little man, this 'slow learner', this 26-year-old actor, this 'crazy fellow', this 'rattle-pated fellow', who, as far as we know, had never killed anything in his life except cats, to kill giants. Was he up to it? He knew that very prominent and powerful men in Richmond and Canada were relying on him. He wanted to meet their expectations. He didn't want to fail them. He didn't want to disappoint them. But could he really do what they were asking of him, with the motley band he had at his command, and not even that entirely? Fortunately for him, he had others to whom he could turn besides his action team. Could he put it all together and actually kill the President of the United States and then say, 'I have done it'? He could and he would.

To better comprehend the relationship between the Confederate leadership and Booth at this time, it is helpful to consider the breadth of the conspiracy of which Booth was the titular head and the multiplicity of events that occurred in Washington on the night of 14 April. We know, of course, that Lincoln was assassinated, that Seward came within an inch of meeting the same fate at the hands of Lewis Powell, and that attempts were almost certainly made on the lives of Johnson, Stanton and Grant, all of which failed. But what is commonly overlooked is that other federal office holders may also have been targeted, and probably were, per the letter from the Confederate agent 'Johnston' quoted by the Union agent in Paris, and per the T.I.O.S. letter, both previously referred to; that there were quite likely Mosby men in the city to help if they were needed in the attack, as evidenced by the numerous whistles that were heard that night in the city (whistles being a favourite means of communication by Mosby men and by Mosby himself), by riders who ignored demands for a password and barrelled through Union pickets amid a hail of gunfire, by suspiciously blasé horsemen who feigned surprise and mocked news of the assassination and attempted assassinations, and by the many incidents of federal pickets being fired upon in the vicinity of the capital; that there were reports of known partisans leaving their homes under suspicious circumstances and returning at ungodly hours, also under suspicious circumstances, one announcing that 'we have done the deed';[38] and that Booth and Herold easily crossed the Navy Yard bridge despite the fact that they crossed after hours and without passes. All of this ties in well with Booth's telling Herold that there were thirty-five involved in his conspiracy and telling Sam Chester that there were between fifty and 100 involved. It also ties in well with Powell's telling Abram Dunn Gillette that he did not know the names of the principal men collaborating with Booth and that others involved had not been apprehended, and telling Thomas T. Eckert that all he could say about others being complicit was that federal prosecutors did not have the one-half of them (conspirators) and that it was his impression that arrangements had been made with others for the same disposition of other federal office holders as he was to make of Seward. And it also ties in well with Arnold saying, in his memoirs, that at some point he realised that Booth was dealing with others besides his action team.

Clearly, a conspiracy of such scope and involving so many players could not possibly have been planned for and carried out without the knowledge, approval and direction of the highest levels of the Confederate government and its Secret Service. Just as clear and certain is the fact that none of it would have been necessary if the Harney mission had been successful. If Harney had not been captured 15 miles from Washington, but had proceeded into the city and successfully planted his bomb or bombs with their timers, thereby destroying much of the government's leadership, what need would there have been for Booth, his team and Booth's other operatives to do anything? None whatsoever. It follows that Booth's work was contingent upon the failure of Harney's, and it follows, therefore, that Booth had to have been advised of, first, Harney's mission, and second, its failure.

The alternative is to believe that there were two parallel conspiracies operating at more or less the same time and targeting more or less the same people and that neither conspiracy was known to the other: one (Harney's) organised, directed and controlled by Confederate leaders and the other a completely independent effort that had nothing to do with Confederate leaders and in fact was completely unknown to them, despite the fact that its titular head and his team and all the other men and women with whom Booth was connected were as well known to Confederate leaders as were any other operatives and teams in the Confederate underground.

The alternative is also to believe that the Confederate government and its Secret Service , with all their resources in money and materiel, in manpower and highly trained and effective agents, including assassins, could not kill the President of the United States, over a period of more than four years, by infecting him with yellow fever, by poisoning him, by shooting him, by blowing him apart, or any other way, but a 26-year-old actor, a 'crazy fellow' and a 'rattle-pated fellow, filled with quixotic notions … a wild-brained boy … a poor, crazy boy …', with help from no one besides a motley crew of amateurs who stayed with him only because of the 'bounty they were receiving at [his] hand', could and did. And not only that, but escaped with his life from the scene of the crime, past 1,700 patrons in the theatre, armed guards, 30,000 Union troops in the area, and the National Detective Police, and then eluded the United States military and intelligence services for twelve days, again, all without help from anyone save David Herold, his co-conspirator, and a few members of the mail line.

These alternatives, I submit, are naïve and patent absurdities.

Chapter Four

The Fourth Smoking Gun: John Harrison Surratt, Judah Philip Benjamin and Henri Beaumont de Sainte-Marie

John Harrison Surratt, Jnr (hereinafter John or Surratt) was the son of John Harrison Surratt, Snr and Mary Elizabeth Surratt (neé Maria Eugenia Jenkins). He was born on 13 April 1844. He had two siblings: Isaac, an older brother who fought for the Confederacy in the Trans-Mississippi, and Anna, an older sister. John, Snr, a heavy drinker, most often in debt and a violent man, died in August 1862, at the age of 49.

Mary was a dyed-in-the-wool Confederate sympathiser.[1] As such, she aided the Confederate cause whenever and wherever she could, was complicit in the events of 14 April 1865, including the assassination of President Lincoln (beyond a reasonable doubt and per the opinion of most assassination historians) and was hanged for her crime on 7 July 1865, in Washington, the first woman in the history of the United States to be executed by the federal government.

By 1853, John, Snr had built an inn and a tavern at a crossroads about 12 miles south of Washington. They are still there. Later in that year, he bought a townhouse at 541 H. Street (now 604 H. Street) in Washington and began renting it out. It too is still there. President Andrew Johnson said that it was here that Mary 'kept the nest that hatched the egg',[2] i.e. used it as a meeting place for the conspirators who plotted Lincoln's murder and the attempted decapitation of the United States government. It is, of course, possible that the inn and the tavern were constructed and the townhouse acquired at the order of, and with the assistance of, the Confederate government and/or its Secret Service. The subsequent use of all this real estate for clandestine Confederate operations tends to render that possibility a likelihood.

At the time of his death, John, Snr was postmaster for the community, then known as Surrattsville, now known as Clinton, Maryland. Given the strong Confederate sympathies of both John, Snr and Mary (and the great majority of the inhabitants of lower Maryland), it is likely that John, Snr was a conduit for communications between Confederate operatives in Washington and Baltimore, and on the Potomac, and Richmond, in addition to other clandestine activities that he likely engaged in. Call it the family business. When he died, his son, John, all of 18 years old, inherited that business. Whether John was recruited by superiors for new work at that time, or merely continued his father's work, or perhaps some of both, is not known. In any case, it wasn't long before John added dispatch delivery to his duties as postmaster. It was dangerous work, but the danger did not deter him; he loved the challenge, being totally committed to the Confederate cause. It should not surprise anyone, however, that on 17 November 1863, federal authorities relieved him of his duties as postmaster, alleging disloyalty. The wonder is that a 19-year-old boy could carry on as he did for as long as he did. Relieved of his duties as postmaster, John turned all his energies to dispatch riding and carrying messages and money between Richmond and Confederate Secret Service operatives in Canada, who were active in Montreal (their headquarters), Toronto, St Catherines, Hamilton and Windsor.

In November 1864, Mary moved, with John and Anna, from the inn and tavern to the boarding house in Washington. Isaac was off fighting a war. Mary leased the inn and tavern to one John M. Lloyd, another heavy drinker. She would regret that, because it was principally Lloyd's testimony, and to a lesser extent the testimony of Louis J. Weichmann, her boarder, at the trial of the conspirators in May and June 1865, that sent her to the gallows.

As a committed spy, John mastered the tools of his craft: chronic lying, cheating, stealing, duplicity, defrauding and deceiving, in addition, of course, to treachery, murder and mayhem. That is to say that in becoming an accomplished agent and spy, he became a thoroughly disagreeable human being, indeed a man wholly without principles, honour, integrity and scruples, in a word – character.

On his voyage to Europe in September 1865, following five months of hiding in Canada after the assassination, where he was protected by Catholic clergy, his clerical protectors placed him in the charge of Dr Lewis J.A. McMillan, the ship's doctor. McMillian was a witness at Surratt's trial in 1867 for complicity in the assassination of Lincoln. His testimony must be regarded as highly credible inasmuch as he did not pursue Surratt for reward money, though he later did lay claim to the same when he realised Surratt's value and the value of the information that had come his way by virtue of having been appointed Surratt's guardian on the voyage to Europe. McMillan described conversations he had had with Surratt aboard the *Peruvian.* Being outside of American jurisdiction, having a misplaced confidence in his listener and being inebriated part of the time (he was a pretty good tippler, brandy being his drink of choice), Surratt let his guard down, confided to McMillan his real name (he was travelling as 'John McCarty', one of his many aliases) and told McMillan about some of his services to the Confederacy. One of his more striking admissions was the fact that he and Booth had spent $10,000 on their conspiracy.[3] That's about $160,000 in 2020 dollars. Where on earth did this unemployed son of a boarding house keeper and his unemployed actor friend get the equivalent of $160,000 if not from the Confederate government and/or its supporters? Bear in mind, in this connection, that by late summer or early autumn of 1864, Booth had turned over all his assets to his mother and his older brother, Junius, because of the treason statute, which provided for the confiscation of assets of traitors. The statute was passed by Congress on 17 July 1862.

Asked by McMillan why he feared a passenger whom he suspected might be an American detective, Surratt answered that he had done more things than McMillan was aware of and that if he knew everything he had done, it would make McMillan stare or gape, or words to that effect.[4] Well, what would make him stare or gape? Carrying money to Canada? Hardly; that is not gape-worthy, nor is it anything that would cause Surratt to flee his country, abandon his mother to the hangman, hide in Canada for five months, seek refuge in Europe and Egypt and remain abroad for nineteen months. No, it would take more than carrying money and dispatches to Canada to make McMillan gape. Here are a few examples of what it took – deeds that Surratt admitted to McMillan, which McMillan testified to at Surratt's trial, which must surely be only the tip of the iceberg and which are gape-worthy:

1. When Surratt, Sarah Slater and four or five other Confederate operatives were making their way to Richmond, in late March 1865 (arriving on the 29th or 31st), they encountered, south of Fredericksburg, a half-dozen emaciated Union prisoners of war who had recently escaped from captivity and were making their way back to Union lines. At Slater's urging, the party shot the prisoners dead in cold blood.[5]
2. Aboard a boat crossing the Potomac with twelve to fifteen comrades, Surratt was hailed by a Union gunboat and ordered to surrender. Surratt and the others agreed to it, but when a smaller boat sent from the gunboat came alongside the Confederate boat for the purpose of arresting its occupants, Surratt and the others treacherously fired into the arresting party, killing some, and then escaped.[6]
3. Upon discovering a Union telegrapher in the process of telegraphing, in a barn, Surratt and his party coolly executed the man on the spot.[7]

McMillan also told the court that Surratt, waving a pistol for emphasis, said that he hoped to God that he would live to see the time when he could serve President Johnson the same way Lincoln had been served.

Surratt was a committed spy by 16 May 1863.[8] John Wilkes Booth was most likely recruited by the Secret Service in early 1864 and was in regular contact with Confederate agents and familiar with their cipher system by the autumn of that year. He met with four Confederate agents at the Parker House in Boston on 26 July, a very portentous meeting, because he began gathering his action team shortly thereafter, in early August. Surratt and Booth made numerous trips to Montreal. Charles Dunham (alias Sanford Conover) testified at the trial of the conspirators that he saw Booth there in late October 1864[9] (we know that Booth was there from 18 to 27 October, so it fits), and saw Surratt there in early April 1865 (we know he arrived there on 6 April[10] and stayed until at least the 10th, so this fits too) and again three or four days after the assassination (i.e. the 17th or 18th, which also fits with Surratt's accounts).[11] James B. Merritt, said to be a Union agent or a double agent, testified that at a meeting held in Montreal about the middle of February, Surratt was mentioned, among others, as one who was 'ready and willing … to engage in the undertaking to remove the President, the Vice President, the Cabinet, and some of the leading Generals; and that there was any amount of money to accomplish the purpose, meaning the assassination'.[12] He added that he had seen Surratt in Toronto and Booth in Canada 'two or three times'. It seems likely, therefore, that Surratt and Booth knew of each other, and perhaps even had some contact, before 23 December 1864, but that is the date a 'chance' meeting of Booth, Surratt, Weichmann and Dr Samuel Mudd took place on a Washington street. Dr Mudd was a landowner in lower Maryland, a slaveholder and part of what was known as the 'mail line' of Confederate operatives between Richmond and Washington. In any case, it was from this time, at the latest, that Surratt became a major player in Booth's scheme to ostensibly kidnap Lincoln, but almost certainly to assassinate him and other federal office holders. It is fair to say, in fact, that he became Booth's right hand, second in command and therefore privy to all of Booth's machinations, his comings and goings, his successes and his failures. It should be added that whatever he didn't learn from Booth himself, for whatever reason, he was quite likely to learn from his mother, who was very close to Booth (she called him 'Pet') and who was, at one time or another, in contact with all the members of his action team except Samuel Arnold and Michael O'Laughlen, two co-conspirators who were Booth's childhood chums from Baltimore and who were the first recruits to his conspiracy.

Demonstrating the degree of his commitment to Booth's conspiracy, Surratt participated in the *Jack Cade* affair, which occurred in January 1865. The affair began when Booth heard, or said he heard, that Lincoln and some guests were going to attend a performance of *Jack Cade* at Ford's Theatre on the 18th of the month. Supposedly, he tried to gather his team for an attempt at kidnapping Lincoln. Surratt asked for three days' leave from his job with the Adams Express Company, telling his superior he had to take his mother to the old home in Surrattsville. His superior turned him down, so his deeply religious mother came and lied to the superior, supporting her son's balderdash, but to no avail.

The opportunity was so important to Surratt that he quit his job. He, Booth and co-conspirator David Herold, a druggist's assistant from Washington, then summoned the rest of the team to action. Booth even tried to enlist his actor friend from New York, Samuel Knapp Chester, in the effort, without success. Surratt and his co-conspirator George Atzerodt, a river rat and carriage painter from Port Tobacco, Maryland, are said to have found a boat that would be suitable for ferrying ten or twelve people across the Potomac. The wheels began to come off the operation when Booth asked his actor friend, John Mathews, for help and received the same response that Chester had given him and when Arnold and O'Laughlen failed to show. Furious with these two unreliable Baltimoreans, Booth proceeded anyway, even ordering a vehicle with side curtains to be parked in the alley. The wheels came off completely when Lincoln did not come. Supposedly, Booth tried to ride out his disappointment by getting drunk.[13]

The foregoing account appears in several secondary sources, and there is some corroboration for the boat story, but the truth is that we don't know how much of this event really happened or, if it happened essentially as described, how much was a bona fide kidnap attempt and how much a cover for assassination. William Hanchett summed the matter up by saying, 'Whatever Booth and his friends were up to in January, there is no real evidence that they planned seriously to capture Lincoln inside the theatre.'[14]

Surratt also participated in the Gautier's Restaurant meeting, which we touched upon in Chapter Two. This was a meeting of Booth and all the members of his action team, including newly arrived Lewis Powell (now using the alias 'Mosby'), a powerfully built man who had acquired a reputation as a tough-as-nails fighter for the cause. He had been dispatched to Booth by the Gray Ghost himself, doubtless on orders from higher authority, for a service deemed more important to the Confederacy than guerilla work in Virginia. Arrangements were made by Surratt himself for Powell's transfer, with help from another agent in Baltimore, David Preston Parr, a china dealer.[15] Also present were Herold, Atzerodt, Arnold and O'Laughlen – seven in all.

Booth called the meeting for the night of 15/16 March and rented a private room at Gautier's for the event. His purpose was to rekindle what he perceived to be a waning interest in the project, to give his team greater cohesion, some of whom barely knew each other, and to put them in readiness for action, which he knew or believed would come soon.

After the last waiter left the restaurant, Booth got down to business. First, they discussed the possibility that their scheme was known to federal authorities. Surratt would later say that everyone but Booth believed it and that the weak-kneed among them felt that this was reason enough for them to abandon their plans, which confirmed to Booth that, in fact, they were all losing heart for the enterprise. Booth met these objections by exploding. Slamming his fist on the table for emphasis, he bellowed, 'Well, gentlemen, if the worst comes to the worst, I shall know what to do.' Booth was by this time heavily under the influence of the evening's libations and it appears, therefore, to be a case of *in vino veritas*, which is to say that he let the cat out of the bag with respect to his true intentions. His outburst was effectively a notice and justification of what was likely to come as well as a shifting of at least part of the responsibility for the same onto his team, a penalty for their wavering and doubts. The outburst, of course, did not help matters, so he sought to mollify the doubters by telling them that others were in place to help with the kidnapping, another reference to 'others' with whom Booth was in contact for the purpose of engineering his decapitation and still more evidence that Booth was merely a pawn, a very valuable one to the Confederacy, but nevertheless a pawn, an agent who was being counselled, instructed, directed and financed at all times by higher authority, indeed authority that ultimately resided in Richmond and Canada.

Booth then assigned each member of the team a role in the 'abduction' from Ford's Theatre. The plan was so bizarre, so plainly unworkable, that it was hard to believe he was serious, which, of course, he wasn't. Arnold pointed out that the entire rationale for the plot had been undercut by Grant's resumption of prisoner exchange in January, which obviously undercut the ostensible purpose of the plot, which was to kidnap the President and then hold him for ransom pending the release of Confederate prisoners of war. He also pointed out that the chances of getting Lincoln past thousands in the audience, armed guards, pursuing cavalry and bridge sentries were near zero and that he wanted a chance for his life. He said to Booth, 'You can be the leader of the party, but not my executioner.' Booth shifted his ground, saying that Southern independence, not release of prisoners, was the real goal of the plot and that it could be achieved by kidnapping Lincoln. With everyone well oiled by this time, Booth threatened to shoot Arnold, reminding him of his oath. Arnold responded by saying that Booth had changed the plan and that for that reason his oath was no longer operative, adding, defiantly, that if Booth wanted to shoot him, he could proceed, but that Booth should remember that 'two can play at that game'. This was enough for Booth to back off. Arnold took advantage of the retreat to tell everyone that if the kidnapping were not accomplished by the end of the week (i.e. the week of 16–22 March), he was out of the conspiracy. The meeting broke up at 5.00 a.m. with the conspiracy intact, but badly shaken by the confrontation between Booth and Arnold.[16]

And then there is the Campbell Hospital episode, also touched upon in Chapter Two. Campbell Hospital, which was sometimes referred to as the Seventh Street Hospital, was located near the Soldiers' Home, to which the Lincolns often repaired in the summer to escape the heat of the city. The home is still there. As with the *Jack Cade* affair, there is a great deal of uncertainty as to what really happened at or about the Campbell Hospital, how it happened and why it happened. Accounts differ substantially and the whole truth, therefore, will never be known. The only certainty is that something happened that involved Booth, Surratt and the rest of the action team, that it happened very soon after the Gautier's Restaurant meeting and that the two episodes are not unrelated.

With Arnold openly threatening to pull out of the conspiracy and with everyone now doubting both the wisdom and the likelihood of success of kidnapping the President, possibly excepting Powell who was too new to the team to learn to doubt, Booth naturally feared that the entire enterprise was in danger of collapse and that some bold action was needed to properly motivate his team and to inspire the newly acquired Powell. To accomplish this, he got word to them that he had received intelligence that on the following day, 17 March, Lincoln was scheduled to appear at Campbell Hospital for a benefit performance of a play and that this was a golden opportunity for them to kidnap the old bird and haul him off to Richmond. ('Received intelligence'? From whom, if not from superiors in the Confederate government or the Secret Service?) Is this seemingly innocuous statement by Booth in fact very telling as to his relationship with the government and its Secret Service and therefore the source of his orders? This line of attack nicely avoided the pitfalls of an abduction in the theatre, which had created such an uproar at Gautier's, and, further, was consistent with their original plan to capture Lincoln on the way to or from the Soldiers' Home. That plan had apparently found greater favour with the team.

At this point all the accounts differ as to how everyone got to the hospital area, when they got there, what they did when they got there and what they did when everything came to an inglorious end and they left the area. Dan, a 'half-witted mulatto' who did chores around the boarding house, gave one account, according to Weichmann in his history of the assassination; Arnold, in his memoirs, gave three accounts, all different from Dan's and Weichmann's accounts and from each other; Surratt's account, given in his 1870 Rockville, Maryland, lecture, is different from all the others; and Atzerodt's account, given in his 6 July 1865 confession, is also different from all the others. It is therefore impossible to know what really happened that day at or near the hospital.[17]

In any case, the episode gave the appearance of being another bust, like the *Jack Cade* affair, because Lincoln did not appear at the hospital, spending the afternoon instead at the National Hotel performing some perfunctory act of patronage. There was irony here, because the National was the hotel where Booth always stayed when he was in Washington.

The belief among some historians, such as Michael Kauffman, and such as this writer, is that, in fact, Booth never received word that Lincoln was going to be at the hospital that day, that he fabricated the story and orchestrated the entire episode for his own purposes, which were, as previously said, to properly motivate his team and thereby to energise his sagging conspiracy, which is further evidence that 'others' were depending upon him to deliver something. If he were truly a lone wolf or a rogue agent, he would have, by this time, folded his tent and gone home. But he was a driven man, because others were driving him and those others, ultimately, had to include a person or persons in very high places. His ego was very much involved, as was his reputation. Both needed vindication. So he would continue, even when the rationale for his conspiracy evaporated and even when faced with rebellion in his ranks.

Booth also accomplished a couple of other things that day, which must also have been in his mind. He retrieved weapons and tools that he had previously given to Arnold and O'Laughlen for safekeeping and he nicely implicated everyone in the conspiracy, in the eyes of the law, so as to minimise the likelihood of their withdrawal from it as well as their cooperation with federal authority. It is interesting to note that Kauffman's and this writer's conclusion that Booth had staged the entire event echoes a conclusion reached 100 years earlier by Arnold. In his memoirs, Arnold wrote that the episode was so demented and foolhardy that 'we concluded that it was done to try the nerve of his [Booth's] associates'.[18]

These three episodes tell us a great deal about Surratt's involvement in Booth's conspiracy. But there is more, including:

1. On the morning of 18 March, after the failed 'kidnapping' attempt at Campbell Hospital, Surratt, Atzerodt and Herold went to the tavern in Surrattsville and deposited there, with John Lloyd, the weapons and tools that Booth had recovered from Arnold and O'Laughlen.[19]
2. It was Surratt who had recruited Atzerodt and Powell to participate in the conspiracy, the former because he knew the Potomac as well as anyone and had made part of his living ferrying people across it, and the latter because he had muscle and daring. And it was Surratt who had arranged for Powell to come to Washington from Baltimore on 14 March and to meet with Booth and the others at Gautier's on the 15th and 16th.
3. It was Surratt who, with Atzerodt's help, acquired a boat from one Richard Smoot, which was capable of carrying a dozen or so men and which was to be used to carry Lincoln across the Potomac, en route to Richmond, after his abduction.
4. And, of course, Surratt had met often with Booth, from 23 December 1864, at the latest, in furtherance of their plans.

It is clear enough from the foregoing that Surratt was a major player in Booth's conspiracy, second only to Booth himself. Recall, too, that he lived with his mother, who kept the boarding house, which, from December 1864 to the date of the assassination, was a beehive of activity, with Confederate couriers, spies, blockade runners and other agents coming and going at all hours, including visits by Booth, Powell, Herold, Atzerodt, Arnold and O'Laughlen. Booth, especially, came often and met with Surratt and his mother to discuss the conspiracy and to formulate their plans. Virtually everything that went on under Mary Surratt's roof, therefore, was known to Surratt, as was virtually every communication between his mother and Booth and between the other members of the team, excepting only Arnold and O'Laughlen, who appear to have visited the boarding house during this period only once, when the team galloped off for Campbell Hospital.

Surratt, in these circumstances, could not help but acquire an encyclopedic knowledge of Booth, his action team and his conspiracy. Along the way, he would quite naturally pick up information relative to other Secret Service operatives and operations. In addition to Sarah Slater, he must surely have known, or known of, and perhaps even had contact with, Belle Boyd, Thomas Nelson Conrad, Benjamin Franklin Ficklin, Rose O'Neal Greenhow, Thomas Harbin, Thomas H. Hines, Augustus Howell, 'mail line' operatives between Richmond and Washington, such as Samuel Cox, Dr Samuel Mudd, Thomas A. Jones, John J. Hughes, Elizabeth Quesenberry, Joseph Baden, William Bryant and Dr Richard Stuart, and many more, some low, some high, in the command structure. Recall, too, that he was exposed to many, probably most, of the Confederate operatives who were engaged in clandestine work and who passed into and out of the boarding house. It was also true that he was a frequent visitor to Dr Mudd's home, a Confederate safe house, near Bryantown, Maryland, which was also heavily trafficked by the Confederate underground, as Mary Simms, one of Dr Mudd's slaves, testified to at the trial of the conspirators.[20] As for his knowledge of other plots, he said, significantly, in his 1870 Rockville lecture, speaking of the events of 1864–5, 'I had good reason to believe that there was another conspiracy afloat in Washington, in fact we all knew it.' Clearly, Surratt had become, by 1864 and 1865, a master of his craft, having an intimate knowledge of not just Booth and his conspiracy, in which he was a major player, but of Confederate clandestine operatives and operations in general.

With whom would he share that knowledge? His superiors, of course, and anyone in the Secret Service who had a need to know, provided he had authority to do this. It seems safe to assume, too, that he would report to intermediaries between him and the highest levels of the Confederate government inasmuch as the highest levels of governments routinely insulate themselves from lower operatives – grunts and hatchet men – with intermediate operatives. Unless, that is, there is evidence that Surratt dealt directly with those highest levels. Is there such evidence? There is indeed. The fact is that Surratt was a courier for Judah P. Benjamin, the Confederate Secretary of State, previously the Confederate Attorney General and Secretary of War. More than that, he met almost weekly with Benjamin in Richmond[21] and quite likely met with Jefferson Davis himself.[22] And more than that, Surratt was, according to one of Benjamin's biographers, Eli Evans, Benjamin's 'most trusted courier'.[23]

Benjamin was a most interesting figure, perhaps the most interesting of all of Davis's cabinet members. Stephen Vincent Benet thought enough of him to describe him this way in *John Brown's Body*:

> Judah P. Benjamin, the dapper Jew,
> Seal Sleek, black-eyed, lawyer and epicure,
> Able, well-hated, face alive with life,
> Looked round the council-chamber with the slight
> Perpetual smile he held before himself
> Continually like a silk-ribbed fan.
> Behind the fan, his quick, shrewd, fluid mind
> Weighed Gentiles in an old balance …

Benet wasn't finished, of course, but that's enough to set the stage for a brief biography.

Judah Philip Benjamin was born on 11 August 1811, in St Croix of the Danish West Indies (now in the US Virgin Islands). His family moved to the United States when he was a child, first to Fayetteville, North Carolina, then to Charleston, South Carolina. At 14, he entered

Yale College, but left two years later without completing his studies. Mystery surrounds the cause of his leaving, but it was later written on good authority that he had been expelled for gambling, which fits with his attraction to that form of recreation throughout his life.

He moved to New Orleans in 1828, where he began the study of law. He was admitted to the Louisiana bar in 1832. The following year, he married Natalie St Martin, a wealthy woman of some notoriety in New Orleans. The marriage was not a happy one: they spent the better part of the next forty years living an ocean apart, she in Paris and he in America, though they did have one child, a daughter, Ninette, and they did manage to see each other about once a year.

Benjamin had a successful law practice for some years in New Orleans, which made him a wealthy man, but he soon succumbed to the lure of politics. In 1851, he was elected to the State Senate and in 1853 to the United States Senate. Clearly, his intelligence and his competence had not gone unnoticed. So competent was he, in fact, that he even managed to maintain a lucrative law practice in Washington when the Senate was not is session.

He defended slavery on the grounds that slaves were property and that the right to maintain that species of property was preserved and protected by the United States Constitution. He, as well as many others in the South, feared a slave insurrection and the massacre of the white population, such as had occurred in Haiti in 1804. Recognising its potential for undermining the legitimacy of the South's peculiar institution, and therefore of the South itself as then constituted, Benjamin was highly critical of Harriet Beecher Stowe's enormously successful novel, *Uncle Tom's Cabin.*

In 1856, he abandoned the Whig Party, or what was left of it after it split on the issue of slavery. This issue, which had bedevilled the Republic since its inception in 1789, became explosive in the decade leading up to the Civil War. He joined the Democratic Party, because he believed it best represented Southern interests.

In 1859, Benjamin was re-elected to the United States Senate. Though he supported secession in principal, believing it was entirely lawful, he felt that resort should be had to it only if all other means and methods of protecting Southern interests failed. Apparently believing that that condition had been met, he resigned his seat in the Senate on 4 February 1861, choosing to stay with his seceded state. He had no illusion, however, that the Southern states could secede from the Union peacefully.

On 25 February, Davis, newly elected President of the Confederate States of America, appointed Benjamin as Attorney General of the new nation. At this stage in the development of this new nation, this office did not give its holder much to do (there was, as yet, no judiciary worthy of the name) and for this reason and others, Davis appointed him Secretary of War in September 1861. This was a highly controversial position, because blame for reversals on the battlefield or at sea was quite likely to be laid at the feet of the Secretary of War, unless there was a very good reason for placing it elsewhere. Human nature being what it is, the fact that he was Jewish made matters worse, because scapegoating lent itself to references to his ethnicity and ancestry. On 17 March 1862, Davis appointed him Secretary of State and it was in this position that he served the Confederacy for as long as it existed.

As Secretary of State, Benjamin exercised ultimate authority over the Confederate Secret Service, including, at least, domestic agents, foreign agents, the Signal Corps, the Torpedo Bureau, the Submarine Battery Service, espionage, the Special and Secret Service Bureau and Secret Service operations in Canada. As previously stated, the Secret Service went into high gear from the spring of 1864 to the spring of 1865, after the failed Wistar and Dahlgren-Kilpatrick raids on Richmond in February and March 1864. This was the year of accelerated and more deadly covert actions in the North, impelled and believed to be legitimised by the raids and directed from politically neutral Canada, where Davis's point men, James Holcombe, Clement Clay and Jacob Thompson (until he was relieved, near the end of the war, and replaced by General Edwin G. Lee) executed plans whose purpose was to accomplish objectives that had been decided upon in Richmond. Let us be clear on this distinction: the objectives were decided upon in Richmond by Confederate political and military leaders who met in the series of high-level conferences that took place in Richmond following the raids.[24] These objectives were then made clear to Holcombe, Thompson and Clay in verbal orders and instructions, because they were deemed to be too sensitive to be committed to writing even in code. For the same reason, these men, in turn, gave verbal orders and instructions to their subordinates as to how to accomplish the objectives. No writings containing these orders and instructions, therefore, will ever be found, because no such writings ever existed. We have some idea of what they were, however, based on the terror and assassination plots that followed the installation of the Confederate leaders' men in Canada.

So there he is – Judah P. Benjamin, second in command of the Confederate States of America and, when Davis went to Tennessee to confer with General Braxton Bragg's recalcitrant subordinate generals, after Chickamauga, briefly first in command.[25] Clearly, he was a man of enormous power and authority, which extended to all Confederate operations, domestic and foreign, other than those that were under the immediate control of other Cabinet members. Clandestine operations, especially, were under his eyes and in his hands, subject only to check by Davis. The notion that the Confederate leaders' appointees in Canada – Holcombe, Thompson and Clay – and those under their command, such as Thomas Henry Hines, Bennett H. Young, John Yeats Beall and Dr Luke P. Blackburn, would initiate and carry out terror and assassination plots against the Union without orders from those leaders, or contrary to their orders, and without following their instructions precisely, is ridiculous. Likewise for John Taylor Wood, Gabriel James Rains, Joseph W. Tucker, John Maxwell, R.K. Dillard, Robert Cobb Kennedy, Robert M. Martin and all other operatives who struck back at the Union, in the only ways and with the only means they felt were available to them at the time, for the death and destruction wrought by Union armies in the South and for the perceived attempt by Union cavalry units to destroy their capital and to murder their leaders.

Intelligence operations, indeed government in general and war-making in particular, are carried out according to the leadership principle. Everyone follows orders, except those who give them. Failure to do so has consequences. Malfeasance, misfeasance and nonfeasance in the execution of orders always has consequences, all negative. A 'rogue agent' is almost an oxymoron, and such a creature is almost unknown. Virtually every aspect of the Confederate year of terror against the North, therefore, unless independent action was expressly authorised, must have been carried out with the knowledge and approval of Confederate leaders.

Further, this is the man – Benjamin – be it ever remembered, who met weekly with none other than John Surratt in Richmond, according to Henri Beaumont de Ste Marie, Surratt's fellow Papal Zouave in Italy, about whom more later, and who dutifully couriered Benjamin's dispatches and the Confederacy's money to Canada.[26] Surratt – the right hand of John Wilkes Booth from December 1864, at the latest. Surratt – he with the encyclopedic knowledge of Booth's action team and their conspiracy, as well as of the Confederate underground in general. Surratt – Benjamin's 'most trusted courier'. There were surely dozens of couriers doing service in the Confederacy, perhaps more if we include those who served officers in the field. Why did Benjamin choose Surratt? Could it have been pure chance that he chose a man who was so close to Booth? Would he not have carefully vetted his couriers or have them carefully vetted? Of course he would. If Surratt's closeness to Booth occurred after the vetting process, would Benjamin not know how and when Surratt and Booth came together and what the consequences of that joining were? And if these were in any way displeasing to Benjamin, would he not drop Surratt as a courier? The fact that he did not can only mean that there was nothing about Surratt, past or present, that displeased him, or in any case, nothing that constituted sufficient cause for him to retain a new courier. Having vetted Surratt, would he then not know of his closeness to Booth and his knowledge, therefore, of what Booth and his team were doing and not doing? Of course he would. Would he not know of Surratt's role in bringing Lewis Powell to Booth? Of course he would. Would he not know that he was the son of Mary Surratt, who owned Confederate safe houses in Surrattsville and Washington, in and out of which a Rogue's Gallery of Confederate agents found their way? Of course he would.

Eli Evans, one of Benjamin's biographers, contends that Benjamin's choice of Surratt was a mistake of judgment and that Davis saw the matter so. Nonsense! Not that men and women who wield enormous power and influence do not make mistakes of judgment; of course they do. But they are most unlikely to make one in their choice of such an important servant or associate as a courier of critically important dispatches and money and they are most unlikely to continue the error if error it is found to be. Far more likely is it that Benjamin chose Surratt, not in ignorance of his connection to Booth, but because of it! Put plainly, Surratt was Benjamin's man in the Booth conspiracy, his pipeline, his conduit. To know what Booth and his team were doing, or, more precisely, to know whether or not Booth, the Confederate agent, was diligently pursuing the goals that had been set for him and was prepared to act if and when called upon by his handlers to do so, Benjamin had only to ask Surratt, which he must have done in every one of the almost weekly meetings he had with him.

Further, is it not simply sensible and rational that Davis himself would sometimes choose to get his information directly from the horse's mouth rather than secondhand from Benjamin, or perhaps to question Surratt, or, for some other reason or reasons, to converse with him? After all, Davis's and Benjamin's offices were under the same roof, in the Confederate White House, only steps away from each other. Yes, it is. In his book, *A True History of the Assassination of Abraham Lincoln and of the Conspiracy of 1865*, Weichmann, who must be regarded as an original source (he lived the story), mentions Surratt's return to the boarding house in the evening of 3 April 1865, en route to Montreal. He wrote, 'I asked him where he had been. "To Richmond," he answered. I then said "Richmond is evacuated. Did you not hear the news?" "No, it is not," he said. "I saw Benjamin and Davis in Richmond, and they told me it would not be evacuated."'[27] The passage is obviously heavy with meaning and it has therefore found its way into the works of many assassination historians.[28] In fairness, Henri Beaumont de Ste Marie stated, in his affidavit to Secretary of State William Seward, in 1866, that when he and Surratt were Papal Zouaves together in Italy, he had asked Surratt if he knew Davis and that Surratt had answered 'No', but that he had acted under the instructions of persons under Davis's immediate orders.[29] Which of the two statements is more credible? The one given to an old acquaintance whom he had not seen in three years and therefore had no particular desire to share secrets with, not knowing how well he could trust him, or the one given spontaneously to a boarder in his mother's boarding house, whom he knew very well and may have had dealings with and at a time when he had no reason whatsoever to fabricate a meeting with Davis inasmuch as a meeting with only Benjamin in Richmond would have quite sufficed to give him the authority he wished to project. Adding Davis to the sentence was therefore unnecessary and for that reason quite credible. Moreover, relative to the issue of the complicity of Confederate leaders in the assassination and attempted assassinations, how much difference, really, does it make if Surratt was following Davis's orders directly or if he 'acted under the instructions of persons under Davis's immediate orders', as he said. I submit: none at all.

Furthermore, which is more rational and believable: that Surratt went weekly, or almost weekly, to Richmond to meet with Benjamin and while in the Confederate White House never met with the Confederate President, who was only steps away and under the same roof, or that he did in fact meet with the Confederate President, perhaps occasionally, perhaps regularly. Davis would have every reason, would he not, to want to tap into the storehouse of Surratt's knowledge of one of the Confederacy's underground teams that just might, if conditions required it, play a major role in the Confederacy's last effort, in the waning days of the war, before final surrender precluded all options, to snatch independence from an apparently hopeless cause. But truly, meetings of Surratt and Davis are of little more than academic interest, because Surratt's meetings with Benjamin, of which there is no doubt, were quite enough to forge a powerful link between the highest levels of Confederate leadership and Booth and his team. There was little, if anything, that Benjamin did not share with Davis. Nevertheless, the evidence favours a conclusion that Surratt and Davis did meet, from time to time, rather than a conclusion that they did not.

What are the chances that Surratt met with Benjamin regularly, and sometimes with Davis, without the parties discussing Booth and his team and their comings, goings and doings? Zero. All later attempts by Surratt to convince his listeners and readers that the Confederate government was completely ignorant of Booth's conspiracy, first to 'kidnap' Lincoln and then to murder him and as many as fourteen, but no less than four, other federal office holders, are not only unconvincing, but utterly feeble, disingenuous and ridiculous. They join the other gratuitous exculpations of the Confederate government's complicity in the assassination of Lincoln, all of which have an odour about them. Here is Surratt's contribution, given in his 1870 Rockville lecture:

> It may be well to remark here that this scheme of abduction was concocted without the knowledge or the assistance of the Confederate government in any shape or form. Booth and I often consulted together as to whether it would not be well to acquaint the authorities in Richmond with our plan, as we were sadly in want of money, our expenses being very heavy. In fact, the question arose among us as to whether, after getting Mr Lincoln, if we succeeded in our plan, the Confederate authorities would not surrender us to the United States again, because of doing the thing without their knowledge or consent. But we never acquainted them with the plan, and they never had anything in the wide world to do with it. In fact, we were jealous of our undertaking and wanted no outside help. I have not made this statement to defend the officers of the Confederate government. They are perfectly able to defend themselves.[30]

This passage drips with falsehood. It is inconsistent with everything we know about Surratt, including his admissions to McMillan aboard the *Peruvian* and to Ste Marie in Italy. Note the telltale signs of falsehood: the fabricated introduction ('It may be well to remark here …'); the excess baggage ('in any shape or form' and 'never had anything in the wide world to do with it', both hyperbolic giveaways); and the unasked-for rationale ('I have not made this statement, etc.'). There are few things as suspicious as an anticipatory defence. Who asked for it? Let the reader decide how believable this statement is, considering that it came from one who had been serving the Confederate cause since he was 18 and had been an active agent of the Confederate Secret Service since May 1863, travelled to Richmond almost weekly to meet with Judah Benjamin and most likely Jefferson Davis too, knew and worked with the many men and women who comprised the mail line, knew and worked with operatives in Baltimore (e.g. David Preston Parr) and New York (e.g. Roderick Watson), and travelled often to Canada to deliver dispatches and money to, and coordinate policy with, Thompson, Clay, Holcombe, et al., and who, after the assassination, left the country for nineteen months, leaving his mother to the hangman. As for the reference to being 'sadly in want of money', it doesn't square with the evidence, which is that all the members of Booth's team had plenty of money during their active period. In fact, Arnold said in his memoirs that:

> The men by whom [Booth] had been surrounded and who had associated themselves with him were, to a great extent, ignorant men. They clung to him for the bounty they were receiving at [his] hand. No labor to perform to earn their living, Booth providing it, and they were willing to let it so continue ...[31]

As to the reference to their fear that if they succeeded, the Confederate authorities might send them back to the United States, would they really risk such an outcome, knowing that if they were sent back they would be looking at a hangman's noose?

We have already discussed the kidnapping ruse in Chapter Two, but part of it bears repeating here. The notion that Booth really planned to kidnap Lincoln is absurd. Did one of his team plan to throw him over his shoulder and then march past 1,700 theatregoers, armed guards and 30,000 Union troops defending the city? What did they plan to do with him even if they had managed the nearly impossible task of getting him safely out of the theatre, into a carriage and across the Navy Yard Bridge? Would Booth show up at the Confederate White House door with Lincoln in handcuffs, to be held pending the release of Confederate prisoners of war, who were already being released pursuant to Grant's January order? Is there anything that sounds realistic about that scenario? Could Booth be confident that he would receive a favourable response from Confederate leaders? *Would* he have received a favourable response from Confederate leaders? Or is it more likely that Confederate leaders, outraged that someone would presume to take upon himself an act of incalculable political and military consequences, would have ordered him to get out of their house, out of their city, out of their state, out of their country, or face a Confederate noose? Assuming that Confederate leaders accepted the fruits of Booth's labor, what would they have done with Lincoln in the face of Northern stonewalling? Pulled out his fingernails? Torn him limb from limb? Obviously not. Manifestly, kidnapping was a ruse, never seriously planned, not, in any case, by Booth and his team.

Surratt's relationship with Benjamin and Davis, then, constitutes half of a fourth smoking gun, because it means that the two highest Confederate leaders (and quite likely, therefore (but by no means necessarily, because the need for airtight secrecy was critical), other Confederate leaders, such as Vice President Alexander Stephens and Secretary of War James Seddon), knew all about Booth, his team and their conspiracy, but did absolutely nothing to stop him. They did nothing, because he was doing exactly what they wanted him to do and what he had been groomed to do from the moment of his recruitment to the Secret Service, namely gathering a team on the pretense of kidnapping Lincoln and then preparing the team, or as many of them as he could, for the more sinister business of multiple assassinations of Union leaders if and when he should be ordered to do so. The kidnapping pretense facilitated recruitment. If he had told his would-be recruits that his purpose was assassination or multiple assassinations, they would have run for cover. He couldn't even get his actor friends Samuel Knapp Chester and John Mathews to come aboard for kidnapping. The other half of this fourth smoking gun will be supplied by Surratt's relationship with Henri Beaumont de Ste. Marie.

One of the more enduring mysteries of the Civil War, one that has provoked endless speculation and debate, is Surratt's whereabouts on the day of the assassination, April 14. 1865. At his trial in Washington, before a civil court, in 1867, five witnesses testified that they saw him in Elmira, New York, on April 13, 14 and 15 April, but fourteen witnesses said they saw him in Washington on the 14th and one witness – Ste Marie – said Surratt told him he was in Washington on that date and that he left the city that night by train, or the following morning, Ste Marie wasn't sure. Ste Marie added that Surratt said he had a hard time doing so, succeeding largely because he was disguised as an Englishman, i.e. wearing English-style clothes.[32] So five witnesses had him in Elmira and fourteen in Washington. It was largely because of this conflict that the jury could not reach a verdict, voting 8-4 for conviction or acquittal, depending on whom one believes.

The prosecution prepared for a second trial, but it never happened; the case petered out after a series of legal manoeuvres dragged on into 1868, after which Surratt emerged, in November 1868, after eighteen months of incarceration, a free man.

Surratt did not testify, because the law in all but one state at that time provided that a defendant in a criminal trial was not a competent witness. From three sources (McMillan's testimony; Surratt's 1870 Rockville lecture; and an interview he gave to journalist Hanson Hiss that appeared in the *Washington Post* on 2 April 1898), however, we have some idea of Surratt's meanderings in March and April 1865. We know that he returned to Washington on 3 April, from Richmond, after delivering dispatches there to Benjamin from the Canadian Cabinet in late March, accompanied by courier Sarah Slater. We know, too, that he left for Montreal the following morning with dispatches from Benjamin for General Edwin G. Lee, who had by this time replaced Jacob Thompson, arriving there on 6 April after a stop in New York to see Booth, who, however, was not there, being in Boston for a performance.

From this point the story gets dicey, because Surratt gave three different versions of where he was and what he did from 6 to 18 April and where and when he heard that Lincoln had been assassinated and what he did when he heard it. In one version, he said he received a 'letter', 'dated New York', from Booth at the beginning of the week (i.e. 10 April, because 9 April was a Sunday), ordering him to return to Washington forthwith because their plans had changed. In response, he left immediately for Washington, but stopped in Elmira, pursuant to instructions from General Edwin G. Lee, to case out the Union prison there with a view towards freeing the Confederate prisoners. This has an odour about it, indeed a terrible one. How on earth did Lee expect to free the heavily guarded prisoners, most of whom, indeed almost all of whom, were emaciated and bedraggled and therefore unfit for fighting, and what on earth was he going to do with them, hundreds of miles inside enemy territory? Further, Surratt arrived in Elmira, he said, on the 12th, three days after General Robert E. Lee surrendered the Army of Northern Virginia to General Grant, and he must surely have known that. Further, Grant had resumed prisoner exchange in January and had set a goal of 3,000 prisoners per week. Further, Surratt had been to Elmira once before for the purpose of casing out the prison, so why was it necessary for him to do it again? Surratt's stated purpose for stopping in Elmira, therefore, assuming he really did, makes no sense at all and we must conclude that he had another purpose or that he really didn't stop there, perhaps even making use of a look-alike.

He may have been trying to establish an alibi, because, in fact, he did claim one at his trial: five witnesses from Elmira put him in that city on the 13th, 14th and 15th of the month. That did not equal the fourteen witnesses who put him in Washington, but it was enough to create a lot of doubt in the minds of the jurors and certainly had much to do with the fact that they failed to convict him. As previously said, it was not the first time he had been in Elmira. In his Hanson Hiss interview, he said that he had, some time earlier, been ordered to go there and case out the prison, that he was there for several weeks, passed out a lot of 'Uncle Sam's gold' and made a host of friends, which, he said, was a good thing, because it saved his life at the trial.

Or, less likely for this hard-as-nails and completely dedicated agent of the Secret Service, he simply may have decided that things were getting too hot for him, and, by extension, his mother, that the Confederacy was a lost cause and that he wanted out, so he made himself comfortable in Elmira. While there, he said, he telegraphed Booth in New York, but was advised that he had already left for Washington. Why did he telegraph Booth? Was it perhaps to tell him that Edwin Lee had ordered him to stay in Elmira to check out the prison and that Booth would have to get by without him in Washington? In any case, he stayed in Elmira, he said, patronising haberdashers and tailors while the Confederacy crumbled.

If he did make it to Washington, as fourteen witnesses alleged, what did he do there to help Booth? We do not have a record of his having done anything. Was he the fellow who was on Grant's train to Burlington, New Jersey? Possibly, but most unlikely, because that fellow thanked God that he had not been successful (in an anonymous letter to Grant which he received a day or two after the assassination), which is totally out of character for Surratt, who would have clicked his heels if he had been successful in assassinating Grant. In any case, on the way back to Montreal a few days after the assassination, he heard of the assassination, he said, while having breakfast in St Albans, Vermont. He returned to Montreal, because he saw a newspaper that gave his name as one of the assassins.[33]

In another version, General Edwin Lee sent him to Elmira to case out the prison about a week after his arrival in Montreal. He says nothing about the 'letter' from Booth ordering him to Washington. While in Elmira, on the 15th, he heard of the assassination. In response, he determined to go to Baltimore 'to find out the particulars of the tragedy', but found that there was no train going south that evening, so he went to Canandaigua, about 60 miles north-west of Elmira, i.e. farther away from Baltimore and giving no particular reason why he would go there, but intending to go from there to Baltimore via Elmira and New York. On Monday, the 17th, still in Canandaigua, he saw his name in a newspaper that identified him as Seward's assassin, so he abandoned his Baltimore plan and headed back to Montreal by way of Albany.[34]

In his third version, he said that after he had rejected Booth's kidnapping proposal, he went to Richmond, where he was ordered by General Wilder to go to Elmira to do his prison thing. He stayed there, he said, for several weeks, after which, his assignment completed, he decided to return to Richmond. On his way to Albany from Elmira, he heard of the assassination. The next day, travelling from Albany to New York, he picked up a newspaper that identified him as an assassin, with a $25,000 reward on his head, so he gave up on Richmond and went to Montreal instead.[35]

Surratt's accounts are so conflicting that we simply do not know what the truth is and almost certainly never will. One is driven to the conclusion that he intentionally sought to sow confusion, for his contemporaries and for posterity. It was said that in old age he began to write his memoirs, but then thought better of it and burned everything he had written. It's just as well; none of it would have been believable anyway, coming from the pen of one who had made lying and deception an art form.

The only certainty is that he remained in Canada for about five months, protected at all times by Catholic clergy, and then sailed from Quebec City to Liverpool, aboard the *Peruvian*, embarking on 16 September

1865. From Liverpool, he made his way to the Continent and ultimately to Italy, finding refuge, cover and anonymity, he thought, with the Papal Zouaves, a unit of the Pope's army, which he joined in January 1866. It was here, however, much to his surprise and chagrin, that he met, once again, Henri Beaumont de Ste Marie, his old acquaintance from Little Texas (also known as Ellengowan, which is sometimes spelled Ellen Gowan), Maryland, near Baltimore. He had also joined the Zouaves, on 9 April of the same year.

Henri Beaumont de Ste Marie, aka Henri Benjamin de Ste Marie, was a strange duck. He was a Canadian with swarthy skin, dark hair and brown eyes. He was said to be handsome, to have polished manners and to be a good conversationalist. He projected intelligence and spoke three languages fluently – English, French and Italian. He also played the guitar and sang the tenor voice. That's all on the plus side. On the negative side, he said and did things that were characteristic of a lightweight, if not a jerk. Canadian lawyers who knew him well said he lied easily and for that reason was not to be taken too seriously.[36]

He was born on 13 May 1835 (per Papal records), in Canada, near Montreal. He was, of course, educated in the Catholic institutions of that very Catholic city. In 1863, not doing anything particularly worthwhile or interesting, he decided to join the Confederate army. He attempted to reach the Confederacy by running the blockade with a ship out of New York, but his ship was captured and he wound up in Fort McHenry as a prisoner of war. He was released, as a British subject, by intervention of an English diplomat.

He later found employment as a teacher in a Catholic parochial school in Little Texas and it was here, on 3 April 1863, that he met and befriended Louis Weichmann and John Surratt, who were in the area visiting their Alma Mater, St Charles College.[37] A local priest arranged the meeting. Ste Marie soon abandoned his position at the Catholic school in Little Texas, saying conditions had become intolerable there, and came to Weichmann, whom he barely knew. Weichmann secured a position for him at St Matthew's Institute in Washington, but within a month, Ste Marie abandoned this position too, for unstated reasons. He then joined the Union army, but quickly deserted, his heart, apparently, being with the Confederate cause. He was obviously a restless and unstable fellow, not really knowing what he wanted. The Confederates, however, were not impressed with him. They thought he was a spy and so threw him into Castle Thunder, the prison in Richmond reserved for political prisoners, spies and traitors. Fortunately for him, he wasn't there long. He learned of and exposed to the authorities a gang of forgers, and for that contribution to the Confederate cause, he was released. Apparently fed up with America's Civil War and its prisons, he returned to Montreal by way of Nassau and England. He was in Montreal when he heard of Lincoln's assassination. No one could ever accuse Ste Marie of not being able to negotiate the world's highways and somehow acquiring the means to do so.

There is little doubt, if any, that Ste Marie pursued Surratt for the reward money offered for his arrest, after he had seen a copy of the many posters that were distributed about the country, and even in Canada, immediately after the assassination. The posters offered $25,000 for Surratt's arrest, an extraordinary sum in those days (about $400,000 in 2020 dollars). In his 1872 petition to the United States Court of Claims for reward money, Ste Marie acknowledged that upon his seeing the reward offer, he put the rest of his life on hold and commenced the pursuit of Surratt. He had his dates wrong, however, averring that he left for Europe on 22 June 1865, upon learning that Surratt had left for Europe on 20 June. He was way off. Surratt actually left for Europe on 16 September that year. Perhaps the fact that the petition was prepared seven years after the facts, time enough for his memory to weaken, had something to do with the dating error. Regardless, it remains nearly certain that Ste Marie was motivated by money, because only that motive explains why he went to the American legation in Rome, as soon as he had made contact with Surratt, to advise them as to where he, Surratt, was.

In any case, he tracked Surratt through England and France and into Italy, where he learned, in March 1866, that Surratt was a Papal Zouave. i.e. a soldier in the Pope's army. Ste Marie promptly joined the Zouaves himself, not knowing that on 24 November 1865, President Johnson had revoked the $25,000 reward offer. Ste Marie made contact with Surratt rather quickly. He was now using the alias John Watson (or Giovanni

Watson). Ste Marie identified Surratt by his proper name and reminded him of their meeting in Little Texas about three years earlier. Surratt made no attempt to conceal his true identity, but begged Ste Marie to keep it secret. He didn't. He went, instead, almost immediately, to General Rufus King, the American Minister to the Papal States, then living in Rome. On 23 April, King wrote to Seward, giving him the information that had come to him from Ste Marie. Here is the letter, with my italics for emphasis:

> Sir:
> On Saturday last, 21st instant, a private in the Papal Zouaves, giving his name as H.B. St. Marie, and claiming to be Canadian by birth, called upon me for the purpose, as he said, of communicating the information that John H. Surratt, who was charged with complicity in the murder of President Lincoln, but made his escape at the time from the United States, had recently enlisted in the Papal Zouaves, under the name of John Watson, and was now stationed with his company, the 3rd, at (Sezze). My informant said that he had known Surratt in America; that he recognized him as soon as he saw him at (Sezze); that he called him by his proper name, and that Surratt, taking him aside, admitted that he was right in the guess. *He added that Surratt acknowledged his participation in the plot against Mr Lincoln's life, and declared that Jefferson Davis had incited or was privy to it.* St. Marie further said that Surratt seemed to be well provided with money and appealed to him as a comrade not to betray his secret; and he expressed an earnest desire that if any steps were taken towards reclaiming Surratt as a criminal, he, St. Marie, should not be known in the matter. He spoke so positively in answer to my questions as to his acquaintance with Surratt, and the certainty that he was the man, and there seemed such entire absence of motive for any false statement on the subject, that I could not very well doubt the truth of what he told me. I deemed

> it my duty, therefore, to report the circumstance to the Department and ask for instructions.
>
> I have the honor to be, with great respect, your obedient servant,
>
> Rufus King

Note that King said that Ste Marie had told him that Davis had 'incited' the assassination or was 'privy' to it, not that he ordered it. Whether or not inciting or being privy to an act means to be complicit in the act cannot be said with certainty. More information is needed. In any case, this sentence from King is incriminating, but it does not constitute a smoking gun, not because it is hearsay evidence, but because it is ambiguous and therefore too weak.

Seward referred the letter to Stanton, who referred it to Judge Advocate General Joseph Holt, one of the prosecutors in the trial of the conspirators. Holt responded to King, asking that he obtain a full statement of Surratt's confession. Over the next couple of months, Seward and King exchanged numerous letters relative to the matter, during which period Surratt led a perfectly normal life in the Pope's army, blithely performing his duties and enjoying his prerogatives, unaware of what Ste Marie, King and Seward were doing behind the scenes. Then, on 10 July 1866, after numerous conversations with Surratt, Ste Marie prepared and executed this affidavit, with my italics for emphasis:

> I, Henri de Ste. Marie, a native of Canada, British America, age thirty three, do swear and declare under oath, that about six months previous to the assassination of President Abraham Lincoln I was living in Maryland, at a small village called Ellen Gowan or Little Texas about twenty five or thirty miles from Baltimore, where I was engaged as teacher, for a period of about five months. I there and then got acquainted with Lewis J. Wiechman [*sic*] and John H. Surratt, who came to that locality to pay a visit to the parish priest.
>
> At that first interview a great deal was said about the war and slavery – the sentiments expressed by these two

individuals being more than strongly secessionists. In the course of the conversation I remember Surratt to have said that President Lincoln would certainly pay for all the men that were slain during the war. About a month after I removed to Washington at the instigation of Wiechman and got a situation as Tutor in St. Mathew's Institute, where he was himself engaged. Surratt visited us weekly, and once he offered me to send me South, but I declined. I did not remain more than one month at Washington, not being able to agree with Wiechman and enlisted in the army of the North as stated in my first statement in writing to General King.

I have met Surratt here in Italy at a small town called Velletri, he is now known under the name of John Watson, I recognized him before he made himself known to me, and told him privately: 'You are John Surratt, the person I have known in Maryland.' He acknowledged he was and begged of me to keep the thing secret. After some conversation, we spoke of the unfortunate affair of the assassination of President Lincoln, and these were his words '*Damn the Yankees, they have killed my mother, but I have done them as much harm as I could, we have killed Lincoln, the niggers' friend.' He then said speaking of his mother: 'Had it not been for me and that coward Wiechman my mother would be living yet. It was fear made him speak, had he kept his tongue there was no danger for him, but if I ever return to America or meet him elsewhere, I shall kill him.'* He then said he was in the secret service of the South, and Wiechman who was in some department there used to steal copies of the dispatches and forward them to him and thence to Richmond. *Speaking of the murder he said they had acted under the orders of men who are not yet known, some of whom are still in New York and others in London*, I am aware that money is sent him yet from London. When I left Canada he said, I had but little money, but I had a letter for a party in London, I was in disguise, with dyed hair and false beard, that party sent me to a Hotel where he told me to remain till I would hear from him, after a few weeks he came and proposed me to go to Spain, but I declined and asked to go to Paris, he gave me seventy pounds with a letter of introduction to a party there, who sent him here to Rome, where he joined the Zouaves, he says he can get money in Rome at any time.

I believe he is protected by the Clergy and that the murder is the result of a deep laid plot not only against the life of President Lincoln, but against the existence of the republic, as we are aware that priesthood and royalty are and always have been opposed to liberty. *That such men as Surratt, Booth, Wiechman and others, should of their own accord plan and execute the infernal plot which resulted in the death of President Lincoln is impossible. There are others behind the curtain who have pulled the strings to make these scoundrels act.*

I have also asked him if he knew Jefferson Davis he said no, but that he had acted under the instructions of persons under his immediate orders, being asked if Jefferson Davis had anything to do with the assassination he said 'I am not going to tell you.' My impression is that he brought the order from Richmond, as he was in the habit of going there weekly, he must have bribed the others to do it, for when the event took place he told me he was in New York, prepared to fly as soon as the deed would be done. He says that he does not regret what has taken place, and that he will visit New York in a year or two, as there is a heavy shipping firm there, who had much to do with the South, and he is surprised that they have not been suspected.

This is the exact truth of what I know about Surratt, more I could not learn being afraid to awaken his suspicions.

And furthermore I do not say.
Henri B. de Ste. Marie

Sworn and subscribed before me at the American Legation in Rome this tenth (10th) day of July A.D. 1866.

Rufus King
Minister Resident[38]

The affidavit obviously contains a lot of valuable information relative to a determination of ultimate responsibility for the assassination of America's sixteenth president, regarded by many as the greatest in American history. In saying 'we have killed Lincoln, the niggers' friend', whom does Surratt mean by 'we'? It is possible, of course, that he is referring to the Confederate Secret Service, of which he was an agent, or even the Confederate States of America, in general, but these are very remote possibilities. Far more likely is it, inasmuch as the admission immediately follows 'I have done them as much harm as I could', that 'we' refers to Surratt himself and Booth, possibly including the action team. As such, it constitutes no smoking gun, because evidence of Surratt's complicity in the murder and attempted murders is already clear and convincing, indeed all but conclusive.

We get closer to a smoking gun with Surratt's statements that '[We] had acted under the orders of men who are not yet known, some of whom are still in New York and others in London' and that '[I] had acted under the instructions of persons under [Davis's] immediate orders.' Orders to Surratt and Booth to murder Lincoln and decapitate Union leadership could not possibly have originated with the 'men' in New York and London and the 'persons under [Davis's] immediate orders', but must have been given to these 'men' and 'persons' by a higher authority. That higher authority, ultimately, could not have been anyone but Davis and/or Benjamin, because they were the *highest* authority, and, in fact, the second statement explicitly names Davis as the higher authority. No one lower in the Confederate hierarchy would have dared to issue such orders without higher authority – orders whose execution would have immense consequences for the Confederacy, greater, in fact, than those resulting from any previous order.

But we arrive squarely at the smoking gun with Surratt's answer to Ste Marie's question as to whether or not Davis had anything to do with the assassination, namely: 'I am not going to tell you.' Ste Marie's question obviously came at Surratt too fast for him to realise that his answer was as good as an affirmative one, because it meant that Surratt knew whether or not Confederate leaders were involved, because otherwise he would have said, simply, 'I don't know', and that Confederate leaders *were* involved, because otherwise he would have said something like 'No, Davis had nothing to do with it' or 'No, Davis is completely innocent' or 'No, the Confederate government had nothing to do with it', or words of similar import. 'I am not going to tell you', therefore, fits only with the Confederate leaders' complicity and Surratt's knowledge of it. Such a conclusion fits perfectly with what we already know, namely that Surratt, who was Booth's second in command in the conspiracy and intimately acquainted with all its details, was Benjamin's 'most trusted courier' and met regularly with Benjamin, and most likely with Davis himself, in Richmond. These two facts, then, taken together, i.e. Surratt's regular meetings with Benjamin and probably with Davis, in Richmond, and Surratt's answer 'I am not going to tell you' in response to Ste Marie's asking if Davis was involved in the assassination, constitute the fourth smoking gun.

We must address the issue of credibility. How believable is the information Ste Marie gave to King? How believable is his affidavit? We have already heard that Canadian lawyers who knew him said he lied easily and was therefore not to be taken too seriously. And we have also seen that he demonstrated a degree of instability when he tried to join the Confederate army by running the blockade, only to wind up in a Union prison; by abruptly abandoning his teaching position in Little Texas and again at St Matthew's Institute; and by joining the Union army and then deserting it, only to wind up in a Confederate prison. Still, none of this precludes his telling the truth if he had no motivation not to. And the fact is that he had none, because it was not necessary for him to incriminate Davis or any other Confederate leader in order to collect the reward money he believed was due to him. The poster provided that $25,000 would be paid for Surratt's apprehension, but it also provided that 'Liberal rewards will be paid for any information that shall conduce to the arrest' of Surratt. The great likelihood is that King advised Ste Marie that the offer of $25,000 had been revoked by President Johnson, but whether or not that destroyed his claim for the same was a question of contract law, inasmuch as Ste Marie had accepted the offer and changed his position in reliance upon it. Ste Marie's claim and the contract issue would eventually go all the way to the Supreme Court of the United States, but this is not relevant to the question before us, which is Ste Marie's credibility as to what he told King and as to what he said in his affidavit to Seward. Inasmuch as the requirements of at least part of the offer, as given in the poster, would have been met by simply advising King of Surratt's whereabouts, and nothing more, which Ste Marie did, a strong presumption of veracity attaches to any additional information he gave King and Seward. This presumption is strengthened by the fact that Ste Marie gave his information, not casually to acquaintances in circumstances that would favour falsehood or exaggeration, but to prominent government officials and under oath. It is also strengthened by the fact that Surratt was a very garrulous fellow, careless with facts he would have been better advised to conceal. In connection with his conversations with McMillan aboard the *Peruvian*, McMillan said, in Surratt's trial:

> I do not remember asking him during the whole passage a half dozen questions, and the reason I did not question him is, that he seemed to be so free in expressing everything that he had done, that I thought he would tell me enough without my questioning him. … He was quite free; seemed to be overflowing with the subject.[39]

Inasmuch as Ste Marie had no motivation to lie, therefore, or even to embellish, is it not rational and reasonable to conclude that in his message to King and in his affidavit, which he prepared pursuant to Joseph Holt's request for 'a full statement of John H. Surratt's confession to H.B. Ste. Marie, verified by oath', he simply recited what had been said to him by Surratt? Do Surratt's words and Ste Marie's relating of the same have the ring of truth? Shall we be surprised that the garrulous Surratt, who had opened up so freely to McMillan aboard the *Peruvian*, and now being so far from American jurisdiction, would acknowledge his participation in the plot against Lincoln's life and declare that Davis had incited it and was privy to it? Surratt had already gone on record with Ste Marie, at their meeting in Little Texas, as to what he thought Lincoln's fate would be, saying to him, then, that President Lincoln would certainly pay for all the men who were slain during the war. His acknowledgement of participation in the plot, therefore, may fairly be interpreted as a fulfillment of that prediction. Is not the fact that Ste Marie used guarded words like 'incited' and 'privy' probative of their truth? If he were inclined to fabricate, he most likely would have said something like 'Davis ordered the assassination', but it would have been highly unlikely for Surratt to say such a thing, so he used guarded words instead, just as he cagily answered Ste Marie's question about Davis's participation in the plot ('I am not going to tell you'). That Ste Marie was almost certainly telling King the truth was confirmed by King himself, who, in his letter to Seward of 23 April 1866, said, 'He spoke so positively in answer to my questions as to his acquaintance with Surratt, and the certainty that he was the man, and there seemed such entire absence of motive for any false statement on the subject, that I could not very well doubt the truth of what he told me.'

Similarly, shall we be surprised that in the affidavit the loquacious Surratt is reported to have said, 'Damn the Yankees, they have killed my mother, but I have done them as much harm as I could, we have killed Lincoln, the niggers' friend,' and, further, that '[We] had acted under the orders of men who are not yet known, some of whom are still in New York and others in London', and, further, that '[I] had acted under the instructions of persons under his [Davis's] immediate orders', and, further, that in response to Ste Marie asking if Davis had anything to do with the assassination, he said, 'I am not going to tell you'. Are these statements not exactly what we should expect from Surratt? The first is pure Surratt, blaming federal law enforcement for killing his mother rather than himself for abandoning her, and, further, expressing his ideology with reference to 'the niggers' friend'. In the second, what would Ste Marie know of men in New York and London if he didn't get it from Surratt? In the third, what would he know of persons under Davis's immediate orders if he didn't get it from Surratt? And in the fourth, is it not sensible that Surratt would not wish to nail the issue down for Ste Marie, who simply wasn't close enough to him to share details of what he knew about the plot. After all, they had had only one previous meeting, in Little Texas three years earlier. He certainly would not say 'Yes' in answer to the question. He could have said 'No', but that would have been too categorical, effectively giving Ste Marie a conclusive answer, which he did not wish to do, and placing himself right in the heart of the conspiracy, an impression he would not wish to create. It would also have invited further questions, which he wished to avoid. So he gave what he thought was a safe answer, not realising that it was as good as an affirmative one.

Is there another source or sources that would tend to confirm the veracity of the information Ste Marie gave to King and the statements he made in his affidavit to Seward that pertain to Surratt's and Davis's complicity in the assassination? There is, and it is nothing less than the works of Surratt himself. Surratt said to a *New York Times* correspondent who interviewed him on 2 April 1867, which interview was published on 8 April, that he manifested:

> no vindictiveness toward the witness for having discovered him to the authorities, but considers him a 'treacherous' fellow, and thinks he was mistaken in his character. [He] says that he had information of Ste. Marie's 'treachery' before it was fully accomplished, and was kept advised from time to time of the steps taken to secure his arrest. Had the actual arrest been delayed one day longer, as [he] had reason to expect it would be, he would have been beyond the reach of his pursuers, his arrangements for desertion and flight being nearly perfected at the time of his arrest.

Further, in his interview with Hanson Hiss, the newspaper reporter, which was published in the *Washington Post* on 3 April 1898, Surratt had this to say about Ste. Marie, in response to Hiss's question as to how Pope Pius IX learned who he was and was thus able to effect Surratt's arrest:

> Through the contemptible treachery of a friend – so called – a Canadian. I had shared my bread and butter, my blanket, and even my shirts, with the man, and had anyone told me he was going to prove as false as he did, I would have scouted the bare suggestion. I have long since learned that no man in this world can be trusted. This man went to

> Cardinal Antonelli and told him my story. Antonelli went with the information to the Pope, who immediately ordered my arrest and strict confinement.[40]

Two points are worth making in connection with both of these interviews.

1. Note that Surratt did not claim that Ste Marie had lied about or fabricated anything, but only that he had betrayed him, a friend who had literally given Ste Marie the shirt off his back. Would Surratt have used the word 'betray' if Ste Marie had done something more than repeat what Surratt had said, i.e. if he had corrupted what he had said? I think not. If Ste Marie had lied about or fabricated something, would not Surratt have said so, calling him a liar, and worse, in the same way he had spoken of Weichmann in his Rockville lecture and in his Hanson Hiss interview. In the former, he said that 'I do pronounce him [Weichmann] a base-born perjurer' and in the latter, he said, 'That man's testimony from beginning to end was outrageously false. He lied, lied, lied from the time he took the witness stand until the time he left it,' and, further, 'Weichmann made up his story out of whole cloth.' Surratt said none of this, or anything like it, with respect to Ste Marie, only that he had betrayed him. Is this not greatly probative of the truth of the information Ste Marie had given to the *New York Times* correspondent and to King and Seward?
2. Note that Antonelli did not tarry; he went directly to the Pope with the information that had come to him from Ste Marie through Rufus King. And note, too, that the Pope himself acted promptly and decisively. Obviously, the Cardinal and the Pope deemed the information to be very profound. Just as importantly, and given the totality of the circumstances attendant to the origin and receipt of the information, they deemed it to be true, true enough, in any case, to justify Surratt's immediate arrest and incarceration. Significantly, too, they would follow through with an order for extradition, despite the fact that no treaty providing for the same existed between the Vatican and the United States. They would make an exception in Surratt's case because of the gravity of the charges.

The rest of the Surratt, Benjamin and Ste Marie story is largely anticlimactic, but let us take each of them to their ends so that nothing that needs to be said remains unsaid.

Surratt was arrested, finally, on orders from Cardinal Antonelli, on 7 November 1866. After his arrest, it was said that he escaped his captors by leaping into a 100-foot ravine, miraculously landing on a 4-foot rock outcropping 35 feet below the precipice. The outcropping may or may not have been covered with barracks filth, depending on whom one believes, which, it was said, broke his fall. Nonsense, of course. A drop of 35 feet to a rock outcropping would kill anyone even if the outcropping were covered with beach balls. One of Surratt's superiors, a Colonel Allet, said, in his report, that the distance from the top of the ravine to the ledge was only 23 feet. And the *New York Times* correspondent who interviewed Surratt on 2 April 1867 wrote that Surratt had read:

> with great apparent interest, the published accounts of his capture and escape, and the official correspondence bearing on those points, and takes great pleasure in criticizing them. The wonderful leap off the precipice in Italy, of which much has been said and written, is a source of great amusement to him. The height which he jumped he describes as about … 12 feet.

So the leap has gone from 35 to 23 to 12 feet. Despite this and other inconsistencies, Surratt used the magnificent leap story as late as 1898 in his Hanson Hiss interview. It was infinitely more heroic than the truth, which, however, finally emerged from one Henry Lipman, a bright fellow from the Netherlands who spoke six languages fluently and who said he knew both Surratt and Ste Marie. He told the *New York Tribune*, in 1881, and later other newspapers, that twelve Zouaves, all friends of Surratt, were ordered to guard him in a dungeon in which he had been placed after his arrest. With their help, Surratt crawled out of the dungeon and into a sewer that emptied into a body of water. The twelve sought to immunise themselves from a charge of complicity by firing at the escapee, all of their shots missing, of course. Lipman added that he got a terrific laugh from the magnificent leap story.[41]

Surratt first went to Naples, then to Malta and finally to Alexandria, where he was again arrested, this time by the American Consul General there, on 27 November. He was placed in an Egyptian jail for three weeks and was then taken aboard the USS *Swatara* for the ride home. He was kept in irons for the entire voyage. *Swatara* was long in crossing – fifty-two days, arriving at Hampton Roads on 16 February 1867.

Even in an American prison, influence was being pushed, and palms were probably being greased, by someone, somewhere, on his behalf, because the *New York Times* correspondent, in his 8 April 1867 article, described Surratt's accommodations as:

> a corridor, fully thirty feet in length and eight feet in breadth, with three large cells, … placed entirely at his disposal – he is provided with a plentiful assortment of books. … Comforts and even luxuries for the toilet are also abundant. His *cuisine* seems to be carefully looked after by friends and no restriction is placed upon the amount or variety that is sent him … [he] has the choicest of domestic cooking, selected with the sole view of pleasing his palate.

His trial, in a civil court, began on 10 June 1867. He was represented by three of the finest criminal lawyers in the country. Surratt said in his Hanson Hiss interview that two friends from Baltimore paid his legal fees, sending him checks for $1,000 and $5,000 at a time, but no one really knows where the money to pay the lawyers ultimately came from.[42] The trial lasted fifty-five days, with three days of deliberations. The jury, which comprised seven men born in the South and five born in the North, deadlocked hopelessly and was thus released by Judge George Fisher. Much legal wrangling followed, but the case was finally dismissed on 6 November 1868, because a statute of limitations had run. Surratt was free.

He had been living as a fugitive and as a defendant for three and a half years. He was a broken man. He spent the next six months recuperating and vacationing in South America. Again, no one knows where the money to pay for this came from. He returned to a more or less normal life in the country he had betrayed. He had seen and done enough for two lifetimes and his many escapes were almost legendary. But he did not escape the judgment of his co-conspirators, all of whom condemned him for saving his own skin, even at the expense of abandoning his mother to a hangman. Outliving almost everyone else in the drama that began in 1862, he died on 21 April 1916, at the age of 72. He was given a High Requiem Mass by St Pius Church in Baltimore, an honour usually reserved for those who have given exceptional devotion or distinguished service to the Church. No evidence worthy of the name has ever been offered to tie the Roman Catholic Church to the assassination and attempted assassinations that occurred in Washington on 14 April 1865. And yet, Surratt's concealment in Canada by Catholic clergy and the help still other clergy gave him in connection with his voyage to Europe and his travels to and residences in England, France and Italy, with his concealment among the Papal Zouaves, with his escape and with his trial, capped by the Solemn High Requiem Mass given to him upon his death, suggest that there is more to the story than we know and that the great likelihood is that we will never know it.

As for Judah Benjamin, written evidence identifying him as the mastermind of the Confederate year of terror against the North is non-existent, for the very good reason that all orders and instructions given to the leading Confederate agents were given verbally, as said, and because virtually all of Benjamin's records and correspondence were consigned to the flames. This was done in two stages: the greater part on 2 April 1865, when the occupation of Richmond by federal forces was imminent and the rest when Benjamin realised there was no hope left for the Confederacy and therefore parted from Davis and other members of the rump Confederate government who were fleeing southwards in the days following the occupation. Benjamin said to a would-be biographer, shortly before his death, that:

> I have no material available for the purpose. I have never kept a diary, or retained a copy of a letter written by me. No letters addressed to me by others will be found among my papers when I die. … I do not want to leave behind me letters and documents to be used in … a work about myself.[43]

It is perfectly obvious that Benjamin was bound and determined to leave nothing behind that could in any way implicate him or other Confederates, especially his superior, Davis, in the Confederate year of terror and assassination plots against the Union (spring 1864 to spring 1865).

In the company of only one person (Colonel Henry Leovy of New Orleans), he attempted to escape a Union hangman, because he knew he had no chance at all against Union retributive justice, especially a prosecution led by the rapacious and vindictive Secretary of War Edwin M. Stanton and especially because he was Jewish. The attempt was an incredible gamble, but he was a gambler, having spent a lot of time, surprisingly for a man of such responsibilities, in Richmond's gambling dens playing poker and faro. It was his purpose to, in his own words, 'get to the farthest place from the United States if it takes me to the middle of China'. Travelling frequently with false documents and in various disguises, he struck first for the Caribbean and then for England. Overcoming extraordinary difficulties and challenges, including swarms of insects, federal patrols, heat, hunger, thirst, shipwrecks, fires at sea and other near misses with death, he made it to England, made contact with other Confederate expatriates and then carved out a successful career as a Queen's Counsel. He even found time to write a treatise on the law of sale of personal property, known as *Benjamin on Sales* or *Benjamin's Sale of Goods*, which is a classic in both Britain and America and is still in use today. For the rest of his life, he never spoke of the American Civil War nor of his role in it, nor did he ever return to the United States, as so many other Confederate leaders who had fled the country did. One reason, surely, was that he really had nothing to return to: his wife and daughter were in France, and Bellechasse, his magnificent sugar plantation near New Orleans, with its 140 slaves, was gone.[44] But another reason, surely, was the knowledge that he had masterminded terror and assassination plots and would not escape the hangman if he returned and was captured.

He died a natural death on 6 May 1884, at the age of 73. He is buried in Paris at the well-known Père Lachaise Cemetery, identified only as 'Philippe Benjamin'.

Summary and Conclusions

Summary

The Black Flag rules. I have already said it, but it bears repeating. All wars – especially civil wars, because one can forgive an enemy, but not a heretic, a traitor or a renegade – sooner or later degenerate into Black Flag warfare. More often sooner than later; all it takes is one excess, in or out of combat, to initiate a cycle of killings and atrocities. And let there be no mistake: There is absolutely no difference, none at all, in the records of the ancient, medieval and modern worlds. We are just as vicious, brutal, sadistic and barbarous now as we have ever been.

The Black Flag in our savage war meant that captives would, in many cases, be killed in cold blood, beheaded, buried alive, impaled to the ground with stakes through their throats or other parts of their bodies, have their genitals severed and placed where nature did not intend them to be, and/or have their eyes gouged or plucked out. But it also meant:

1. Prisoner of war camps in which the prisoners died like flies from abuse and neglect;
2. Massacres (killing of unarmed prisoners and civilians);
3. The depredations of psychopathic killers;
4. The burning of cities;
5. The pillage and plundering of non-combat areas;
6. Insurrections; and
7. Biological and chemical warfare.

Targeted killings, i.e. assassinations, were very much a part of this scene, and always have been and always will be a part of armed conflict, even if we are all tan, speak Esperanto and convert to one religion, and even if the exponential growth of our population ceases, and even if the depletion of the world's resources slows, none of which will happen in the time left to our species, which cannot be long. Polarisation and conflict are what we do. We are a pugnacious animal. We had to be to survive our long evolutionary trek.

The list of assassinations is endless, and all of them in some degree altered the course of history. In our own time, these have been the most significant: Franz Ferdinand (whose murder ignited the First World War), Mahatma Gandhi, John F. Kennedy, Malcolm X, Martin Luther King, Robert F. Kennedy, Indira Gandhi, Yitzhak Rabin and Benazir Bhutto.

There were at least a dozen attempts on Lincoln's life during his time in office as president, both before and after the Wistar and Dahlgren-Kilpatrick raids. Even the food that was gifted to him upon his nomination and election was found to be poisoned. In addition to the attempts made during his terms, attempts were made when he travelled from Springfield to Washington for his first Inauguration, including Cipriano Ferrandini's well-planned Baltimore Plot, which was foiled only by great ingenuity. Lincoln received an estimated 10,000 death threats during the time he was in office according to Horace Greely, publisher of the *New York Tribune*. Lincoln kept an envelope in his desk, labelled 'Assassinations', which contained about eighty of the threats that he or his Secretaries (Hay, Nicolay and Stoddard) deemed serious enough to keep a record of. Contrary to the conventional wisdom, he went to great lengths to secure better protection for himself when he went, reluctantly (so as not to disappoint the people), to Ford's Theatre to see *Our American Cousin* on the night of 14 April 1865, an outing that was probably arranged by treacherous office holders in the government. Assassination hung over his head like a dark cloud and he knew it. And so did his best friend and self-appointed bodyguard Ward Hill Lamon, who said so more pointedly. Most regrettably, Lincoln sent Lamon to Richmond on business on the 12th. Before he left, Lamon asked his best friend to promise him that he would avoid public places, *especially the theatre*, in his absence. Lincoln said he would do the best he could 'towards it'.

As for Davis, there was an attempt by a Belgian (First Lieutenant Victor Vifquain) and two Frenchmen (Captain Alfred Cipriani and Lieutenant Armond Duclos) (who, appropriately, used pseudonyms from *The Three Musketeers*) to capture him in April 1862. It failed.[1] There do not appear to be any other attempts to capture him, nor is there evidence of an attempt to assassinate him until the raids on Richmond. But Wistar's and Dahlgren's orders were quite enough for him, for the Confederate political and military establishment, and for the Southern press and people, to change the character of the war after early March 1864, by raising the Black Flag to a level that had not previously been seen in the war, bad as it already was.

It can be seen, therefore, in light of the foregoing, that the attempts on the lives of Lincoln, Johnson, Seward, Stanton and Grant, at least, and perhaps as many as ten other Union leaders, were of a piece with that which had preceded them.

If we are going to correct the historical record, or at least to shed greater light on it, we must deal in hard facts, not fancy, fantasy, surmises, suppositions or theories. So let us do that. Here are the hard facts, summarised from the foregoing Introduction and Chapters One to Four.

Holcombe's, Thompson's, Clays' and Blackburn's verbal orders from Davis, and therefore their purpose and objective, were to kill Lincoln. That conclusion is beyond a reasonable doubt. There is not a word in the record to indicate that kidnapping ever entered their minds. The evidence for this is right in the transcripts of the trial of the conspirators and in the letter to Davis from Kensey Johns Stewart. The transcript not only records Hyams's testimony, which is damning in the extreme, but also the fact that in all the recorded and reported conversations between Confederate operatives in Canada, there is one reference to 'abduction' and dozens of references to assassination. There is a very good reason for this: 'abduction' would have been incredibly difficult and would have done the Confederacy no good at all, even if the abductors had pulled off the all-but-impossible task of doing it, according to Davis himself and according to top Secret Service agent Thomas Nelson Conrad, who said that 'a child could conclude … that [kidnapping] would have accomplished no tangible good for the Confederacy'. Let us put aside the fact that they also tried to spread pestilence in the North, though it does indicate the lengths to which Confederate leaders were willing to go to even the score with the North and to reverse the direction of the war. If they were willing to kill thousands of innocents – maybe more – to bring the war home to the North, just as Union armies and the orders of the highest levels of the federal government had brought it home to the South, would they hesitate to kill the author of all their losses and of all the suffering and grief of the Southern people? Let us, rather, speak only of their designs on Lincoln. Infecting him with yellow fever from 'infected' shirts was their weapon of choice to assassinate him and they neither used nor needed John Wilkes Booth for the purpose.

Lewis Powell was ordered, or at least strongly urged, by Booth, on three occasions during the period January to March 1865 to kill Lincoln, not to kidnap him. Remember that this was the period during which Booth, as he later wrote in his diary, had no purpose other than to kidnap Lincoln, which we now know was a ruse to facilitate recruitment to his team and to conceal his much more sinister purposes. Powell failed to deliver on all three occasions, in two cases because he had more brains than Booth and in the third case because Lincoln was not alone, being accompanied by Eckert. Would Booth have urged Powell to kill Lincoln if his orders from Confederate leaders were only to kidnap him? Would Powell have even considered killing Lincoln, and, on at least one occasion, put himself in a position to do so, if his orders were only to assist Booth with kidnapping? The point is that, as with Holcombe, Thompson, Clay and Blackburn, Booth's orders were to kill Lincoln, not to kidnap him, and Powell had to have known that killing was to become his business too, and these facts had to be known to Confederate leaders inasmuch as they were the authors of the orders and inasmuch as Booth, as their agent, was at all times following their orders, and inasmuch as Powell, the Mosby Ranger, could not have joined Booth's team without their approval. These conclusions are beyond a reasonable doubt.

Thomas F. Harney's mission was to kill Lincoln and as many other federal office holders as could be lured into a wing of the White House prior to blowing it up. Not a word written about the mission or its principals has anything to do with kidnapping. As with Holcombe,

Thompson, Clay, Blackburn, Booth and Powell, it was a 'hit' mission, pure and simple, all the way. It failed, by chance, but that fact in no way alters the purpose of the mission, which, because it involved not only the Secret Service's Torpedo Bureau, but also trainmen, post commanders, guides, other agents and the Gray Ghost himself, had to have been known to, and approved, directed and controlled by, Confederate leaders. These conclusions are beyond a reasonable doubt.

By Surratt's own admission (to Ste Marie in Italy), he and Booth killed Abraham Lincoln ('We have killed Lincoln, the niggers' friend'). They didn't kidnap him. They didn't attempt to kidnap him. To Ste Marie, Surratt said nothing whatsoever about kidnapping. Kidnapping was obviously not on the agenda, indeed had never been on the agenda, regardless of the ruse that was marketed to conceal the real agenda. It seems likely that the ruse was crafted and sold to Booth by the agents he met at the Parker House in Boston in July 1864, after which he began to gather his team, partially blinding them with the blather about kidnapping, which he said was a legitimate act of war. In addition to being Booth's right hand and companion in conspiracy, Surratt was Judah P. Benjamin's 'most trusted courier'. Benjamin was second only to Davis in authority and power in the Confederacy. Of all the dozens of candidates – perhaps hundreds – whom Benjamin had to choose from for the position of his personal courier, this second most powerful officer in the Confederacy chose the man who was closer to Booth than anyone else in his action team was – closer, in fact, than anyone in Booth's life was, except for family members, but perhaps including these inasmuch as all of them were Unionists. The Benjamin-Surratt-Booth connection is entirely too striking to have been a coincidence, and even in the extraordinary unlikelihood that it was a coincidence, that still wouldn't keep Surratt from discussing with Benjamin and Davis matters pertaining to Booth and his team and their doings. The connection, rather, demonstrates the need for Benjamin to have a pipeline to Booth, and vice versa, someone to deliver messages from Benjamin or Davis to Booth and to receive messages from him for Benjamin and Davis, which in turn demonstrates the control of Booth by Confederate leaders. Surratt's almost weekly meetings with Benjamin, and occasional meetings with Davis, are clear and convincing evidence of the purposeful link between Benjamin, the orchestrator of the Confederacy's response to Wistar-Dahlgren-Kilpatrick, and Booth, the 'crazy fellow', the 'rattle-pated fellow, filled with quixotic notions … [the] wild-brained boy', who, because of these attributes, had to be monitored closely.

The striking relationship between Benjamin, Surratt and Booth accords well with Ste Marie's affidavit of 10 July 1866 to Seward, in which he quoted Surratt's admissions to him that 'We', i.e. he and Booth, 'have killed Lincoln, the nigger's friend' and that they 'had acted under the orders of men who are not yet known, some of whom are still in New York and others in London' and 'persons under [Davis's] immediate orders'. The relationship between Benjamin, Surratt and Booth also accords well with Surratt's response to Ste Marie's asking him if Davis had anything to do with the assassination, namely, 'I am not going to tell you', which is as good as an affirmative answer, because it means that Surratt knew and that Confederate leaders *were* complicit, otherwise he would have said either 'I don't know' or 'No, Davis had nothing to do with it'. The Benjamin-Surratt-Booth relationship, together with Ste Marie's affidavit, is again proof beyond a reasonable doubt that the orders given to Holcombe, Thompson, Clay, Blackburn, Booth, Surratt, Powell and Harney to kill Lincoln and the other targeted office holders came from Confederate leaders, because only Confederate leaders had the authority and the power to order these men to kill Union leaders.

Conclusions

I have said that it is my purpose in writing this book to attempt to shed light on the issue of ultimate responsibility for the assassination and the attempted assassinations that occurred on 14 April 1865 in Washington. I proposed to do so by proving, beyond a reasonable doubt, that, consistent with the law of complicity (that anyone complicit in a crime is as guilty of it as the principal offender), Confederate leaders, principally President Jefferson Davis, Secretary of State Judah P. Benjamin, head of the Canadian contingency of the Confederate Secret Service Jacob Thompson and his successor General Edwin G. Lee, Charles A. Dunham and George N. Sanders, were ultimately responsible for the events of that fateful night. That fact probably has much to do with the fact that Benjamin, Thompson and Sanders fled the country after the assassination. Benjamin never returned. Thompson returned after four years, when it was safe to do so, after living in style in Europe on Confederate money that he had secured in Canada before departing. Sanders drifted back after about seven years, in time to die in New York City in 1873. Davis fled too, but he never left the country. He wanted to reach Texas to carry on the war from there and to pass into Mexico only if he had to. He was apprehended near Irwinville, Georgia, and manfully surrendered when he realised that all was lost. The business about his wearing women's clothing is nonsense; he had on a black shawl that his wife, Varina, had placed across his shoulders to protect him from the weather.

Let us not mince words: the object, always, was to kill Lincoln, the perceived author of all the South's loss, pain and suffering. More than a dozen attempts on his life had been made from the date of his election to the date of Booth's deed. The means to that end was not important. Whether it was accomplished by disease, poisoning, gunshot or explosion was immaterial, as long as it was accomplished. Whether it was accomplished by Holcombe, Thompson, Clay, Blackburn, Hyams, Booth, Surratt, Powell or Harney, or anyone else for that matter, was immaterial, as long as it was accomplished. Let us express Booth's role, inasmuch as it was he who succeeded where all others had failed, as a three-premise syllogism, as follows:

> Confederate leaders knew all about Booth and his team (per Surratt, Harbin, Jones).
> Confederate leaders knew that kidnapping Lincoln would do them no good at all (per Davis, Conrad).
> Confederate leaders did nothing to stop Booth.

I submit that one, and only one, conclusion can be deduced from this three-premise syllogism, and it is that: Booth's purpose was not kidnapping, and Confederate leaders knew it.

Did John Wilkes Booth kill Lincoln? Of course he did, but he was far from alone. He was not a half-mad actor who, proceeding with no more help than he received from his action team, murdered Lincoln because he was consumed by personal hatred of the man and because he was traumatised by the South's loss of the war. That is a gigantic myth that took root after the collapse of the case against Davis and Canadian Cabinet members, as unindicted co-conspirators, in the trial of the conspirators in May and June 1865, and that has persisted into our own time despite its demonstrated falsity. He was, rather, a dedicated agent of the Confederate Secret Service who did indeed hate Lincoln, and blacks too, indeed the entire Union cause, and was indeed traumatised by the demise of the Confederacy, but who, as a dutiful agent, was following orders that came to him from the highest levels of the Confederate government and its Secret Service. But let us not be too judgmental: the evidence is strong that major figures in the Lincoln Administration, perhaps Lincoln himself, had ordered the same fate for Davis and his cabinet. Though the author of that order could not know it at the time, he was in fact signing death warrants. It was war. The Black Flag had long since been raised. Though a Code regulating the usages of war was in existence for the Union, there was none for the Confederacy. But, truly, how much would it have mattered? The passions of armed conflict are rarely constrained by such Codes of permitted and prohibited conduct. The accounts of the depredations of psychopathic killers in the Civil War and the armed conflicts that led up to it make one's skin crawl. Wars are fought because both sides want something badly and will therefore do anything to prevail. Not 'almost anything', but *anything* they are capable of doing. And they did. Codes be damned.

The only real difference between the Union and the Confederate efforts to decapitate their enemy's government was that one failed utterly and the other was partially successful. Unfortunately for the South and therefore for the Union, the effects of the partial success are still being felt today.

References

Preface

1. Lamon, p. 47.
2. Crook, pp. 74–6.
3. *New York Sunday Telegraph*, 23 May 1909.
4. *New York Herald*, 16 April 1865.

Introduction

1. Hanchett, 'The Lincoln Assassination Revisited', *North and South*, Vol. 3, No. 7, Sept. 2000, pp. 33–9.
2. Current (Review of *Come Retribution*), *Illinois Historical Journal*, Vol. LXXXII, No. 4 (Winter 1989), p. 271.
3. Sears, 'The Case for a Confederate Conspiracy', *The Washington Post*, 19 Dec. 1988, p. D3.
4. Winkler, pp. 255–7, 260, 261.
5. Edwards and Steers, eds., *The Lincoln Assassination*, pp. 193, 709.
6. Official Records, Ser. 1, Vol. XLIII, Pt. II, p. 935.
7. Roth, ed., p. 57.
8. Burkhardt, p. 46.
9. Chamlee, p. 501.
10. Weichmann, pp. 32, 430; Pitman, ed., p. 114; Oldroyd, pp. 163, 164; Kauffman, *American*, pp. 154, 155.
11. Evans, p. 390.
12. McLoughlin, pp. 141–3.
13. Oldroyd, p. 178; Weichmann, p. 128.

14. Interview in 1885 of Thomas Harbin by George Alfred Townsend, *Cincinnati Enquirer*, 18 April 1892.
15. *Ibid.*; Tidwell, Hall and Gaddy, p. 342.
16. Tidwell, Hall and Gaddy, pp. 342, 345, No. 41; Stewart, p. 108.
17. Arnold, p. 45.
18. *Impeachment Investigation*, p. 674.
19. *Ibid.*
20. Chamlee, p. 455.
21. Ibid. p. 462.
22. Titone, pp. 319, 329.
23. *Ibid.* p. 335; Rhodehamel and Taper, p. 119.
24. Roscoe, p. 502; Tidwell, Hall and Gaddy, pp. 262, 263.
25. Higham, pp. 137, 138.
26. Clarke, *John Wilkes Booth*, pp. 85, 87; Kauffman, *American*, pp. 130, 131.
27. Pitman, ed., p. 44.
28. Edwards and Steers, eds., *The Lincoln Assassination*, p. 727.
29. *Ibid.* p. 38.
30. Pitman, ed., p. 236; Steers, ed., *The Trial*, p. XXX.
31. Poore, ed., Vol. II, pp. 269, 270; Steers, *Lincoln Legends*, p.169.
32. Weichmann, pp. 32–5.
33. Pitman, ed., pp. 170, 171.
34. *Ibid.* p. 39.
35. Jones, pp. 39–62.
36. Clarke, *John Wilkes Booth,* pp. 104–10.

Chapter One

1. Basler, ed., p. 203.
2. Varon, pp. 114, 115.
3. *Ibid.* p. 114.
4. *Ibid.* p. 115; Joseph George, Jnr, 'Black Flag Warfare: Lincoln and the Raids Against Richmond and Jefferson Davis', *Pennsylvania Magazine of History and Biography*, 115, No. 3, July 1994, pp. 301, 303, 304; Tidwell, Hall and Gaddy, p. 247.

5. Varon, p. 117.
6. Wistar, p. 87.
7. George, Jnr, Joseph, 'Black Flag Warfare: Lincoln and the Raids Against Richmond and Jefferson Davis', *Pennsylvania Magazine of History and Biography*, 115, No. 3, July 1994, pp. 303, 304.
8. Sears, pp. 230–4.
9. Catton, pp. 7, 8.
10. Varon, p. 139; *Battles and Leaders*, p. 96; 'The Dahlgren Papers Revisited', originally published by *America's Civil War*, Online, 12 June 2006.
11. Sears, p. 241; James O. Hall, 'The Dahlgren Papers: A Yankee Plot to Kill President Davis', 22 *Civil War Times Illustrated* 30 (Nov. 1983), p. 31.
12. Records of the Adjutant General's Office, 1780s – 1917, Entry 721, Serial 60, RG 94, National Archives; *Richmond Examiner*, 1 April 1864; *Southern Historical Society Papers*, Vol. 3, p. 221; Steers, *Blood*, p. 45; *Battles and Leaders*, p. 96; Hall, 'The Dahlgren Papers: A Yankee Plot to Kill President Davis', 22 *Civil War Times Illustrated* 30 (Nov. 1983), pp. 30–9; Varon, p. 139; Tidwell, Hall and Gaddy, pp. 243–5.
13. Daniel, pp. 176, 177.
14. Tidwell, Hall and Gaddy, p. 245.
15. Catton, pp. 13, 14.
16. Varon, p. 140.
17. Catton, p. 17; van der Linden, p. 96.
18. Butler to Wistar, 4 February 1864, Benjamin F. Butler, *Private and Official Correspondence of Gen. Benjamin F. Butler*, ed., Jesse Ames Marshall, Plimpton Press, 1917, Vol. 3, pp. 373, 374; Baker, pp. 199, 200.
19. Tidwell, Hall and Gaddy, pp. 247–51.
20. Davis, Jefferson, Vol. 2, p. 507.
21. Manuscript Collections, Virginia State Library and Archive, Richmond.
22. Horan, pp. 67, 68, 92; van der Linden p. 105; Schultz, p. 207; Thomas Hines Papers, Margaret L. King Library, University of Kentucky, Lexington.
23. Van Doren Stern, pp. 242–6; Tidwell, Hall and Gaddy, pp. 201–203.
24. Singer, p. 92.

25. Van Doren Stern, pp. 202, 203; Tidwell, Hall and Gaddy, pp. 199, 200, 202, 203.
26. Van Doren Stern, pp. 219–29.
27. Tidwell, Hall and Gaddy, pp. 162–7.
28. Van Doren Stern, p. 208.
29. *The War of the Rebellion*, Ser. 1, Vol. 42, Pt. 1, pp. 954–6; Morris Schaff, 'The Explosion at City Point', in Van Doren Stern, pp. 230–5.
30. Van Doren Stern, pp. 257–67; Pitman, ed., pp. 29–31.
31. Tidwell, Hall and Gaddy, pp. 162, 163; Van Doren Stern, p. 208.
32. Pitman, ed., pp. 54–7; Poore, Vol. 2, pp. 409–19.
33. *Ibid.*
34. Tidwell, Hall and Gaddy, pp. 185–7; Steers, *Blood*, pp. 53, 54.
35. Horan, pp. 67, 68, 92; van der Linden p. 105; Schultz, p. 207; Thomas Hines Papers, Margaret L. King Library, University of Kentucky, Lexington.

Chapter Two

1. 'Death of Miss Seward', Obituary, *Baltimore Sun*, 31 Oct. 1866.
2. Statement of Mary Branson, LAS File, M-599, R3, National Archives.
3. Ownsbey, p. 30.
4. *Ibid.* pp. 160, 161.
5. *Ibid.* p. 161; *Philadelphia Weekly Times*, 3 June 1882.
6. *Ibid.* p. 163; *Ibid.*
7. Pitman, ed., p. 24.
8. Ownsbey, pp. 28, 29, 203.
9. *Ibid.* p. XIII.
10. Stewart, p. 138
11. *Trial of John H. Surratt*, Vol. 1, p. 275; Edwards and Steers, eds., *The Lincoln Assassination*, pp. 1382, 1383.
12. Bates, p. 377
13. Conrad, p. 75.
14. Louthan, 'A Proposed Abduction of Lincoln'; Andy Turner, *A Proposed Abduction of Lincoln*.

15. Conrad, pp. 68–70
16. *Ibid.* p. 75
17. Arnold, p. 4.
18. Pitman, ed., pp. 380, 390; Harris, p. 310; Hanchett, p. 239.
19. Bates, p. 384; Ownsbey, pp. 67, 68.
20. Steers, ed., *The Trial*, p. CVI.
21. Pitman, ed., p. 24.
22. *Ibid.* pp. 380, 390.
23. Ingraham, Prentiss, 'Pursuit and Death of John Wilkes Booth', *The Century*, Vol. 39 (n.s., Vol. 17), No. 3, Jan. 1890.
24. Pitman, ed., pp. 28, 29, 377.
25. *Ibid.*
26. Ownsbey, p. 40.
27. Bates, pp. 384–8.
28. *Trial of John H. Surratt*, Vol. 1, pp. 332, 334, 335, 340, 341, 485.
29. *Impeachment Investigation*, p. 673.
30. *Ibid.* p. 674.
31. *Ibid.*
32. Pitman, p. 97.
33. *New York Times*, 8 July 1865.
34. Edwards and Steers, eds., *The Lincoln Assassination*, pp. 727, 728.
35. McLoughlin, pp. 141–3.
36. *Impeachment Investigation*, p. 674.
37. Edwards and Steers, eds., *The Lincoln Assassination*, p. 674.
38. Pitman, ed., p. 44.
39. Chamlee, p. 462.
40. Arnold, p. 45.
41. Chamlee, p. 455.
42. *Ibid.* p. 462.
43. 'The Execution', *Boston Post*, 8 July 1865; Ownsbey, p. 139.
44. *New York Times*, 8 July 1865.
45. 'The Execution', *Boston Post*, 8 July 1865; Ownsbey, p. 139.
46. Ownsbey, pp. 139, 203.
47. *Ibid.* p. 139
48. *Ibid.* p. 203.

Chapter Three

1. Singer, pp. 124–30; Goetz, p. 198.
2. Tidwell, Hall and Gaddy, p. 419.
3. Goetz, p. 199.
4. *Ibid.*; Frank Harney's Compiled Service Record, Tidwell Research Papers, Surratt Society.
5. Tidwell, Hall and Gaddy, p. 157.
6. Singer, p. 18; *New York Herald*, 19 and 20 May, 1863.
7. Edwards and Steers, eds., *The Lincoln Assassination*, pp. 637, 638.
8. Pitman, ed., p. 44.
9. Tidwell, Hall and Gaddy, pp. 411, 412.
10. Hertz, Preface; Roscoe, p. 533.
11. Higham, pp. 236, 237.
12. Official Records, Ser. I, Vol. XLIII, Pt. II, p. 935.
13. Tidwell, Hall and Gaddy, p. 415; Goetz, p. 201.
14. Weichmann, p. 128; Oldroyd, p. 178.
15. Singer, p. 135; Tidwell, Hall and Gaddy, p. 463.
16. Guttridge and Neff, pp. 52, 53, 252.
17. Swanson, pp. 214, 215; Tidwell, Hall and Gaddy, pp. 461–3, 467; Steers, *Blood*, p. 189; Steers, *Encyclopedia,* pp. 79, 80; Singer, p. 139.
18. Tidwell, pp. 183, 184.
19. *Ibid.* pp. 162–4; Goetz, p. 201.
20. Tidwell, p. 164.
21. Tidwell, Hall and Gaddy, p. 419.
22. Singer, pp. 134–7.
23. *Ibid.* p. 140; Goetz, p. 210.
24. Tidwell, p. 175.
25. Singer, p. 139.
26. *Trial of John H. Surratt*, Vol. 1, pp. 471, 476.
27. *Ibid.* p. 483.
28. Loux, pp. 206–208.
29. Weichmann, p. 433.
30. *Trial of John H. Surratt*, Vol. 1, pp. 461 et seq., 493.
31. Weichmann, pp. 428 et seq.

32. *Ibid.* pp. 441 et seq.
33. Alford, *Fortune's Fool*, p. 260.
34. Loux, pp. 206–209.
35. *New York Sunday Telegraph*, 23 May 1909.
36. Pitch, p. 89; Reck, pp. 68, 77.
37. Pitch, pp. 89, 113; Reck, pp. 68, 77, 96, 112; 'John Wilkes Booth', *Daily Constitutional Union*, 15 April 1865; Grant, p. 155; Bryan, p. 179; Good, p. 173; *Boston Herald*, 11 April 1897.
38. *Baltimore Sun*, 18 April 1865; Kauffman, *American*, p. 73; Edwards and Steers, eds., *The Lincoln Assassination*, pp. 538, 598–600.

Chapter Four

1. Weichmann, p. 20.
2. Kunhardt and Kunhardt, p. 204.
3. *Trial of John H. Surratt*, Vol. 1, p. 483.
4. *Ibid.* Vol. 1, pp. 463, 479.
5. *Ibid.* p. 467.
6. *Ibid.* pp. 468, 480.
7. *Ibid.* p. 468.
8. Chamlee, p. 501.
9. Pitman, ed., p. 28.
10. *Ibid.*
11. *Ibid.* p. 31.
12. *Ibid.* p. 35.
13. DeWitt, pp. 25–7; Oldroyd, pp. 274–6; Roscoe, pp. 72–5.
14. Hanchett, p. 119.
15. Steers, *Blood*, p. 83.
16. Arnold, pp. 25, 26, 48, 135, 136, 148, 149; Weichmann, pp. 431, 432.
17. Weichmann, p. 101, 386, 432; Arnold, pp. 27, 35, 49, 149, 150; Oldroyd, p. 134; Kauffman, *American*, p. 185.
18. Arnold, p. 149.
19. Kauffman, *American*, pp. 187, 188.
20. Pitman, ed., p. 170.

21. McLoughlin, pp. 141–3.
22. Weichmann, p. 128.
23. Evans, p. 390.
24. Tidwell, Hall and Gaddy, pp. 247–51.
25. Evans, p. 241.
26. *Ibid.* pp. 389, 390.
27. Weichmann, p. 128.
28. Oldroyd, p. 178; Jampoler, p. 54.
29. McLoughlin, pp. 141–3.
30. Weichmann, p. 433.
31. Arnold, p. 127.
32. *Trial of John H. Surratt*, Vol. 1, pp. 492, 493.
33. *Ibid.* p. 472.
34. Weichmann, pp. 433–8.
35. *Ibid.* p. 445.
36. Jampoler, pp. 92, 104, 105.
37. *Ibid.* p. 106.
38. McLoughlin, pp. 141–3.
39. *Trial of John H. Surratt*, Vol. 1, p. 480.
40. Weichmann, p. 446.
41. Jampoler, pp. 114, 115.
42. Weichmann, p. 451.
43. Evans, p. 398.
44. *Ibid.* p. 47.

Summary and Conclusions

1. Vifquain, Victor, *The 1862 Plot to Kidnap Jefferson Davis*, ed. by Jeffrey H. Smith and Phillip Thomas Tucker, Stackpole Books, Mechanicsburg, Pa., 1998.

Bibliography

Books

Alford, Terry, *Fortune's Fool: The Life of John Wilkes Booth*, New York: Oxford University Press, 2015.

__________, ed., *John Wilkes Booth: A Sister's Memoir*, Jackson: University Press of Mississippi, 1996.

Arnold, Samuel, *Memoirs of a Lincoln Conspirator*, ed. Michael W. Kauffman, Bowie, MD: Heritage Books, Inc., 1995.

Baker, Lafayette C., *History of the United States Secret Service*, Philadelphia: L.C. Baker, 1867.

Basler, Roy P., ed., *Collected Works of Abraham Lincoln*, New Brunswick, NJ: Rutgers University Press, 1953.

Bates, David Homer, *Lincoln in the Telegraph Office*, New York: The Century Co., 1907.

Berry, Randall Alan, ed., *Shall We Gather At The River, The Unwritten History Of The Assassination Of Abraham Lincoln*, Ada, OK: ECO/ Living Art Publishing, 2011.

Booth, John Wilkes, *'Right or Wrong, God Judge Me': The Writings of John Wilkes Booth*, eds. John Rhodehamel & Louise Taper, Urbana-Champaign: University of Illinois Press, 1997.

Bryan, George S., *The Great American Myth*, Chicago: Americana House, Inc., 1940.

Burkhart, George S., *Confederate Rage, Yankee Wrath: No Quarter in the Civil War*, Carbondale: Southern Illinois University Press, 2007.

Catton, Bruce, *A Stillness at Appomattox*, Garden City, NY: Doubleday & Company, Inc., 1953.

Chamlee, Roy Z., *Lincoln's Assassins: A Complete Account of Their Capture, Trial and Punishment*, Jefferson, NC: McFarland & Company, Inc., Publishers, 1990.

Clarke, Asia Booth, *John Wilkes Booth: A Sister's Memoir*, ed. Terry Alford, Jackson: University Press of Mississippi, 1996.

__________, *The Unlocked Book*, New York: Arno Press, 1938.

Conrad, Thomas Nelson, *A Confederate Spy*, New York: J.S. Ogilvie Publishers, 1892.

Crawford, J. Marshall, *Mosby and His Men*, New York: G.W. Carleton & Company, 1867.

Crook, William H., *Through Five Administrations: Reminiscences of Colonel William H. Crook, Body-guard to President Lincoln*, comp. and ed. by Margarita Spalding Gerry, New York: Harper & Brothers, 1910.

Cumming, Carman, *Devil's Game*, Urbana-Champaign: University of Illinois Press, 2004.

Daniel, John M., *The Richmond Examiner During The War*, New York: Printed for the author, 1868.

Davis, Jefferson, *The Rise and Fall of the Confederate Government*, New York: D. Appleton & Company, 1881.

Davis, William C., *An Honorable Defeat: The Last Days of the Confederate Government*, New York: Harcourt, Inc., 2001.

Edwards, William C. & Edward Steers, Jnr, eds., *The Lincoln Assassination: The Evidence*, Urbana and Chicago: University of Illinois Press, 2009.

Eisenschiml, Otto, *Why Was Lincoln Murdered?*, Boston: Little, Brown & Company, 1937.

Evans, Eli N., *Judah P. Benjamin: The Jewish Confederate*, New York: The Free Press, a division of Simon & Schuster, Inc., 1989.

Flower, Frank A., *Edwin McMasters Stanton*, Akron, OH: Saalfield Publishing Co., 1905.

From War Department Files, Statements Made by the Alleged Lincoln Conspirators Under Examination, 1865, Clinton, MD: The Surratt Society, Nov. 1980.

Gerry, Margarita Spalding, ed., *Through Five Administrations: Reminiscences of Colonel William H. Crook, Body-guard to President Lincoln*, New York: Harper & Brothers, 1910.

Goetz, David, *Ever the Gray Ghost: Colonel John Singleton Mosby and the Lincoln Conspiracies*.

Good, Timothy S., *We Saw Lincoln Shot: One Hundred Eyewitness Accounts*, Jackson: University Press of Mississippi, 1995.

Grant, Julia Dent, *The Personal Memoirs of Julia Dent Grant*, ed. John Y. Simon, Carbondale: Southern Illinois University Press, 1975.

Guttridge, Leonard F., & Ray A. Neff, *Dark Union: The Secret Web of Profiteers, Politicians and Booth Conspirators That Led to Lincoln's Death*, Hoboken, NJ: John Wiley & Sons, Inc., 2003.

Hall, James O. & Michael Malone, *John Wilkes Booth: Following the Money Trail*, Clinton, MD: the Surratt Society, 2003.

Hanchett, William, *The Lincoln Murder Conspiracies*, Urbana-Champaign: University of Illinois Press, 1986.

Harris, Thomas M., *The Assassination of Lincoln: A History of the Great Conspiracy*, Berwyn Heights, MD: Heritage Books, Inc., 1989.

Hatch, Frederick, *Protecting President Lincoln: The Security Effort, the Thwarted Plots and the Disaster at Ford's Theatre*, Jefferson, NC: McFarland & Company, Inc., Publishers, 2011.

Headley, John W., *Confederate Operations in Canada and New York*, New York: Neale Publishing Co., 1906.

Hertz, Emmanuel, *The Hidden Lincoln*, New York: the Viking Press, 1938.

Higham, Charles, *Murdering Mr Lincoln: A New Detection of the 19th Century's Most Famous Crime*, Beverly Hills, CA: New Millennium Press, 2004.

Horan, James D., *Confederate Agent*, New York: Crown, 1954.

Impeachment Investigation: Testimony Taken Before the Judiciary Committee of the House of Representatives in the Investigation of the Charges Against Andrew Johnson, Second Session, Thirty-Ninth Congress, and First Session, Fortieth Congress, 1867, Washington, DC: Government Printing Office, 1867.

Jampoler, Andrew C.A., *The Last Lincoln Conspirator: John Surratt's Flight From the Gallows*, Annapolis, MD: Naval Institute Press, 2008.

Jones, Thomas A., *J. Wilkes Booth*, Chicago: Laird & Lee, 1893.

Kauffman, Michael W., *American Brutus: John Wilkes Booth and the Lincoln Conspiracies*, New York: Random House, 2004.

__________, ed., *Memoirs of a Lincoln Conspirator*, Bowie, MD: Heritage Books, Inc., 1995.

Kunhardt, Dorothy Meserve & Philip B. Kunhardt, Jnr, *Twenty Days*, Secaucus, NJ: Castle Books, a division of Book Sales, Inc., 1965.

Lamon, Ward Hill, *Recollections of Abraham Lincoln 1847–1865*, Lincoln: University of Nebraska Press, 1994.

Larson, Kate Clifford, *The Assassin's Accomplice: Mary Surratt and the Plot to Kill Abraham Lincoln*, New York: Basic Books, a Member of the Perseus Books Group, 2008.

Laughlin, Clara M., *The Death of Lincoln*, New York: Doubleday, Page & Company, 1909.

Leech, Margaret, *Reveille in Washington, 1860–1865*, New York: Harper & Brothers, 1941.

Lewis, Lloyd, *The Assassination of Lincoln: History and Myth*, Lincoln and London: University of Nebraska Press, 1929.

Logan, John A., *The Great Conspiracy: It's Origin and History*, New York: A.R. Hart & Co., 1886.

Mahoney, Ella V., *Sketches of Tudor Hall and the Booth Family*, Belair, MD: Tudor Hall, 1925.

McLoughlin, Emmett, *An Inquiry Into the Assassination of Abraham Lincoln*, New York: Lyle Stuart, Inc., 1963.

Meade, George Gordon, ed., *The Life and Letters of George Gordon Meade, Major-General United States Army*, New York: Charles Scribner's Sons, 1913.

Mills, Robert Lockwood, *It Didn't Happen The Way You Think*, Bowie, MD: Heritage Books, Inc., 1994.

O'Neal, Michael, *The Assassination of Abraham Lincoln: Opposing Viewpoints*, San Diego: Greenhaven Press, Inc., 1949.

Official Records. The War of the Rebellion: A Compilation of the Official Records of the Union and Confederate Armies, Washington, DC: Government Printing Office, 1881–1901.

Oldroyd, Osborn H., *The Assassination of Abraham Lincoln: Flight, Pursuit, Capture and Punishment of the Conspirators*, Washington, DC: O.H. Oldroyd, 1901.

Ownsbey, Betty J., *Alias 'Paine'*, Jefferson, NC: McFarland & Company, Inc., 1993.

Pendel, Thomas Franses, *Thirty-Six Years in the White House, A Memoir of the White House Doorkeeper*, New York: The Neale Publishing Company, 1902.

Pitch, Anthony, *They Have Killed Papa Dead!*, Hanover, NH: Steerforth Press, 2008.

Pitman, Benn, ed., *The Assassination of President Lincoln and the Trial of the Conspirators*, Cincinnati: Moore, Wilstach & Baldwin, 1865.

Poore, Ben: Perley, ed., *The Conspiracy Trial for the Murder of the President and the Attempt to Overthrow the Government by the Assassination of its Principal Officers*, Boston: J.E. Tilton & Company, 1865.

Prentiss, Ingraham, M.B. Ruggles & Edward P. Doherty, *Pursuit and Death of John Wilkes Booth*, New York, Century Company, 1890.

Reck, W. Emerson, *A. Lincoln: His Last 24 Hours*, Columbia: University of South Carolina Press, 1987.

Rhodehamel, John & Louis Taper, eds., *'Right or Wrong, God Judge Me': The Writings of John Wilkes Booth*, Urbana and Chicago: University of Illinois Press, 1997.

Ripley, Edward H., *The Capture and Occupation of Richmond, April 3, 1865*, Whitefish, MT: Kessinger Publishing, 2007.

Roscoe, Theodore, *The Web of Conspiracy*, Englewood Cliffs, NJ: Prentice-Hall, Inc., 1959.

Roth, Margaret Brobst, ed., *Well Mary: Civil War Letters of a Wisconsin Volunteer*, Madison, WI: 1960).

Schultz, Duane, *The Dahlgren Affair: Terror and Conspiracy in the Civil War*, New York: W.W. Norton, 1998.

Simon, John Y., ed., *The Personal Memoirs of Julia Dent Grant*, Carbondale: Southern Illinois University Press, 1975.

Singer, Jane, *The Confederate Dirty War: Arson, Bombings, Assassination and Plots for Chemical and Germ Attacks on the Union*, Jefferson, NC: McFarland & Company Inc., 2005.

Smith, Henry Bascom, *Between the Lines: Secret Service Stories Told Fifty Years After*, New York: Booz Brothers, 1911.

Smoot, Richard Mitchell, *Shall We Gather At The River, The Unwritten History Of The Assassination Of Abraham Lincoln*, ed. Randall Alan Berry, Ada, OK: ECO / Living Art Publishing, 2011.

Starkey, Larry, *Wilkes Booth Came to Washington*, New York: Random House, 1976.

Steers, Edward, Jnr, *Blood on the Moon*, Lexington: The University Press of Kentucky, 2001.

___________, *His Name is Still Mudd*, Gettysburg, PA: Thomas Publications, 1997.

___________, *Lincoln Legends: Myths, Hoaxes and Confabulations Associated With Our Greatest President*, Lexington: The University Press of Kentucky, 2007.

___________, *The Escape and Capture of John Wilkes Booth*, Gettysburg, PA: Thomas Publications, 1983, 1992.

___________, *The Lincoln Assassination Encyclopedia*, New York: Harper Perennial, 2010.

___________, ed., *The Trial: The Assassination of President Lincoln and the Trial of the Conspirators,* Lexington: The University Press of Kentucky, 2003.

Steers, Edward, Jnr & Harold Holzer, eds., *The Lincoln Assassination Conspirators*, Baton Rogue: Louisiana State University Press, 2009.

Steers, Edward, Jnr & William C. Edwards, eds., *The Lincoln Assassination: The Evidence*, Urbana and Chicago: University of Illinois Press, 2009.

Stewart, John, *Confederate Spies at Large*, Jefferson, N.C. and London: McFarland & Company, Inc., 2007.

Stoddard, William O., *Abraham Lincoln: The True Story of a Great Life*, Fords, New York: Howard & Hulbert, 1884.

___________, *Inside the White House in War Times: Memoirs and Reports of Lincoln's Secretary*, Michael Burlingame, ed., Lincoln: University of Nebraska Press, 2000.

Swanson, James L., *Manhunt: The 12-Day Chase for Lincoln's Killer*, New York: Harper Perennial, 2006.

Teillard, Dorothy Lamon, ed., *Recollections of Abraham Lincoln*, by Ward Hill Lamon, Chicago: A.C. McClurg & Co., 1895.

The Assassination and History of the Conspiracy: A Complete Digest of the Whole Affair From Its Inception to Its Culmination, Sketches of the Principal Characters, Reports of the Obsequies, Etc., Cincinnati: J.R. Hawley & Co., 1865.

The War of the Rebellion: A Compilation of the Official Records of the Union and Confederate Armies, Washington, DC: Government Printing Office, 1881–1901.

Tidwell, William A., *April '65: Confederate Covert Action in the American Civil War*, Kent, OH: The Kent State University Press, 1995.

__________, James O. Hall & David Winfield Gaddy, *Come Retribution: The Confederate Secret Service and the Assassination of Abraham Lincoln*, Jackson: University Press of Mississippi, 1988.

Titone, Nora, *My Thoughts Be Bloody,* New York: Free Press, a division of Simon & Schuster, 2010.

Trial of John H. Surratt in the Criminal Court for the District of Columbia, Washington, DC: Government Printing Office, 1867.

Trudeau, Noah Andre, *Out of the Storm: The End of the Civil War, April–June, 1865*, Boston: Little, Brown & Company, 1994.

Turner, Andy, *A Proposed Abduction of Lincoln*, Gatehouse Press (Online), 23 July 2012.

Turner, Thomas R., *The Assassination of Abraham Lincoln*, Malabar, FL: Krieger Publishing Company, 1999.

__________, *Beware the People Weeping: Public Opinion and the Assassination of Abraham Lincoln*, Baton Rogue: Louisiana State University Press, 1982.

Van der Linden, Frank, *The Dark Intrigue: The True Story of a Civil War Conspiracy*, Golden, CO: Fulcrum Publishing, 2007.

Van Doren Stern, Philip, *Secret Missions of the Civil War*, New York: Wings Books, 1959, 1987.

__________, *The Man Who Killed Lincoln*, New York: Dell Publishing Company, Inc., 1955.

Varon, Elizabeth R., *Southern Lady, Yankee Spy*, New York: Oxford University Press, 2003.

Vifquain, Victor, *The 1862 Plot to Kidnap Jefferson Davis*, ed. by Jeffrey H. Smith & Phillip Thomas Tucker, Mechanicsburg, PA.: Stackpole Books, 1998.

Wearmouth, John M. & Wearmouth, Roberta J., *Thomas A. Jones: Chief Agent of the Confederate Secret Service in Maryland*, Port Tobacco, MD: Stonesthrow Publishing, 1995.

Weber, Jennifer L., *Copperheads: The Rise and Fall of Lincoln's Opponents in the North*, New York: Oxford University Press, 2006.

Weichmann, Louis J., *A True History of the Assassination of Abraham Lincoln and of the Conspiracy of 1865*, New York: Vintage Books, a division of Random House, 1975.

Winik, Jay, *April 1865: The Month That Saved America*, New York: HarperCollins, 2001.

Winkler, H. Donald, *Lincoln and Booth: More Light on the Conspiracy*, Nashville, TN: Cumberland House, 2003.

Articles

Brennan, John C., 'Why the Attempt to Assassinate Secretary of State William Seward', *Surratt Courier*, January 1987.

Current, Richard N., (Review of *Come Retribution*), Illinois Historical Journal, Vol. LXXXII, No. 4 (Winter 1989).

'The Dahlgren Papers Revisited', *America's Civil War*, Online, 12 June 2006.

'The Execution', *Boston Post*, 8 July 1865.

George, Joseph, Jnr, 'Black Flag Warfare: Lincoln and the Raids Against Richmond and Jefferson Davis', *Pennsylvania Magazine of History and Biography*, 115, No. 3, July 1991.

Gillette, Daniel, 'The Last Days of Payne', *New York World*, 3 April 1892.

Hall, James O., 'The Dahlgren Papers: A Yankee Plot to Kill President Davis', *Civil War Times Illustrated* 22 (November 1983).

__________, 'The Mercy Recommendation for Mrs Surratt: The Holt-Johnson Controversy', *Surratt Courier* 15, No. 8 (August 1990).

__________, 'The Mystery of Lincoln's Guard', *Surratt Society News* 7, No. 5 (May 1982).

Hanchett, William, 'The Lincoln Assassination Revisited', *North and South*, Vol. 3, No. 7.

Ingraham, Prentiss, 'Pursuit and Death of John Wilkes Booth', *The Century*, Vol. 39 (n.s., Vol. 17), No. 3, January 1890.

Interview in 1885 of Thomas Harbin by George Alfred Townsend, *Cincinnati Enquirer*, 18 April 1882.

Lange, James E.T. & Katherine DeWitt, Jnr, 'Who Ordered Lincoln's Death', *North and South*, Vol. 1, No. 6, June 1998.

Louthan, Henry T., 'A Proposed Abduction of Lincoln', *Confederate Veteran*, April 1903.

Martin, Paul, 'Lincoln's Missing Guard', *Smithsonian.com, History and Archeology*, 8 April 2010.

McElfresh, George W., 'Guarding Mr Lincoln', *The Ohio Soldier*, Chillicothe, OH: 28 April 1888.

McPherson, James M., 'A Failed Richmond Raid and Its Consequences', *Columbiad: A Quarterly Review of the War Between the States*, 2, No. 4 (Winter 1999).

Ruggles, M.B. & Edward P. Doherty, 'Pursuit and Death of John Wilkes Booth', *The Century Magazine*, Vol. XXXIX, N.S., Vol. XVII (November 1889–April 1890).

Sears, Stephen W., 'The Case for a Confederate Conspiracy', *The Washington Post*, 19 December 1988, p. D3.

Taylor, W.H., 'A New Story of the Assassination of Lincoln', *Leslie's Weekly*, Washington, DC: Library of Congress, 3 March 1920.

'The Dahlgren Papers Revisited', *America's Civil War*, Online, 12 June 2006.

'The Execution', *Boston Post*, 8 July 1865.

Thomas, Emory M., 'The Kilpatrick-Dahlgren Raid', *Civil War Times Illustrated*, 17 (April 1978).

Tidwell, William A., 'The Man Who Shifted the Blame', *Civil War Times Illustrated*, Vol. 40, Issue 3, June 2001.

Miscellaneous

An Act Relative to the Election of a President and Vice President of the United States and Declaring the Officer Who Shall Act as President in Case of Vacancies in the Offices Both of President and Vice President, 1 Stat. 259, §9–10 (1 March 1792).

Demond, Frederick A., Letters to Finis L. Bates, E.H. Swaim Papers, Washington, DC: Georgetown University Library Special Collections Research Centre.

Doherty, Edward, Statement, 29 April 1865, M619, 456: 274–284, Washington, DC: National Archives.

__________, to Andrew Johnson, 23 December 1865, M619, 455:769–775, Washington, DC: National Archives.

Eckert, Major Thomas T., Testimony of, *Judiciary House Committee, House of Representatives: The Impeachment Committee Investigation*, Washington, D.C., Government Printing Office, 1867.

Forbes, Charles, Affidavit, 17 September 1892, Chicago Historical Society.

Leale, Dr Charles A., Letter to General B.F. Butler, 20 July 1867, Washington, DC: Library of Congress.

__________, *Lincoln's Last Hours*, Address delivered before the Military Order of the Loyal Legion of the United States, New York Commandery, February 1909; *Harpers Weekly*, 13 February 1909.

__________, *Report of Dr Charles A. Leale (On Death of President Lincoln)*, 15 April 1865.

Rathbone, Major Henry R., Affidavit of 15 April 1865, Washington DC: National Archives.

__________, Affidavit of 17 April 1865, Washington DC: National Archives.

__________, Statement, Ford's Theatre Archives.

Swaim, E.H., Collection, Papers, Washington DC: Georgetown University Manuscripts, Georgetown University Special Collections Research Centre.

Thomas Hines Papers, Margaret L. King Library, Lexington: University of Kentucky.

Thompson J., Secret Agent of the Late Confederate Government, Stationed in Canada, for the Purpose of Organizing Insurrection in the Northern States and Burning Their Principal Cities, Report to Hon. J.P. Benjamin, Secretary of State. Toronto, C.W., 3 December 1864. Endorsed 'Rec'd 13 Feb'y '65. J.R.B.', Canadian Institute for Historic Microreproductions, ©1987.

Newspapers

Baltimore Sun, 18 April 1865.
Baltimore Sun, 31 Oct. 1866.
Boston Herald, 11 April 1897.
Boston Post, 8 July 1865.
Cincinnati Enquirer, 18 April 1892.
Daily Constitutional Union, 15 April 1865.
New York Herald, 16 April 1865.
New York Herald, 19 May 1863.
New York Herald, 20 May 1863.
New York Sunday Telegraph, 23 May 1909.
New York Times, 8 April 1867.
New York Times, 8 July 1865.
Philadelphia Weekly Times, 3 June 1882.
Richmond Examiner, 1 April 1864.
Washington Post, 19 Dec. 1988.

Index